MW00616887

Training for Catastrophe

Training for Catastrophe

Fictions of National Security after 9/11

LINDSAY THOMAS

University of Minnesota Press
Minneapolis
London

The University of Minnesota Press gratefully acknowledges the financial assistance provided for the publication of this book by the University of Miami College of Arts & Sciences.

"A Litany for Survival," from *The Black Unicorn* by Audre Lorde, copyright 1978 by Audre Lorde. Reprinted by permission of W. W. Norton & Company, Inc.

Portions of chapter 3 were previously published in a different form in "Forms of Duration: Preparedness, the *Mars* Trilogy, and the Management of Climate Change," *American Literature* 88, no. 1 (2016): 159–84.

Copyright 2021 by the Regents of the University of Minnesota

All rights reserved. No part of this publication may be reproduced, stored in a retrieval system, or transmitted, in any form or by any means, electronic, mechanical, photocopying, recording, or otherwise, without the prior written permission of the publisher.

Published by the University of Minnesota Press
111 Third Avenue South, Suite 290
Minneapolis, MN 55401-2520
http://www.upress.umn.edu

ISBN 978-1-5179-0985-7 (hc)
ISBN 978-1-5179-0986-4 (pb)

Library of Congress record available at https://lccn.loc.gov/2020053618

Printed in the United States of America on acid-free paper

The University of Minnesota is an equal-opportunity educator and employer.

UMP BmB 2021

To my family

Contents

Preface

I submitted the final manuscript version of this book to the publisher on January 31, 2020. At that time, there were no known cases of COVID-19 in the United States and "only" about 7,818 worldwide.[1] Things rapidly deteriorated from there, and what had seemed like a remote possibility at the end of January—that the SARS-CoV-2 virus would cause a global pandemic—was by mid-March a reality. In the time since, the virus has spread across the globe and killed, at the time of this writing in mid-August 2020, more than 165,000 people in the United States alone. People are, rightly, blaming the Trump administration for these deaths. In particular, many have wondered why the administration wasn't better prepared for this disaster, and the concept of "preparedness" has become a topic of everyday conversation.

In the months since I sent the manuscript off, it has been unsettling to see its central theme take on new life in global politics. For the past two decades, the national security paradigm known as preparedness has been a mainstay of U.S. national security policy, although it tends to emerge into public view only in times of national disaster. The domestic component to the U.S. war on terror, preparedness moved to the center of U.S. policy after September 11, 2001. Placing emergency management and institutional readiness at the forefront of national security, it emphasizes readiness and response over prevention because it assumes that the national security threats for which people need to prepare—including everything from natural disasters to industrial accidents to terrorist attacks—cannot be prevented. One of my arguments in the following pages is that, with this presumption of the inevitability of future disaster, the discourse of preparedness naturalizes disaster by making it un-remarkable, conditioning citizens to accept catastrophe as part of everyday life.

This acceptance, of late, has been pushed nearly to a breaking point. Interestingly, however, what has brought people to this brink is not only the global pandemic itself but the Trump admin-istration's lack of response to it. The administration's dismantling of the nation's disaster preparedness infrastructure has become major news as outlets have published countless articles and think pieces documenting the administration's many failures to prepare.[2] Writers have devoted much attention to detailing federal pandemic preparedness exercises from the past two decades; to lamenting the firing of Timothy Ziemer, the senior administration official in charge of pandemic response, and the dismantling of his pandemic preparedness team in 2018; and to examining the failures to secure needed medical equipment in a timely manner. These nuts and bolts of logistics and procurement rarely receive this kind of critical attention—unless, of course, things go wrong.

The criticisms of the Trump administration's deadly mishan-dling of the disaster seemed to crystallize for a moment in mid-July in the form of a quote falsely attributed to secretary of education Betsy DeVos. After an interview with CNN in which DeVos was asked if schools should return to remote learning if they experience an outbreak, a meme cropped up on Facebook mocking DeVos for allegedly responding, "You can't plan for something that hasn't hap-pened yet." Although the meme turned out to be a misleading para-phrase of her actual words, criticism of DeVos spread rapidly across social media networks.[3] Critics jumped on the logical incongruity inherent in the false statement; obviously, one plans for something precisely because it hasn't happened yet. This basic principle is the foundation of all preparedness, not to mention the dictionary defi-nition of to plan. In mocking DeVos, her critics took on a position of knowingness in the face of her apparent incompetence. How-ever, the expertise they claimed was not knowledge of what would happen but of the meaning of preparedness itself. This criticism of DeVos—coming from the left and center of the political spectrum—was motivated by the same impulse behind the articles and think pieces questioning why the Trump administration was not prepared for the COVID-19 pandemic. It is an impulse that emphasizes the value of expertise and professionalism, including carefully crafted and thoroughly tested disaster preparedness plans, as the answer to the incompetence many members of the Trump administration have displayed.

None of this criticism is wrong. However, writing this book has also made clear to me the danger of a response from the left that criticizes the administration by calling for more preparedness. Ultimately, as *Training for Catastrophe* will argue, it is this kind of criticism that upholds and reasserts the logic of preparedness as a national security paradigm. This logic insists, no matter how many failures of preparedness people are forced to endure, that while specific people can certainly fail at preparedness, preparedness itself can never fail. More and better preparedness is always the answer.

While the Trump administration has failed outrageously at the particular duties of care, of procurement, and of foresight, it has also normalized preparedness in its most extreme form. National disaster preparedness is at root a liberal phenomenon, a product of the Cold War national security state that took on disaster response as a responsibility of the federal government, thereby promising citizens some small means of protection from disasters beyond their control. After 9/11, as preparedness transformed into the centerpiece of U.S. national security, this promise transformed as well. Under the George W. Bush and Obama administrations, by relying on the imaginative tools and techniques of fiction, preparedness took on a newly neoliberal form: while citizens should accept that any federal response to disaster was performed to protect them, the individual citizen is just as responsible for preparing for and responding to disasters as the federal government. We all now "share" that responsibility. The neoliberalization of preparedness emptied out the promise of collective protection and recovery. This is the form of often violent neglect described and critiqued in this book.

But as Trump's presidency drags on, it becomes clearer that this paradigm is shifting again. Or, more precisely, it becomes clearer that certain latent tendencies are surfacing with greater frequency. Although many of the preparedness materials created by officials from previous administrations that I discuss in this book are still in use today, the Trump administration's blatant xenophobia, indefinite detention of migrants, deliberate mismanagement or destruction of immigration policy, construction of a border wall, deployment of a national police force, and malignant mishandling of the COVID-19 pandemic—to name just a few examples—have revealed the hostility at the root of this national security paradigm. Many U.S. citizens now fully understand what it means to include both the agency responsible for disaster management, FEMA, and the agency responsible for immigration and customs, ICE, under the same umbrella national security organization, the Department of Homeland Security. This organization is technically neither a law enforcement agency nor a military unit, yet it retains nearly unchecked power to act as both within the borders of the United States. As the justification at home for endless war abroad, preparedness has always concerned itself with delineating who is deserving of its supposed protections, with policing the border of whose lives matter. What those in the United States who have been fortunate enough not to have to face before are witnessing now is not the failure of preparedness but rather its apotheosis. It is a glimpse of what those who live in the midst of ongoing U.S. military action abroad, or those who are Black or Indigenous or brown or poor within the United States, must endure every day: expulsion from the homeland.

Although this book was completed in the midst of a historic pandemic, its origins lie in the years following the attacks of September 11, 2001. I remember vividly the feeling of tectonic shift as I watched the country's response to 9/11 unfold, and I have been trying to understand the nature of this change ever since. This effort informs my critique of preparedness. I argue that preparedness operates according to a racial logic that marks some as deserving of security and others as undeserving. I show how preparedness, through its deployment of fiction, trains those it considers citizens to accept some disasters as part of everyday life and to respond to them with the calm, cool competence of the preparedness professional. Part of this training involves learning not to recognize some disasters as disasters—learning not to recognize the racial violence of the "active shooter," for example, as a symptom of the disaster of white supremacy. The techniques through which this training happens are often subtle, and they depend on a fascinating and bizarre philosophy of fiction with a long history in U.S. national security, all of which the following pages will detail. But perhaps the actions of the Trump administration have made this training's end game easier for some of us to see. Echoing Walter Benjamin's famous dictum that "*the logical outcome of fascism is an aestheticizing of political life*," the preparedness materials I discuss in this book produce a similar outcome by utilizing the aesthetic tools and strategies of fiction.[4] The creeping fascism of the Trump administration is the latest expansion of this work, begun at least two decades ago.

Introduction

Prepare Yourself

In 2007, the U.S. Department of Homeland Security (DHS) invited writers from the science fiction think tank SIGMA to the Science and Technology Stakeholders Conference in Washington to discuss possible future threats to national security. SIGMA, which describes itself as "a group of science fiction writers who offer futurism consulting to the United States government and appropriate NGOs," was founded in 1992 by science fiction writer and engineer Arlan Andrews, then an American Society of Engineers Senior Fellow at the White House.[1] The group includes more than forty science fiction writers who volunteer to consult with government agencies and provide them with, as the SIGMA website puts it, "the imagination that only speculative writers can provide."[2] SIGMA has consulted for the U.S. Department of Energy, the U.S. Army and Air Force, NATO, and a host of nongovernmental organizations, but its participation in the 2007 DHS conference—and its subsequent participation in the 2008 and 2009 meetings—garnered national attention. Newspapers reported on the "unlikely" partnership between the national security community and science fiction writers, highlighting the "crazy ideas" and "wild imaginations" of the "futuristic yarn-spinners" of SIGMA.[3] They also focused on the gadgets and devices the writers cooked up in conversation with national security officials, like a cell phone that could detect biochemical attacks and a brain-scanning device for bomb-sniffing dogs. In general, the coverage of SIGMA's involvement with DHS emphasized the seeming incongruity between the science fictional ideas the SIGMA writers devised and the serious business of national security, treating SIGMA's participation as, at best, an amusing curiosity.

DHS officials, however, took the collaboration more seriously—they hoped the SIGMA writers would help them concoct scenarios of future disaster to use in training exercises. The involvement of sci-fi writers, officials anticipated, would help to remedy what the 9/11 Commission, convened to investigate the terrorist attacks of September 11, 2001, called "a failure of imagination" in the national security community.[4] As DHS communications officer Chris Christopher described the reasons for SIGMA's involvement in the conferences, "if you think what you've always thought, you'll get what you've always got."[5]

These comments from national security officials reflect the national security state's investment in the power of fiction, a power misunderstood by the news outlets covering the conferences, which treated SIGMA's involvement with DHS as "unlikely" and "crazy." The post-9/11 U.S. national security state takes fiction very seriously, and the consequences of this attitude toward fiction are profound. The collaboration between the SIGMA writers and DHS signals a desire on the part of the national security community to harness the professional production of fiction to create knowledge about future threats. That the form this fiction takes is "science fictional" is almost incidental. DHS is not necessarily interested in gadgets like brain-scanning devices; DHS is interested, however, in creating knowledge about things that haven't happened—about what it terms "the future," and what I call fiction. The best way to create this knowledge, DHS claims, is to enlist the help of people who create futuristic fictions for a living: science fiction writers.

The seriousness with which national security organizations and agencies approach fiction is perhaps best captured by former secretary of defense Donald Rumsfeld's well-known articulation of the concept of "unknown unknowns." At a news briefing on February 12, 2002, in what many now see as a defining moment in the development of the United States' post-9/11 national security paradigm, Rumsfeld outlined his epistemology of national security threats:

Reports that say that something hasn't happened are always interesting to me, because as we know, there are known knowns;

there are things we know we know. We also know there are
known unknowns; that is to say we know there are some things
we do not know. But there are also unknown unknowns—the
ones we don't know we don't know. And if one looks throughout
the history of our country and other free countries, it is the latter
category that tend to be the difficult ones.[6]

Later, reflecting on unknown unknowns in Errol Morris's documentary *The Unknown Known* (2013), Rumsfeld states that "you can only
know more about those things by imagining what they might be."[7]
Rumsfeld positions *imagining* threats as equivalent to *knowing* about
threats; knowing about what we don't know we don't know, in other
words, requires a specific kind of engagement with the imagination
that Rumsfeld refers to in this film as military "intelligence." Echoing
the 9/11 Commission, Rumsfeld also states in the documentary that
his greatest fear as secretary of defense was "the danger that we can
be surprised because of a failure of imagining what might happen."
Such a failure of the imagination, Rumsfeld claims, is exactly what
happened with the September 11 attacks on the World Trade Center
and the Pentagon. We did not imagine that they could happen, so we
were not prepared when they did. The danger for Rumsfeld, in other
words, arises not from not knowing but rather from failing to imagine what we don't know about because it hasn't happened. While we
can't know what will happen in the future, he claims we should try
to imagine everything that could possibly happen so that we can prepare ourselves for any outcome. Rumsfeld's remarks, coupled with
SIGMA's involvement with the national security community, stage
a central concern of this book. They illustrate a specific practice of
contemporary national security: the use of fiction to produce knowledge about possible future threats.

   Training for Catastrophe focuses on how, in the wake of the September 11 attacks, U.S. national security agencies and organizations
utilize this mode of knowledge production as the cornerstone of the
national security paradigm known as preparedness. Preparedness,
the domestic component of the U.S. war on terror, is modeled after
counterterrorism efforts. Like the military doctrine of preemption,
which espouses the need to act on national security threats before
they fully materialize, it emphasizes action before the fact by training people to imagine and respond to disasters before they happen.[8]

However, preparedness does not restrict itself to counterterrorism alone; under preparedness, natural disasters, industrial accidents, disease outbreaks, and terrorist attacks all constitute threats to national security and therefore events for which citizens should learn to prepare. As a national security paradigm designed mainly for use within the "homeland," preparedness supports the waging of endless war abroad by providing its ready-made justification. If we are not safe at home, as preparedness clearly implies, then, it also states, we need to eliminate the sources of the threats—which ultimately originate elsewhere or from "other" people—that endanger us. The potential sources of these threats are as theoretically limitless as the disasters for which people should prepare. While discussions of preemption, counterterrorism, and national security generally are familiar to literary and cultural studies, preparedness as such remains understudied in these fields.[9] This book not only brings the resources of literary and cultural studies to bear on the national security paradigm of preparedness; it also demonstrates how preparedness matters to these fields by focusing on the national security paradigm's investment in fiction. By examining materials produced by or adjacent to national security agencies—including policy documents, workplace disaster training manuals, emergency management textbooks, training exercises, political speeches, preparedness plans, online games, graphic narratives, and political thrillers—as aesthetic objects in their own right, I show how these preparedness materials use fiction toward certain political ends.[10] The value the federal government places on state-sponsored fictions used for national security purposes positions the national security state as an important producer of fiction within the contemporary culture industry.

Training for Catastrophe investigates the philosophy of fiction driving the ostensibly practical, fact-based discourses of contemporary U.S. national security and connects it to the ideology underlying preparedness. This philosophy is one in which fictional events are just as important as actual events, even though they are explicitly named and acknowledged as fiction. In the context of preparedness, using fictional disasters to produce knowledge about what might happen means insisting both that these disasters are imagined and unreal and that they are phenomena we can observe empirically and gather "intelligence" about, as Rumsfeld put it. Preparedness operates, in other words, not by tricking people into believing that fictional disasters have actually happened, or even that they could actually happen, but rather by asking people to treat explicitly fictional events as if they are real. In this way, preparedness operates as part of a political project to depoliticize disaster, and preparedness materials employ seemingly apolitical formal elements of fiction or concepts related to fiction, such as realism, genre, character, and plot, to advance this project. I refer to this mode of persuasion as training.

Preparedness training focuses on teaching people to regard disaster as normal. This normalization positions events like natural disasters, industrial accidents, and disease outbreaks as equivalent to terrorist attacks: all are threats to national security, all are inevitable or unstoppable, and all should be expected as part of daily life. Training people to respond to all disasters in similar ways, preparedness materials argue, will help protect the homeland, enable rapid response to disaster, and ensure that communities will bounce back stronger than ever. But this normalization of disaster does not actually extend to all disasters, and preparedness training is not addressed to all people. The flip side of preparedness discourse's insistence that some disasters are normal is its refusal to engage with other disasters. Preparedness training is designed to uphold the ethnonationalism of the national security state—to protect whiteness, and to protect the homeland as an implicitly white space—by teaching people to ignore or deny the existence of the many disasters of white supremacy. As disasters that help maintain, instead of threaten, the boundaries and membership of the homeland, these disasters fall outside the purview of preparedness. The refusal of preparedness materials to prepare people for these disasters is just as important to understanding preparedness as a national security paradigm as is its emphasis on preparing people for hurricanes and chemical spills.

This book articulates an overlooked use of fiction today: its role in generating consent for national security policies and practices. In a time when the teaching and study of fiction are generally denigrated and defunded, and popular discussions of fiction's social roles are often restricted to the realms of leisure or entertainment,

I follow the federal government in insisting on the importance of fiction to the production not just of political subjects but also of political paradigms more generally. This reliance on fiction forms a foundation of the post-9/11 security state through almost two decades of war on terror. *Training for Catastrophe* thus advances the argument that preparedness materials should be understood not necessarily as literature but rather as an integral part of twenty-first-century American literary history.

Preparedness and the Securitization of Disaster

Scholars in the interdisciplinary field of security studies have produced a large body of scholarship on preparedness. Working largely in the social sciences, including political science, anthropology, sociology, and cultural geography, these scholars have focused on preparedness as a policy program. They have investigated the history of preparedness and traced its development throughout the latter half of the twentieth century; they have critiqued its emphasis on individual action and responsibility and connected it to the larger forces of neoliberalism; and they have theorized its relationship to older forms of speculative managerial practices like insurance.[11] Generally, they have defined preparedness through its emphasis on the enactment of possible future catastrophes to prepare people to respond to the emergence of these disasters. Because the probability and severity of such events cannot be calculated, preparedness emphasizes institutional readiness and emergency management rather than prevention. Officials undergo training in how to handle a variety of potential catastrophic threats—terrorist attacks, natural disasters, industrial accidents, pandemics—using the same protocols for response. They also undergo training in how to develop procedures for determining who the first responders on the scene should be, what resources should be sent where, and how best to protect and ensure the continued functioning of vital infrastructure during and after a disaster. Preparedness is also public facing. As the many training exercises created by the federal government for use in workplaces and schools demonstrate, preparedness training is often designed for members of the general public. To develop the best practices for response, this training is not concerned with prediction or probabilistic calculation so much as it is with imagi-nation. As Andrew Lakoff writes, preparedness exercises "[enact] a vision of the dystopian future in order to develop a set of operational criteria for response."[12] Along with preemption and the environ-mental doctrine of precaution, it is a mode of what Ben Anderson has called "anticipatory action," or a rationality of governance that uses the future or a range of possible futures to justify action in the present.[13] As Louise Amoore puts it, preparedness and related re-gimes of security are concerned with "the governing of emergent, uncertain, *possible* futures."[14]

While this study is bound to a specific historical and national context—the United States after September 11, 2001—I also want to resist the notion that the attacks of September 11 changed every-thing for the United States.[15] Scholars have traced the emergence of what we now know as preparedness, for instance, at least as far back as the early Cold War.[16] During the Cold War, state and local officials realized they could use techniques from nuclear prepared-ness and civil defense exercises to prepare for natural disasters, and attempts were made as early as the late 1940s and 1950s to integrate civil defense and natural disaster response.[17] This integration was formally established at the federal level in the 1970s through a series of legislative acts and institutional reorganizations. In 1972, the De-fense Civil Preparedness Agency was created as a separate defense agency within the Department of Defense, a reorganization that formally expanded the agency's responsibilities to include "helping communities plan and prepare for peacetime disasters."[18] In 1976, Congress passed an amendment to the 1950 Federal Civil Defense Act mandating that all resources required and maintained under the Federal Civil Defense Act could be used to mitigate the effects of natural disasters. And in 1979, Congress moved the responsibil-ity for managing natural disasters and other "peacetime" disasters under the purview of the newly created Federal Emergency Man-agement Agency (FEMA).[19]

The establishment of FEMA formalized a shift in the federal government's conceptualization of disaster that had been slowly occurring throughout the Cold War. Since its inception, FEMA has practiced "all-hazards planning," a core tenet of modern emergency management. All-hazards planning promotes the generalization and standardization of disaster response, treating many different disasters in the same way by identifying how phenomena as varied as earthquakes, floods, and industrial accidents share similar response and management needs.[20] It focuses not on the prevention of these disasters but rather on preparing for their eventual occurrence. The national security community primarily associated all-hazards planning with natural disasters throughout the 1980s and thus understood it as an application of techniques borrowed from the realm of national security and applied to the realm of emergency management. However, the end of the Cold War accelerated the blurring of these two realms. This "new era" in national security, as one White House report published in 1990 put it, brought with it the so-called proliferation of national security threats, which included not only things like terrorist attacks but also natural disasters and disease outbreaks.[21] Throughout the 1990s, government officials began to understand these events not just as natural disasters but also, and more importantly, as security threats.[22]

Conceptualizing hurricanes as "security threats" epitomizes the movement from all-hazards planning to preparedness as it is practiced today.[23] This way of thinking about disasters—what scholars in security studies often refer to as the securitization of disaster—was institutionalized after the attacks of September 11, 2001, with the passing of the USA PATRIOT Act in October 2001 and the establishment of DHS in 2002. The creation of DHS, and the incorporation of the Federal Emergency Management Agency into DHS, installed preparedness and related forms of anticipatory action at the center of U.S. national security and military policy. This brief history highlights the fact that preparedness policies and plans were able to so swiftly dominate all aspects of U.S. national security after 9/11 because they were already well established within national security agencies and organizations. The formation of DHS in 2002 represents a moment of coalescence, not creation. It brought together formerly distinct institutions and agencies, each with its own history, policies, and practices of national security, and standardized their approaches. In other words, after 9/11, preparedness and related forms of anticipatory action no longer constituted just one possible approach to U.S. national security; they constituted the most ubiquitous approach.[24]

Preparedness and the Use of Fiction

The post-9/11 era of preparedness has been remarkably imaginatively productive. While scholarship on preparedness in security
studies discusses speculation as a more general cognitive mode or
philosophy of security, this work rarely takes preparedness materials themselves and the fictions they produce as its primary objects of
study. Likewise, while recent years have witnessed growing interest
in national security among scholars in literary studies, the majority
of this work examines novels or films that contextualize or critique
national security, not national security materials as such.[25] *Training for Catastrophe*, however, takes the "science fictional" quality of
preparedness materials themselves as its starting point. Preparedness training exercises and other materials work not by controlling
the future to ensure an event does not happen but rather by prolif-
erating many possible "futures" in the present to habituate people
to these events. Like speculative and science fiction, that is, these
materials "ope[n] up a future," or many futures, by producing them
in the here and now.[26] The fictional disasters these materials create and document to train people in emergency response include
everything from fictional terrorist attacks to imagined earthquakes,
tsunamis, and hurricanes to science fictional zombie pandemics. I
show how these preparedness materials, even when not discussing
or creating explicitly fictional disasters, utilize concepts and techniques from fiction to train people to respond to potential future
disasters in particular ways. By paying attention to the function of
concepts like characterization and emplotment in preparedness
training materials, this book reveals how the national security state
puts fiction to work for its own purposes—how it produces actual
fictions of its own, and how it borrows concepts and techniques
from the group of cultural activities we might call "fiction making"
more generally.[27]

Far from denigrating fiction for its unreality or uselessness, national security agencies and organizations believe fiction is an important way of learning about the world. Indeed, this investment
in the pedagogical value of fiction is what ties preparedness to literary criticism and what makes preparedness an important site
of study for literary scholarship in particular. The budget for DHS

offers one way of understanding how much the contemporary U.S. national security state values fiction.[28] In 2017, for example, the total enacted budget for DHS—including its subsidiary agencies, such as FEMA and Immigration and Customs Enforcement (ICE)—was $41.1 billion. About $420.3 million of that was earmarked for both "preparedness and protection" and "education, training, and exercises." If we expand that category to include the budget for preparedness training grants to federal, state, and local agencies and nongovernmental organizations ($2.75 billion), the total amount budgeted for preparedness training in 2017 was about $3.17 billion. By comparison, the total 2017 enacted budgets for the National Endowment for the Arts (NEA) and the National Endowment for the Humanities (NEH) were each $149.8 million, or a combined total of $299.6 million.[29]

Obviously, these are general figures, and not all of the money in these budgets is used for creating or discussing fiction. But as the budget for funding preparedness training at the state and local levels demonstrates ($2.75 billion), preparedness training designed and funded by federal agencies doesn't occur only in governmental contexts. It occurs in workplaces, schools, and local communities. In fact, much of preparedness training in nongovernmental or non-policy-related contexts in the United States is organized, designed, or funded by DHS or one of its subsidiaries. The potential audience for preparedness training, in other words, extends not just to government officials but also to many broad segments of the general public. From this perspective, DHS is the largest federal funder of and advocate for the value of fiction in the United States today.

There is nothing unusual, of course, about the use of fiction in political discourse, and many have emphasized the importance of myth, fantasy, and fiction to contemporary American politics in particular. For example, Donald Pease, building on Jacqueline Rose's work on the role of fantasy in public and private life, has used the term *state fantasy* to describe the phenomenon by which "the state's rules and norms can be experienced as internal to the citizens' desire."[30] State fantasies are not delusions or mystifications but rather representations of "the relationship with the national order that US citizens want to have."[31] Similarly, Timothy Melley has argued that fiction is essential to understanding the post–World War II U.S. national security state because during the Cold War, "certain forms of fiction became crucial in helping Americans imagine, or fantasize about, US foreign policy."[32] As the national security state became more secretive in the second half of the twentieth century, Melley argues, the public sphere of state policy gave way to "the covert sphere," a "cultural imaginary shaped by both institutional secrecy and public fascination with the secret work of the state."[33] The covert sphere is dominated by narrative fiction that provides people with a way to "know" about the secret activities of the state without actually knowing about them, and that provides the state with plausible deniability. For both Pease and Melley, fiction is a form of "unknowing" or "half-knowledge" akin to Fredric Jameson's concept of the political unconscious.[34] It acts as a representation of or a mechanism for forging a national unconscious, a way of knowing via denial and repression, without holding that knowledge in one's consciousness—"the stuff of dreams, fantasies, troubled awakenings," as Melley puts it.[35]

This association of fiction with the Jamesonian political unconscious is not what I mean when I talk about how preparedness uses fiction, however. Rather than a kind of unknowing or half-knowledge, fiction for the national security state is a technique of knowledge acquisition. Preparedness materials make use of fiction to produce knowledge about things that haven't happened and to perform their political work. "Literary" concepts like realism, genre, character, and plot give officials the means to claim to know about these events, lend preparedness training exercises realism without plausibility, train people to think about disaster according to specific genre conventions, enable the characterization of citizens of the homeland as heroes, and make it possible to imagine terrorist attacks that haven't happened as plots.[36]

The many uses to which preparedness materials put fiction revolve around the normalization of disaster, both potential and actual. From one perspective, many, influenced by Giorgio Agamben, have connected this normalization of disaster to a broader characterization of the U.S. national security state since the beginning of the Cold War: as existing in a permanent state of exception. For Agamben, the state of exception is both within and outside of the rule of law, a situation in which "the emergency becomes the rule, and the very distinction between peace and war . . . becomes impossible."[37] The state of exception is characterized by an expansion of executive power to coincide with the executive's (nominally reserved and time-limited) wartime or emergency powers. Scholars have argued that, in the U.S. context, the ideological shift to a permanent state of exception began after World War II with the signing of the National Security Act of 1947. This shift has justified war elsewhere in the name of security at home.[38] From this perspective, the normalization of disaster by preparedness materials is one aspect of the ideological project of the state of exception; it is yet another way in which the exception becomes the rule by immersing citizens in the rhythms and habits of constant emergency.[39]

The concepts of biopolitics and necropolitics also provide ways of understanding the normalization of disaster as part of the everyday, bureaucratic work of governing that the security state performs. For Michel Foucault, biopolitics operates at the level of the population and describes methods of regulating and controlling it to proliferate life.[40] In a well-known critique of this concept, Achille Mbembe argues that biopower does not sufficiently account for the death-dealing power of the modern state, or what he terms *necropolitics*.[41] Following from Foucault and Mbembe, scholars have emphasized the security state's insidious investment in the valorization of life at home to justify unending violence elsewhere. Biopolitics and necropolitics have thus provided a rich theoretical framework for understanding how the national security state seeks to render some lives killable so that it may foster and manage the lives of others.[42]

Neither Agamben's state of exception nor Foucault's biopolitics nor Mbembe's necropolitics, however, fully accounts for the specificities of the subject's encounter with preparedness materials themselves. By focusing on what actual preparedness materials aim to do, or on the modes of thought and action they encourage, *Training for Catastrophe* shifts the site of its interventions from the conceptual frameworks that inform national security to the materials that describe the everyday practices of preparedness. These materials are contradictory and often highly weird, a complexity that can get lost in more abstract accounts of national security. Fictions produced by the national security state are always stranger and more complicated than the national security state can admit, and because of this complexity, preparedness materials reward close analysis. Indeed, one of the contentions of this book is that close analysis of the aesthetics, form, and rhetoric of these materials is necessary to understand how preparedness actually works.

In highlighting the practices of preparedness, this book also argues for a shift in understanding the affective valence of this national security paradigm. Generally speaking, because catastrophes and disasters are defined as unforeseen, sudden events that fundamentally disrupt the normal flow of life, the affects and emotions usually associated with catastrophe include fear, anxiety, and trauma.[43] When scholars have written about affect and post-9/11 U.S. national security, they have tended to do so in these terms. For example, Brian Massumi argues that preemption "ingrain[s] in the bodies of the populace" an "anticipatory affective response to signs of fear even in contexts where one is clearly in no present danger," abstracting fear so that its "quality suffuses the atmosphere."[44] This, Massumi writes, "has obvious political control benefits"; people's fear legitimates the threat of catastrophe itself, regardless of whether any "actual" catastrophe materializes, because one always could have materialized.[45] Richard Grusin also identifies fear as integral to what he terms *premediation,* "a form of medial preemption" that seeks to mediate future disasters or violent events by depicting them—on the news, in the media more generally, and in movies and television shows—before they occur in the present. As a logic of twenty-first-century media, premediation is prophylactic: it seeks "to maintain a low level of fear in the present" so as "to prevent a recurrence of the kind of tremendous media shock that the United States and much of the networked world experienced on 9/11."[46] Grusin argues that premediation has the effect of preparing "the media public" to accept future events, such as the War in Iraq, "as a *fait accompli*" before such events actually happen.[47] In these accounts, fear is the prevailing instrument of political power.

I argue, however, that fear is not the only, or even the most salient, affective mechanism through which preparedness performs its political work. Rather than emphasizing the shock of unexpected disaster or the terror of violent acts, preparedness materials advance an understanding of catastrophe as expected and as recurring; rather than fostering fear, they teach people how to control their fear so as to act when faced with disaster. Preparedness training is about habit formation, and preparedness materials emphasize their own version of what Lauren Berlant has termed *crisis ordinariness*, a conception of normal, everyday life that focuses on processes of living on in the catastrophic present.[48] Such processes include learning techniques of what Berlant calls "neutralizing affect management," a kind of "ordinary compartmentalization" that can elicit a wide range of behaviors and feelings, including "coasting, skimming, browsing, distraction, apathy, coolness, counter-absorption, assessments of scale, picking one's fights."[49] Catastrophes are violent and disruptive upheavals, yes, but preparedness materials emphasize time and time again that they are also ongoing, ordinary facets of everyday life. This is why preparedness as a whole is so invested in the concept of resilience, which DHS defines as "the ability to withstand and recover rapidly from deliberate attacks, accidents, natural disasters, as well as unconventional stresses, shocks and threats to our economy and democratic system."[50] As Deepa Kumar has argued, the concept of resilience is "a form of emotion management" for the post-9/11 national security state; it emphasizes the control and management of fear so that people can bounce back stronger than ever from disaster.[51]

The corollary to the argument that preparedness materials teach people to regard disaster as normal, however, is that they also teach them to ignore and deny other kinds of disasters. As Joseph Masco puts it, U.S. national security "works to leave unaddressed the increasing vulnerability and insecurity of everyday American life."[52] Indeed, the making ordinary of catastrophe that preparedness materials carry out is centered on developing practices of affective management that make the effects of specific kinds of catastrophes in some places and for some people easier to handle. This book argues that how preparedness materials train people to distribute their attention and what they direct them to pay attention to have much to do with who preparedness materials imagine as the target of their address: the people of the homeland. The people of the homeland are those whose lives are deemed worth protecting, and they thus provide much of the ideological justification for the practices of the national security state. Although preparedness materials claim that they refer to "the nation" or "the people" as a unified, post-racial whole, I follow Kumar and others in emphasizing that the phrase "the people of the homeland" always already refers to a specific audience: the people of the homeland are implicitly white.[53] Preparedness materials never explicitly name their target audience as white, of course; rather, they address themselves to whiteness in general and in the abstract, while also depicting people of color as happy citizens of the homeland. Like many products of contemporary corporate and governmental discourse, their celebration of and commitment to an official liberal politics of multiculturalism protects them from charges of explicit racism while upholding the inherent ethnonationalism of contemporary U.S. national security.[54] These materials are therefore able, in Rey Chow's terms, to "pose as a liberalist alibi against violence" at the same time as they make violence against (implied nonwhite) others possible.[55]

I am indebted to scholars of color who have shown how seemingly invisible racialized practices, policies, and philosophies of the national security state structure its very existence. For instance, Kumar has excavated the long history of Islamophobia that has served as the cornerstone of U.S. and European empire.[56] Jasbir K. Puar has argued not only that counterterrorism discourses are implicitly racialized and sexualized in the contemporary U.S. security state but also that these discourses "illuminate the production of imbricated normative patriot and terrorist corporealities that cohere against and through each other."[57] In her study of the connections between twenty-first-century humanitarianism and the U.S. national security state, Inderpal Grewal shows how contemporary security institutions exercise both military might and soft power to extend empire and argues throughout that the soft power of these institutions "gain[s] traction because of [their] histories of white racial, masculinized sovereignty."[58] And addressing the lack of discussion of race within surveillance studies specifically, Simone Browne emphasizes that "the surveillance of blackness [is] often unperceivable within the study of surveillance," even while Blackness is "that nonnameable matter that matters the racialized disciplinary society." To name Blackness as integral to understanding practices of surveillance and therefore national security is, as Browne puts it, to "factor in how racism and antiblackness undergird and sustain the intersecting surveillances of our present order."[59] The work of these scholars challenges the absence of discussions of race and white supremacy in much of the scholarship about national security from security studies and places racialization at the center of the U.S. national security state.

Processes of racialization within national security, I show, draw on techniques often associated with the realm of the aesthetic, specifically those related to structures of address and figuration. By addressing themselves not necessarily to white people specifically but rather to whiteness more generally, preparedness materials are able to simultaneously be for "everyone" while also working as vehicles of white identification and subject formation. These materials position (always implied) whiteness as the universal target of address that includes anyone and everyone. Whiteness is usually, though not exclusively, only referred to or depicted in an abstract way in these materials, a way that attempts to maintain its distance from specific bodies or subject positions. But by relying on techniques drawn from fictions of all kinds, these materials also encourage specific subjects to identify with whiteness. They figure whiteness through the depiction of generic individuals, individuals meant to stand in for "anyone." These particular yet generic individuals, or, as I refer to them, characters, are vehicles for white identification that do not require explicit acknowledgment as such. Preparedness materials therefore not only address themselves abstractly to whiteness; they are also populated by nonraced but implicitly white figures.[60] These rhetorical and aesthetic techniques serve to differentiate the target audience for preparedness from "others" who are undeserving of the supposed protections of the national security state. Preparedness materials rely on these distinctions about whose lives matter for their political efficacy.

It is this political efficacy that is the target of this book's critique. I am not arguing that preparing for disasters is "bad" or that the government should stop doing it. Nor am I arguing, however, that people can or should improve the national security paradigm known as preparedness by encouraging the state to make, or by making themselves, more effective preparedness materials—whether "more effective" materials means materials that are more carefully constructed, more scientifically informed, more realistic, or more inclusive. Instead, I examine this concept of efficacy itself. As Sara Ahmed brings to our attention, "to exercise means to put into active use."[61] This book focuses on how materials like preparedness training exercises use fiction. To emphasize the use of fiction is to ask what fiction makes happen; more precisely, it is to ask what national security agencies believe fiction can make happen. These questions echo the connections between fiction and efficacy that have long been central to literary theory and practice, as well as literary scholars' more recent investment in the uses of fiction and literature more generally. Much of this scholarship has considered the force of fiction in reshaping the individual reader.[62] Joshua Landy's articulation of the value of reading (literary) fiction comes closest to how I argue the U.S. national security state understands the value of fiction and fictionality. Landy examines a selection of what he terms *formative fictions*, or "texts whose function it is to fine-tune our mental capacities." These fictions, he argues, equip readers with *"know-how," "skills,"* and training, "present[ing] themselves as spiritual exercises" or as "spaces for prolonged and active encounters that serve, over time, to hone our abilities and thus, in the end, to help us become who we are."[63] Preparedness shares with this understanding of the use of literature a project of training its audience, the conceit that it can imbue a reader or subject with the right "know-how" and "skills" for life as a citizen of the homeland. In this way, preparedness materials use fiction not only to address particular groups of people but also to call out to and isolate members of these audiences—to form individual subjects as such.

Preparedness is a paradigm of national security that speaks to and protects whiteness and that focuses mainly on individual response to disaster. As such, it is designed to make the collective political action that is necessary to meaningfully confront the many disasters with which people both in the United States and abroad are increasingly faced—some of which are disasters created and perpetuated by the national security state itself—seem undesirable, impossible, or irrelevant. Preparedness training teaches (some) people not just that it is their individual responsibility to prepare for and respond to coming catastrophe but also that such preparation and response are the only ways to deal with disaster. Your town was torn apart by a hurricane and your power was out for months? Preparedness training materials tell you to make sure that next time you have enough water and food to last two weeks. There was another "active-shooter event" at a school? Preparedness training materials tell you to teach students to hide in a closet. Preparedness training does not address the systemic nature of these disasters or teach people how to understand, for example, the changing climate at the root of the increased frequency and intensity of tropical storms or the white supremacy and misogyny at the root of many mass shootings. It is not designed to teach people to consider the political solutions to these political problems. Instead, it is designed to make such problems seem beyond the realm of politics altogether. This is what it means not only to treat disasters like security threats but also to treat security threats like disasters. Preparedness training makes events like mass shootings and terrorist attacks seem as natural as hurricanes or earthquakes. As Robert P. Marzec argues, the post-9/11 U.S. national security state "generates a political form of action that considers itself to be postpolitical."[64] Preparedness, document after document implies, is just about disaster response, not prevention, not quality of life, not social welfare, not justice.

Training for Catastrophe centers on the role of fiction in U.S. political life today. Readers of fiction, particularly of speculative and science fiction, have long emphasized its revolutionary potential to imagine alternative possibilities. Jameson, for example, has argued that science fiction and other speculative genres are "the answer to the universal ideological conviction that no alternative is possible, that there is no alternative to the system." This is because, Jameson contends, these genres allow us "to think the break" between their worlds and ours—to imagine different ways of life that throw the contingencies of present configurations of power into greater relief.[65] The U.S. national security state utilizes this same capacity to constrain political action. The fictions of preparedness also aim to imagine otherwise, "to think the break" between our world and the one to come. But the outcome of this imagining, in the context of preparedness, looks quite different from what critics and authors of science and speculative fiction have often described. David Palumbo-Liu has perhaps put it best: "today," he writes of post-9/11 U.S. national security broadly, "we find the deployment of Imagination for particular, antihumanistic purposes that channel the Imagination into specifically strategic and destructive modes of thinking, even while appropriating the rhetoric of the aesthetic."[66] I investigate preparedness, ultimately, by pushing this rationality to its limits.

The Plan

Chapter 1, "Training in an Empiricist Epistemology of Fiction," develops a foundational concept important for understanding preparedness training in general: what I call preparedness's *empiricist epistemology of fiction*. This phrase describes a way of thinking about fiction that, on one hand, insists it is unreal and imaginary and, on the other, assumes it depicts empirical phenomena we can analyze and that have consequences in reality. This epistemology aligns broadly with the epistemology of scientific modeling, on which the empiricist epistemology of fiction implicitly draws for its authority. However, its positivism is directed not toward prediction but rather toward simulation. The chapter begins by analyzing congressional hearing reports about the failed response to Hurricane Katrina to demonstrate this approach to fiction in action. I then turn to an oddly philosophical graphic narrative about earthquake preparedness to explore how preparedness materials encourage people to feel about this empiricist epistemology of fiction. The chapter's final section connects this understanding of fiction to preparedness's overall philosophy of training. By situating rhetoric about training from preparedness documents within existing scholarship in cultural studies about training, I show that being trained in preparedness means learning to respond to disaster out of habit. This conception of training turns our attention to its force in the present rather than its projections of the future. Preparedness training involves an experience of temporal dislocation that positions the present as unending.

While chapter 1 argues that an empiricist epistemology of fiction is a core tenet of the rationality of preparedness, chapter 2, "Realism: Consenting to the Possibilistic Logic of Preparedness," demonstrates how this rationality informs the aesthetics of preparedness materials. I focus in this chapter on Cold War–era nuclear disaster scenarios, a FEMA natural disaster training exercise, and a military zombie preparedness scenario. Building on scholarship about the relationship between realism and science fiction, I investigate what preparedness materials mean when they claim to be "realistic." The chapter's first section explores the disaster scenarios of Herman Kahn, a Cold War–era nuclear strategist who developed and popularized the disaster scenario for use in national security contexts. Kahn redefined the meaning of "plausibility" in these contexts to mean "anything that is possible," and chapter 2 positions this redefinition as foundational to the meaning of realism within preparedness. Next, I show how contemporary preparedness training exercises push this understanding of realism further by training their participants to consent to the reality of the fictions they enjoin them to enact. Preparedness training materials are designed to invite people to play along and to accept the events they depict as being just as real as actual events—without requiring participants to believe in the actuality or even potential actuality of these events. For preparedness, chapter 2 reveals, there is no actionable difference between fictional and actual events.

Chapter 3, "Thinking Generically: The Professional Management of Disaster," focuses on genre. Although preparedness materials themselves do not necessarily constitute their own genre, and while they incorporate elements from many different recognizable genres of fiction, they do train people to understand disaster according to specific genre conventions, a process I call *thinking generically*. This chapter argues that the term *generic* best captures the oscillation between *universality*, claiming to address anyone and everyone, and *particularity*, creating through this address the figure of the implicitly white professional, that preparedness materials enact. The chapter focuses on materials about professional training in preparedness, including the writing of former national security official Richard Clarke, author of several Tom Clancy–esque novels about terrorist attacks as well as a nonfictional memoir about September 11, 2001; FEMA's popular Active Shooter training exercise; and FEMA guidelines on how to design training exercises. Thinking generically is one mechanism through which people are trained to adopt a "professional" attitude toward disaster, regardless of whether they are in fact professional emergency managers or national security officials. The final part of the chapter considers what happens when training in thinking generically ostensibly fails by revisiting the reports about the federal failure to respond effectively to Hurricane Katrina discussed in chapter 1. Paradoxically, this failure can never be a failure of preparedness itself—even when it obviously is—if the generic expectations the training materials set up are met. But though preparedness materials, by their own logic, can never fail to train people, these reports argue that individual people can fail to be trained. Preparedness materials refer to these people, who are implicitly nonwhite, as "unprofessional." Taken together, the materials examined in this chapter reveal the people to whom preparedness addresses itself and who constitute the homeland as preparedness imagines it: "professionals," figures aligned with whiteness.

Whereas the first three chapters explore how preparedness uses fiction, the last two probe the limits of these uses by turning to preparedness discourse's own vocabulary—resilience and plot. These last two chapters also each end with a coda that rereads some of the preparedness materials discussed in that chapter in conjunction with Audre Lorde's "A Litany for Survival" and Jordan Peele's *Get Out*, respectively. These materials offer alternatives to the conceptions of security proffered by the state.

Chapter 4, "Character: The Resilience of the Hero," investigates one of the professional's supposedly most important moral virtues: resilience. Although preparedness materials seem to extol this quality, examining such materials closely reveals the range of contradictory attitudes they take toward resilient individuals. Emphasizing the origins of the term *resilience* in materials science and engineering, I argue that this affective range results from the paradoxical ways that resilient individuals are figured as both human and inhuman, as people worth emulating and as endlessly adaptable and flexible things. Resilience is discomfiting for preparedness materials, in other words, because of its relation to the state of being an object. Chapter 4 therefore relocates the oscillation between the general and the specific unearthed in chapter 3's discussion of genre to a discussion of character—a figure both general and specific, both person and thing. I trace the most resilient of characters, the hero, as it appears in three different examples of public-facing preparedness materials: in online games designed by or in consultation with FEMA about teaching children how to prepare for natural disasters;

in speeches by presidents on the anniversaries of the September 11, 2001, terrorist attacks; and in a comic published by the Centers for Disease Control and Prevention (CDC) as part of its popular zombie pandemic public awareness campaign. These materials all emphasize, paradoxically, the disintegration of the concept of the individual person under preparedness. Everyone becomes a character type—the hero—defined by her relationship to survival and death, especially when survival looks like something very close to death. The figure of the zombie pushes this understanding of heroism to its limit, as zombies, with their exceptional capacities for survival, become the emblematic characters of preparedness. Unlike the implicitly white professional of chapter 3, the figure of the zombie is historically and culturally aligned with Blackness, and the CDC narrative exemplifies how preparedness materials revile those who survive past all expectation. The chapter ends with a coda that rereads the CDC zombie preparedness materials—and the value of resilience—in the wake of Audre Lorde's 1978 poem "A Litany for Survival" to recover a different understanding of the value of survival by and for those who "were never meant to survive."[67]

Chapter 5, "Looking for the Plot: Counterterrorism and the Hermeneutics of Suspicion," turns to another formal preoccupation of preparedness materials through an examination of the workings of plot. Defining plot, pace Peter Brooks, as an interpretive activity, the chapter focuses on the tendency within counterterrorism discourse to imagine terrorist attacks as plots. I track how three different kinds of counterterrorism preparedness materials attempt to teach people to read for the plot: the infamous 2007 "radicalization model" created by the New York Police Department (NYPD), which is meant to describe the trajectory along which a Muslim person travels on his way toward committing a terrorist act; DHS's well-known "If You See Something, Say Something" public awareness campaign; and the Department of State's failed "Think Again Turn Away" public awareness campaign. The NYPD radicalization model and the "If You See Something, Say Something" campaign both address themselves to the people of the homeland, while the "Think Again Turn Away" campaign addresses itself to people outside the homeland considering joining Islamic terrorist groups. Reading these materials as inversions of one another highlights how the national security state uses the imaginative formations of plots and plotting to substitute objects and actions like backpacks and researching things on the internet for the figure of the terrorist, disavowing the racialization of that figure by this discourse. While chapter 4's consideration of resilience witnessed the disintegration of the category of personhood, chapter 5 shows how preparedness relies on substituting things for persons. The coda argues that the 2017 film *Get Out*, however, subverts the structure of seeing and saying implied by counterterrorism materials. I show how the film, like most horror films, also trains its viewers, like counterterrorism materials, to look for the plot (one of its taglines, not coincidentally, was "Say Something"). In critiquing the fantasy of control presented by counterterrorism materials produced by the state, *Get Out* offers a fantasy of the national security state turned against itself.

Training for Catastrophe ends by asking what to do with its arguments about preparedness. Despite the best efforts of some academics and policy makers alike, preparedness—and the related military doctrine of preemption—continues to dominate U.S. national security policy. Indeed, preparedness discourse seems to imagine that preparedness will continue forever, despite any critique. Accordingly, the book's epilogue, "The Uses of Fiction," turns to world building of a different kind, activism against the national security state, to emphasize the kind of action necessary to end the post-9/11 national security regime. It makes a case for understanding the creation of fiction as a collective endeavor and its effects and values as social rather than individual. Part of the work of preparedness training is to make the end of the current U.S. national security regime seem (for some people) undesirable, or, if not that, then unimaginable. My hope is that readers of this book will find a way to imagine otherwise.

1

Training in an Empiricist Epistemology of Fiction

The rationality of preparedness is fundamentally speculative. As I discussed in the introduction, preparedness and the associated military doctrine of preemption seek to manage and contain, as Donald Rumsfeld put it, "unknown unknowns," or those threats "we don't know we don't know" about.[1] With these words, Rumsfeld revealed the central place of epistemology and questions about what we know, what we might know, and what we cannot know within national security policy in the United States. Scholars have likewise tended to focus their discussions of preparedness and preemption on epistemology, specifically on uncertainty. For example, Brian Massumi, whose work on affect and national security has been widely influential, emphasizes that "the epistemology of preemption is . . . unabashedly one of *uncertainty*." He writes that this uncertainty arises "not due to a simple lack of knowledge" but rather because "the nature of the threat cannot be specified" and "this lack of knowledge about the nature of the threat can never be overcome."[2] Likewise, Ben Anderson, whose scholarship focuses on affect and emergency, writes that preparedness training scenarios are designed to explore "the contingency and complexity of an event—the uncertain character and effects of a 'catastrophic terrorist attack' as it unfolds to damage and destroy life."[3] Rumsfeld himself probably puts it best when he states that "the challenge" of our new post–Cold War age is "to defend our nation against the unknown, the uncertain, the unseen, the unexpected."[4]

This book shifts the frame of this discussion from uncertainty and unknowability to fiction. I emphasize that the production of fiction is one of the primary techniques for managing and controlling the uncertain and the unknown within preparedness discourse.[5] Focusing on fiction, however, does not mean leaving questions of epistemology behind. Rather, in this chapter, I show how government officials, policy makers, and emergency managers use fiction as a tool to produce knowledge about and therefore train people to respond to unknown threats. The exact nature of the threats for which preparedness exercises seek to train people may be unknown, in other words, but they are not unimagined. In fact, national security agencies and organizations devote much of their time, energy, and financial resources to this kind of imagination.

In attempting to manage and control the unknown, preparedness materials adopt what I call an empiricist epistemology of fiction, a stance that acknowledges the imaginative character of fiction at the same time as it treats fictional events as empirical phenomena. Broadly speaking, *empiricism* refers to the theory that knowledge derives primarily from sensory experience. As historians of science Steven Shapin and Simon Schaffer emphasize, empiricism depends "upon the generation of matters of fact that [are] objects of perceptual experience."[6] Likewise, historians of science Lorraine Daston and Peter Galison have argued that "empiricism in the service of scientific objectivity . . . demanded that the variability of observed phenomena be carefully heeded, rather than abstracted from or idealized."[7] To say that the rationality of preparedness depends on treating fictional disasters as empirical phenomena, then, is to say that this rationality insists on the existence of these disasters as independent phenomena that can be experienced as such, just like disasters that have actually occurred, and that can therefore become the basis of knowledge claims.

This understanding of fictional events as having an objective reality all their own does not conflict, in the context of preparedness, with the concomitant understanding of fiction as imaginative, or as describing events that are made up and have not actually occurred. The rationality of preparedness depends on both of these understandings of fiction at once. This empiricist epistemology of fiction is not unique to preparedness, however. Generally speaking, understanding projected possibilities as both unreal and empirical is also common, if implicitly, in practices of scientific modeling. Understood in this light, fictional disasters function as models of what could or what is likely to happen, and like scientific models, they are unreal in that they describe or enact things that don't actually exist. As the statistician George E. P. Box famously quipped, "all models are wrong," meaning models are, at best, only abstractions of real phenomena, not accurate representations of them.[8] In abstracting these phenomena, however, scientific models also make them available to sensory experience and observation—they make them objects of knowledge. As Box also said, although "all models are wrong, some are useful."[9] The equation of scientific models and fiction has also become more popular of late in philosophy of science, literary criticism, and popular discourse more generally. Philosopher Roman Frigg's article "Models and Fiction" is frequently cited in discussions of this view. Frigg claims that "scientific modelling shares important aspects in common with literary fiction," including that both fiction and models are "hypothetical systems" that are "not *defined* in contrast to truth" but rather are defined according to their shared "function to serve as . . . prop[s] in a game of make-believe."[10] Similarly, literary scholar Jesse Oak Taylor has argued that we can read some novels as models, particularly as models of climate change, because novels, like models, mediate climate change, which is the only way to experience that phenomenon. As Taylor writes, climate change "literally cannot be experienced firsthand," and so "mediation and modeling provide our only evidence of its existence."[11] Novels thus "provid[e] a model not merely of the climate 'as it is' but of the relationship between the climate as it is and the atmosphere as it is experienced."[12] Finally, in a piece recently published in the *New Yorker*, author Jonathan Franzen writes that while "scientists rely on complicated atmospheric modelling" "to project the rise in global mean temperature," as a writer of fiction, he does his "own kind of modelling" to produce stories. As he puts it, "I run various future scenarios through my brain."[13]

Importantly, the equivalence of fiction and scientific models described above is based on epistemological, not ontological, similarities. Like the sources cited in the previous paragraph, preparedness materials do not claim that the fictions they depict and enact are predictions of reality. Preparedness materials readily admit that the fictional disasters they depict and enact are "wrong," or not necessarily indicative of what may happen in reality. Just as a model that predicts the path of a hurricane is not the same thing as the actual path that hurricane takes, preparedness materials emphasize again and again that the fictional disasters they depict are different from actual disasters. Instead, these materials claim that fictional disasters, like scientific models, are tools of knowledge acquisition. Emergency managers and officials use exercises involving fictional hurricanes, for example, to determine how best to respond in the event of an actual hurricane, including where to send supplies, how to evacuate people to safety, and how to restore power and telephone service. This ordinary and commonsensical approach to training people how to handle things that haven't happened or with which they don't already have experience is what it means to use fiction to produce knowledge. Fictional disasters are acknowledged as unreal: everyone knows that the "facts" about a hurricane designed for use in a training scenario aren't real facts because the hurricane didn't actually occur. Fictional disasters are also, however, treated *as if* they are real events for the purposes of pedagogy: nevertheless, a hurricane preparedness exercise treats such information as facts from which people can learn meaningful and useful knowledge.[14]

This empiricist philosophy of fiction implicitly aligns the fictional disasters of preparedness with scientific practice and expertise. As we will see throughout the next three chapters of this book, preparedness materials often rely on the language of science and scientific reasoning to position the fictions they create as authoritative. Treating fiction as simultaneously real and unreal—like scientists treat models—is one way of creating this authority. However, the authority of preparedness materials to depict "future" disasters does not ultimately rest on such claims to supposed scientific authority. In chapter 2, for example, we will see how far-fetched or completely impossible disasters, such as zombie apocalypses, also provide fertile ground for preparedness training exercises. And in chapter 3, we will explore the fact that a conception of generic professionalism is more important to preparedness than expertise. Despite their claims to the contrary, preparedness materials are more interested in producing the right attitudes and thoughts about di-

saster in the people they train than they are in producing scientifically informed disaster response protocols. Preparedness training,
in other words, is a process of manufacturing consent among participants, specifically the consent, however implied or nominal, to
continue waging endless war "elsewhere" in the name of national
security. This book will show how this consent hinges on the conception of fiction at the heart of preparedness: its empiricist epistemology of fiction.

This chapter begins by examining congressional hearing reports
about the federal failure to respond effectively to Hurricane Katrina
to demonstrate how this empiricist epistemology of fiction operates. I then turn to an oddly philosophical graphic narrative about
earthquake preparedness that instructs the preparedness trainee in
adopting the right attitude toward the empiricist epistemology of
fiction. This attitude depends not on claims to scientific knowledge
but rather on a nihilistic acceptance of, paradoxically, the futility
of preparedness. The chapter's final section connects the empiricist
epistemology of fiction to the overall philosophy of training that
preparedness materials articulate. What does it mean to undergo
training in the context of preparedness? I argue that preparedness
training is a process of ongoing habit formation that relies on persuasion instead of coercion to teach people to respond to disasters in
the correct ways. This conception of training turns our attention to
its force in the present rather than its depictions of the future. Preparedness training, as we will see, aims not just to persuade people
to think and act in certain ways but also to last forever.

"The Simulation Became Reality":
The Rationality of Preparedness

In July 2004 in southeast Louisiana, one year before Hurricane Katrina would hit, FEMA sponsored a large hurricane preparedness
training exercise that brought together more than three hundred
local, state, and federal emergency response officials. The fictional
hurricane created for the exercise, Hurricane Pam, was designed
as a Category 3 hurricane that, in the information given to participants, caused 10 to 20 feet of flooding throughout most of New
Orleans and that affected more than 1 million people, resulting in

175,000 injuries and more than 60,000 deaths. The point of the exercise was for participants to use this fictional information about a fictional hurricane to develop comprehensive plans at the state and local levels for responding to actual hurricanes.

After FEMA's disastrous failure to respond to Hurricane Katrina only one year later, the Senate Committee on Homeland Security and Governmental Affairs held a hearing about the Hurricane Pam exercise as part of its efforts to determine the reasons behind FEMA's failure. During this hearing, exercise participants, emergency managers, and senators alike defended the Hurricane Pam exercise by positioning it as epistemologically equivalent to Hurricane Katrina. The hearing transcript's appendix, for example, includes a table that compares the "projected consequences for Hurricane Pam and actual results produced by Katrina" (Figure 1).[15] This table, which refers to these "projected consequences" as "data," is meant to provide evidence of Hurricane Pam's effectiveness because of how it "actually and eerily predicted" the effects of Katrina (4). Participants in the hearing repeatedly say things like "Katrina was a 'replication' of Pam," "Pam became Katrina," Pam was "a dry run for the real thing," and "the simulation became reality" (4, 2). As Joe Lieberman put it during the hearing, if Katrina had made a direct hit on New Orleans instead of landing about fifteen miles to the east of the city, "67,000 deaths would have resulted" because "that is what the Pam exercise projected" (4).

Something more than analogy is happening here. By this logic, Hurricane Pam was not merely like Hurricane Katrina. Rather, the statements hearing participants made emphasize both that there is actually no epistemological difference between a fictional hurricane and an actual hurricane in the context of preparedness (the fictional Hurricane Pam predicted the effects of actual Hurricane Katrina, so the simulation "became" the reality) and that Hurricane Pam is of course fundamentally different from Hurricane Katrina (Katrina wasn't an exact replica of Pam, obviously, and we are lucky that it wasn't). Hurricane Pam is therefore evidence both of what *would* happen in the future and of what *could* or *might* happen in the future.

This is preparedness's empiricist epistemology of fiction in action. On one hand, Hurricane Pam, a fictional hurricane, is treated like a directly observable phenomenon from which participants

"Hurricane Pam" Data	Actual Results from Hurricane Katrina
20 inches of rain	18 inches of rain
City of New Orleans under 10–20 feet of water	Up to 20 feet of flooding in some areas of New Orleans
Overtopping of levees	Levees breached
Over 55,000 in public shelters prior to landfall	Approximately 60,000 people in public shelters prior to landfall
Louisiana Offshore Oil Port (LOOP) shut down pre-landfall and back on in 2–3 days after storm—LOOP handles 12% of US crude oil imports	The LOOP was inoperable from August 29 to September 2 (5 days)
9 refineries shut down during storm	7 refineries in LA shut down during the storm
57 chemical plants shut down during storm. Many flooded and with no power	More than 50 chemical plants shut down during the storm
Over 1.1 million Louisiana residents displaced (500,000 households affected & 230,000 children)	1 million Gulf Coast residents displaced for the long-term; majority are LA residents
Leeville Bridge on LA 1 collapsed (west of city)	New Orleans Twin Span bridge collapsed in sections (east of city)
20,000 boat-based rescue missions and about 1,000 helicopter-based rescue missions	33,500 US Coast Guard missions; 9,313 National Guard missions; 2,911 DoD active duty missions. The Louisiana Department of Wildlife and Fisheries have rescued more than 16,000 people.
786,359 people in Louisiana lose electricity at initial impact	881,400 people in Louisiana reported to be without electricity the day after impact
Over 12.5 million tons of debris	22 million tons of debris in LA; 12 million tons in Orleans Parish; clean up could take up to 2 years
Coastal marsh erosion	Coastal erosion caused by Katrina at landfall equaled one year of erosion in that area (25 square miles a year)
Sewage treatment facilities not working in the metropolitan area	Sewage treatment facilities not working in the metropolitan area
233,986 collapsed buildings	250,000 homes destroyed

Figure 1. Comparisons between fictional Hurricane Pam and actual Hurricane Katrina included as Table 1 in the congressional hearing report on the effectiveness of the Hurricane Pam exercise.

can collect data, measure outcomes, and draw conclusions. This understanding of fiction echoes how emergency management textbooks—materials designed to turn students of emergency management into professional planners and managers—understand fiction. These textbooks emphasize that "hypothetical scenarios" provide the same kind of knowledge about how to respond to disasters as historical case studies; they are in fact the "corollary" of such case studies, because both fictional scenarios and historical case studies "can help trainees to learn to analyze events or situations in depth."[16] The epistemological equivalence between fiction and nonfiction—or even fiction and reality—is also implicit in how such textbooks explain the value of training exercises based on fictional scenarios. Because "it serves little good to wait until [an actual disaster event] occurs" to test preparedness plans, training exercises serve as a way "to evaluate the efficiency and effectiveness of the plan and its components and to test the systems, facilities, and personnel involved in implementing the plan."[17] Exercises therefore act as a "substitute for 'battlefield experience'"; they are just like the real thing, epistemologically speaking, only repeatable and finetunable.[18] Like participants in the hearing about the Hurricane Pam exercise, emergency management educational materials emphasize that fictional scenarios and exercises provide information that is functionally equivalent to that provided by real disasters. Students and trainees can therefore act on this information when formulating preparedness plans.

At the same time, preparedness materials also allow for and even rely on the distance that separates fiction from reality, the distance that defines fiction-making as a speculative enterprise. This distance has nothing to do with the perceived realism of fictional events—with whether we think they are likely to happen—only with the fact that fiction, by definition, describes made-up events and people. Just as we know when we read a novel that no matter how realistic that novel is, the events it describes have not and will not necessarily happen, preparedness materials also emphasize that there is no necessary connection between the disasters they describe or depict and what may happen in the future. Preparedness is not about predicting the future or preventing disasters, emergency managers proclaim over and over—it is about imagining possibilities. As one emergency management textbook puts it, hypothetical scenarios "free [trainees] from the constraints of preconditioned outcomes."[19] There is never any necessary relation between what people imagine and what might happen, preparedness materials insist again and again; in fact, the disasters people imagine, simply because they are by definition imaginary events, will never happen exactly as they are imagined. Preparedness's empiricist epistemology of fiction maintains that while it's true that Hurricane Pam can provide us with data that we can use to measure the effectiveness of preparedness plans, for example, it is also true that these "data" need not have any relation to actual events in order to be effective as a training device. Exercises are, after all, only "substitute[s] for 'battlefield experience.'"

This way of understanding fiction is not an inconsistency on the part of preparedness materials, nor does it involve tricking or deluding people into believing something false. It's also not a symptom of some kind of undecidability between fact and fiction. Rather, it is fundamental to this national security paradigm. Security studies scholar Andrew Lakoff accurately defines preparedness as "a form of rationality for approaching questions of domestic security in the United States," but it is important to remember that this rationality is speculative and therefore fiction-friendly.[20] It relies on fiction-making as a form of knowledge production while also declaring itself to be a "science and knowledge-based" approach to disaster management.[21] This is paradoxical, but it's not a contradiction: it is what defines the rationality of preparedness *as a rationality.* Unlike other speculative modes of reasoning, such as probability theory, preparedness is not concerned with techniques for discerning what is likely to happen. Although certain kinds of preparedness materials sometimes employ probabilistic methods, preparedness materials are not usually interested in trying to assess the likelihood of specific future disasters. Rather, as we will see in chapter 2, preparedness materials are concerned with possibility; they focus on imagining and experiencing future disasters, no matter how likely or unlikely such disasters may be. The facts on which they depend include both facts about things that have actually happened and facts about fictions, about things that haven't actually happened and that never will. As we will see throughout this book, preparedness materials need to have it both ways. Fiction needs to be a real, tangible thing that trainees can experience and examine and from which they can learn, but it also needs to remain fictional, exciting but unreal, engaging but safe, always about to occur—never the way things actually are but only what they are always about to become if we don't act soon.

Living As-If

I have been arguing that the power of fiction to both inform and engage is at the center of preparedness as a paradigm of national security. But however much preparedness materials emphasize what people can learn from fictional disasters, they emphasize how people should feel about these disasters more. I want to turn our attention now to a very different kind of preparedness material: the strange graphic narrative *A River in Egypt*, published in the 2008 volume *The L.A. Earthquake Sourcebook*. This volume is the result of a three-year public awareness and preparedness campaign created and led by students and faculty at the Art Center College of Design in Los Angeles, with funding from FEMA, the California Governor's Office of Emergency Services, State Farm Insurance, and others.[22] While not a training exercise itself, *A River in Egypt* is a philosophical meditation on the underlying logic of preparedness training, and it builds its plot around describing the correct attitude toward preparedness's empiricist epistemology of fiction. If preparedness materials claim that fiction is both real and unreal, that fictional disasters are both empirical and speculative phenomena, then how should people think and feel about these disasters, and about the imperative to prepare for them?

A River in Egypt depicts a debate between the protagonist, Marty, seemingly a stand-in for the narrative's author Marty Kaplan, and his unnamed "friend" about the value of earthquake preparedness.[23] While Marty feels good about all he has done to prepare his house and his family members for a potential earthquake, his friend exclaims that he is "so in denial," asking Marty if he truly believes that "all this boy scout stuff is gonna save your ass from the BIG ONE?"[24] What unfolds is Marty's defense of preparedness, to which I will turn later. Interspersed between the pages of the graphic narrative is a document titled "The 7 Steps to Earthquake Preparedness," an earthquake preparedness plan developed for the 2007 Dare to Prepare earthquake safety campaign by the Earthquake Country Alliance, a public–private partnership funded by the California Institute of Technology, the County of Los Angeles, FEMA, the American Red Cross, and others.[25] While *A River in Egypt* is centered on a story about the value of preparedness itself, "The 7 Steps to Earthquake Preparedness" provides practical advice on concrete steps the reader can take to prepare herself and her home for earthquakes, including "identify potential hazards in your home and begin to fix them," "create a disaster-preparedness plan," and "create disaster supplies kits" (291, 295, 298). Together, these pieces provide not only a rationale for preparedness but also practical guidance in earthquake preparedness. The interlacing of these two documents reminds us that preparedness does not just describe an abstract rationale or paradigm; it also describes, perhaps even more importantly, sets of practices, operations, and procedures. Receiving training in preparedness involves learning these practices so that one can understand, or at least consent to, the rationale.

Marty's defense of preparedness to his friend hinges on his realization that "luck is a part of life" (305). "We know we can be hit by lightning, or some blood vessel in our brain can burst," he exclaims, but that doesn't mean that we should "let the fear rule us" (311). His friend calls this denial, which the friend defines as "living in an earthquake zone" or "putting your roots down in paradise even though you know that being here is asking for it, bucking the odds, licking the razor" (313). For the friend, denial means willfully ignoring the probability or even the possibility that a big earthquake will occur in southern California. But Marty insists that "it's not denial if you also accept and prepare for what can happen! It's not denial if you've done everything you can!" (311). It's not denial, in other words, if you prepare for it—if you act *as if* a big earthquake is going to occur, regardless of whether it does. Marty compares this stance to that of Sisyphus as his friend reads from Camus's *The Myth of Sisyphus*: "One must imagine Sisyphus happy," the friend quotes (311). Because "randomness" and "chance" are "our lot in life, good or bad," Marty explains, we have to learn to "get on with our lives" and "treasure every moment because you never know what could happen" (311, 308). Like Sisyphus, we have to "live as-if. . . . As if we're immortal. As if our gods will protect us. As if our prayers matter" (311). That's all we can do, Marty insists. Just "prepare. Until the end of time. That's all there is" (314). For Marty, learning to "live as-if" means both acting as if an earthquake will occur—taking concrete steps to prepare yourself, your family, and your home—*and* continuing on with daily life as if an earthquake won't happen or "as if we're immortal" and "as if our gods will protect us." This is the attitude preparedness demands. Not only should you treat fictional disasters as if they are real and as if they are not; you should also adopt a corresponding attitude toward disaster. You should simultaneously be willing to prepare "until the end of time" and put the impending disasters for which you are preparing in the back of your mind.

This attitude normalizes disaster—and, importantly, disaster preparedness itself—as just a part of everyday life. Throughout the piece, Marty equates earthquakes with examples of individual "bad luck" like car accidents, cancer, getting hit by lightning, or bursting a blood vessel in your brain (307, 311). Such comparisons suggest that dying or sustaining an injury from an earthquake is no different than dying or sustaining an injury from one of any of the other myriad hazards of daily life. It's also important to note that Marty extends this normalization to disaster preparedness itself. He emphasizes that, precisely because you never know when disaster will strike, preparedness training itself should just be a normal part of everyday life. As Marty puts it, you have to "take every precaution you can and then you just have to go on with your life" (313). "The 7 Steps to Earthquake Preparedness," the earthquake preparedness plan interspersed between the pages of *A River in Egypt*, reiterates this point. The last page of the last step in the plan—"7. When safe, continue to follow your disaster-preparedness plan"—is arranged in *The L.A. Earthquake Sourcebook* opposite the last page of *A River in Egypt*, where Marty states that preparedness is "all there is" (314, 315). The last paragraph of the plan begins, "Once you have recovered from the earthquake, go back to Step 1 and do the things you did not do before, or do them more thoroughly" (315). In telling people to start planning all over again after they have recovered from a disaster, "7 Steps" suggests that preparedness is indeed, as Marty puts it, "all there is"—that it continues "until the end of time" and that's just how life is (314). Here Marty articulates a theme of preparedness discourse, one that many of the materials discussed in this book will repeat: preparedness training is a cycle from which there is no exit. Planning leads to training, which leads to more planning, on and on and on, positioning preparedness as the horizon of daily life itself.

The normalization of preparedness that the interconnected presentation of these two documents creates is echoed by the comic's form. Like many graphic narratives, *A River in Egypt* often breaks from the familiar panel structure of comics, making free use of the space of the page. This happens during the moments in the narrative when Marty's friend is describing all of the terrible things for which no amount of preparedness training—or, in the words of the friend, no amount of "boy scout stuff"—can prepare him (Figure 2) (298). In these pages, the friend unspools nightmare scenario after nightmare scenario, and the format of these pages echoes this uncontrolled chaos. Images pile up on top of one another, and the forward movement through narrative time that the panel structure enables breaks down. Indeed, these extradiegetic pages are difficult to locate in time, as they occur outside of the conversation between Marty and his friend that forms the main timeline of the narrative.[26] In contrast, the pages where Marty asserts his argument about the value of preparedness are more regularly structured, utilizing panels and gutter space to control and direct the flow of the narrative (Figure 3) (311). What's more, the structured pages depict two men sitting, talking, and drinking beer—the very definition, it seems, of "normality" itself—while the unstructured pages depict the postapocalyptic nightmares of Marty's friend, featuring giant fires, piles of bodies, and strangely lively decomposing corpses.

The contrast between these pages gives visual form not necessarily to the rationality of preparedness but rather to how people are supposed to feel about it. The artist, Darren Ragle, deploys the self-reflexivity scholars have identified as one of the hallmarks of the comic form. As Hillary Chute has argued, because they juxtapose images and text in often incongruous ways, graphic narratives are "highly conscious of the artificiality of [their] selective borders"; likewise, Joseph Darda has emphasized that the tension created between image and text in graphic narratives "highlights

Figure 2. Chaotic page from *A River in Egypt,* a graphic novel by Martin Kaplan with visuals by Darren Ragle, from *The L.A. Earthquake Sourcebook.* Courtesy of the USC Annenberg Norman Lear Center.

Figure 3. Controlled page from *A River in Egypt*, a graphic novel by Martin Kaplan with visuals by Darren Ragle, from *The L.A. Earthquake Sourcebook.* Courtesy of the USC Annenberg Norman Lear Center.

the constructedness of representation in general."²⁷ While any art form can be self-reflexive, these scholars argue that self-reflexivity is inherent in the comic form itself. In literally containing Marty's arguments about the value of preparedness, *A River in Egypt* makes the visual argument that preparedness can contain and control the chaos of disasters large and small—that it can give form and meaning to the formlessness of everyday life.

The contrast between these pages also leads us to another way of understanding what Marty means when he says that we need to "live as-if." A crucial component of living as-if for Marty is, as I have discussed, "tak[ing] every precaution you can and then you just have to go on with your life" (313). By "going on with your life," Marty explains, he means "treasur[ing] every moment because you never know what could happen" (308). As his friend quotes from Camus, "one must imagine Sisyphus happy" (311). Living as-if, then, is not only about living as if disasters both will and won't happen, and as if disaster preparedness is a normal part of life. It's also about living as if disaster preparedness makes a difference—as if it *can* in fact order and make sense of the world, as it literally does on the pages of the comic, even though we may think it won't. It means living "as if our gods will protect us" and "as if our prayers matter," even though they do not. This is an attitude of resignation, but it's described in the comic as a happy, willing sort of resignation. Preparedness, *A River in Egypt* tells us, means living as if it makes you happy, like Sisyphus, to keep "pushing [your] boulder up the mountain, knowing it will always go rolling down again" (311). It doesn't matter if it *actually* makes you happy to do this; what matters is that you live as if it does, regardless of the outcome.

This is what makes *A River in Egypt* such an utterly bizarre—and honest—example of preparedness discourse. It's strange not because it emphasizes contentment and enjoyment; as we will see in the next chapter, this is common among some preparedness materials. Rather, it's strange because it baldly declares this contentment and enjoyment, in true existentialist fashion, to be a form of necessary, albeit knowingly impossible, wish fulfillment. As Camus writes in the sentence before the one Marty's friend quotes from *The Myth of Sisyphus*, "the struggle itself toward the heights is enough to fill a man's heart."²⁸ Notice that it's "the struggle" here that is important, not actually attaining a level of preparedness. This struggle—the struggle to prepare "until the end of time," because "that's all there is," while also "treasur[ing] every moment"—is all that is available to us in what Marty describes as a "broken" world (34). In this way, *A River in Egypt* actually acknowledges Marty's friend's argument about the uselessness of preparedness in the face of major disasters. As we will see throughout this book, a kernel of this acknowledgment is present in many preparedness materials, but they usually aren't as explicit about it as *A River in Egypt* is. The comic emphasizes that while there may be nothing you can actually do to prepare for the "big one," it's nevertheless preparing itself that's important. It's what gives your life meaning and what fills your heart. Living as-if is about adopting the right attitude not only toward disaster but also toward disaster preparedness itself. It's about learning to live as if you like it.

"We Test Plans, but We Train People"

The methods through which people are supposed to learn to live as-if, or to learn to adopt the correct attitude toward disaster and preparedness itself, are those taught via preparedness training. The corollary to the empiricist epistemology of fiction preparedness materials espouse is an emphasis on response, on translating what people learn from fictional disasters into action. FEMA emphasizes that training people is just as important—if not more important—than developing response plans: as they put it, "we test plans, but we train people."[29] The many different federal programs and institutes designed to teach people how to respond to disasters of all kinds are evidence of this commitment. Such programs and institutes, all housed under or connected to DHS, include FEMA's Emergency Management Institute, the National Domestic Preparedness Consortium, the Center for Domestic Preparedness, and the National Training and Education Division, to name just a few. These programs and institutes train officials across federal, state, and local governments in emergency management and preparedness, and many of them also provide courses, programs, and grants for preparedness training in workplaces, schools, and local communities. As discussed in the introduction, preparedness training therefore represents an extension of the power of the U.S. national security state into the everyday lives of people living in the United States, not just government officials.

But what does it mean to undergo training in the context of preparedness? Given the obvious relationship between preparedness and militarism, an initial answer to this question might focus on a military conception of training. Such an answer might conceptualize training as something close to how Michel Foucault describes discipline in *Discipline and Punish*: as "an art of correct training" that involves "the coercion of individuals."[30] For Foucault, training is a process of "mastering [the body], making it pliable, ready at all times, turning [learned behavior] silently into the automatism of habit."[31] As the phrase "automatism of habit" indicates, a machinic vocabulary infuses Foucault's descriptions of training. Training is a "mechanics of power" that operates on the body "at the level of the mechanism itself" and produces "an efficient machine."[32] And when one is trained, one "learn[s] the code of the signals and respond[s] automatically to them."[33] Understanding preparedness training in this way would emphasize how it strives to teach people to respond to disaster in particular ways automatically, without thinking.

However, this militaristic understanding of training is insufficient for understanding what training means in the context of preparedness. When preparedness materials discuss training, they do not describe it as a mechanistic or automatic process, and, unlike military training, they do not seek to coerce individuals so much as they seek to convince them. Manuals and handbooks about how to design and conduct preparedness training exercises use terms like "on-the-spot correction" and "coaching" as synonyms for training; they emphasize that one of the trainer's roles during an exercise should be to "help the players resolve conflicts and feel comfortable"; and they state that one of the main purposes of training exercises is "to explore, innovate, and build team cohesiveness."[34] These materials also insist that one of the essential ingredients of a successful training exercise is "a committed group of people," and they enjoin exercise facilitators to emphasize "the positive aspects of the group's efforts" when giving postexercise feedback.[35] They repeat over and over again that the evaluation phase of the exercise, when exercise participants offer their feedback on overall exercise design, execution, and outcomes, is just as important as the exercise itself. "The evaluation and action steps following the exercise are perhaps the most critical," one presentation on exercise design emphasizes; and as one handbook states, "no amount of exercising will be constructive unless each exercise is followed by a structured evaluation that enables the emergency management organization to identify successes and shortfalls."[36] As these examples show, preparedness materials describe training as a process of self-formation that involves dialogue, critique, and collaboration. For preparedness, training for catastrophe is not about turning individuals into unthinking robots. It's about learning established protocols and procedures—how best to respond to disaster—and, more importantly, learning to carry out these protocols and procedures in concert with others, to give and receive constructive feedback, and to feel in control while doing so.

This conception of training is more closely aligned with how Sara Ahmed has described the process of conforming to what she terms the *social will*. For Ahmed, the social will is "a will that speaks the language of 'ought to,' or 'should,' or even . . . the language of 'must.'"[37] More purposive and directed than Pierre Bourdieu's *habitus*, Ahmed's social will nevertheless retains the sense, like *habitus*, of something in between freedom and coercion, of something like what Bourdieu describes as "embodied history, internalized as a second nature and so forgotten as history."[38] Training is the process through which, as Ahmed puts it, social "willing becomes 'my own' through the work of adjustment."[39] Such adjustment is not necessarily conscious, but it isn't necessarily involuntary, unconscious, or automatic either. Rather, it is an example of acquiring "habits of the will," which are formed by directing the will "in the right way, so that it does right of its own accord."[40] Another way of describing this is to say that training involves learning to adopt certain habits of the will so that they align with the social will. It is about agreeing, again and again, to adopt the right attitude, to become disposed toward certain ideas and sensations so that such ideas and sensations become habitual, ordinary, routine—but also so that they come to feel, through this process, like one's own. It is a process of being pressed, but in such a way that the pressing feels more like self-conscious tweaking or fine-tuning than an imposition.[41] It is a form of self-discipline, but one that feels, in certain contexts, like improvement.

To understand preparedness training as a process of learning to adopt the "social will" as one's own is to emphasize the volition and consent of the trainee. People who undergo preparedness training do not become automatons who have ceded control over their own actions. Rather, the process of training itself is designed to accord with the trainee's sense of his own autonomy.[42] In stressing the consent of the trainee, however, I do not mean that people always consciously "choose" to undergo preparedness training or, conversely, that they always have the option not to undergo training if they don't want to participate. Often, preparedness training is simply part of your job, or just another day at school, or only a trip to the airport. Rather, I mean that sometimes acting in accordance with your own will feels more like going with the flow, or just not resisting, not making a fuss, getting through the day. As I will argue in chapter 3, preparedness training is designed to produce such feelings. What's more, sometimes acting in accordance with your own will doesn't feel like choosing to act at all. It just means doing what you think is right, or proper, or responsible. As Ahmed writes, sometimes "we become willing by learning not be conscious of an agreement."[43]

Thinking of preparedness training as composed of procedures for generating consent also throws the accepted temporality of training into question. Training is generally understood as future oriented. Patrick Crogan, for example, writes, "In general terms, we can say that training is future directed to the extent that it is about developing proficiencies in order to better execute some task. Military training is about improving skills so that one may survive to attain an effective level of control over the event space."[44] Training as Crogan describes it is not the same as actually performing that task. Instead, training means becoming proficient in a particular skill or set of skills so that when, at some future date, you are asked to utilize these skills "for real," you will be able to do so competently. It occurs separately from the actual execution of the skills you are trying to master in both space and time: it takes place before the events for which you are training and in a controlled environment where you can make mistakes with little consequence.

Yet, as *A River in Egypt* makes clear, preparedness training is directed toward the present. It is indistinguishable from the events for which one is training because the training itself is the goal. DHS, for example, recommends that all federal organizations and agencies develop "a progressive, multi-year [preparedness] exercise program" that involves "a series of increasingly complex exercises, with each successive exercise building upon the previous one until mastery is achieved."[45] The temporality of such a "progressive" exercise program seems linear, but DHS's emphasis on continuous improvement means that although the stated goal of each exercise is to "identify capability gaps" and the "corrective actions" needed to address those gaps so as to eliminate them, in practice the actual goal is only to create more opportunities for the continual examination of training exercise outcomes and the continual management of personnel.[46] Particular training courses and programs come to a close, but as soon as they end, they beget more training courses and programs; there is no way to "graduate" from preparedness training, not really and for good, because there are always new ways to improve and new skills and techniques to learn and review. Eric Cazdyn calls this temporal mode the "new chronic," emphasizing how it "extends the present into the future, burying in the process the force of the terminal, making it seem as if the present will never end."[47] Each exercise produces some fresh disaster, and so participants must handle disasters—and their responses to them—over and over, returning to the scene of catastrophe again and again. What happens as you train for the "future" is what is happening now, in the present of your training. Preparedness training therefore unceasingly returns you to the "undying present" at the same time that it styles this present as the future, as that which is not yet happening but may at any moment.[48] In addition to learning to adjust your own will to the will of others by force of habit, preparedness training involves this temporal dislocation, this experience of the future in the present and of the present as that which stretches, unending, into the future.[49]

The design of preparedness training exercises themselves exacerbates this feeling of temporal dislocation. Preparedness training exercises like the Hurricane Pam exercise are supposed to induce failure. The motivation behind preparedness training exercises isn't only to teach people how to respond to disaster but also, as DHS puts it, to "assess and validate capabilities, and address areas for improvement."[50] Exercises are "useful tools" that help people to both "practice and refine" their responses to disasters.[51] They are designed, in other words, to identify what isn't working in the preparedness protocol or plan, so that this point of failure can be identified and improved. DHS therefore encourages exercise designers to conceive of exercise evaluation and improvement planning as part of the training exercise process itself. Materials for an online course on exercise evaluation designed by FEMA's Emergency Management Institute, for example, state that exercise evaluation "is part of an on-going process of improvements to preparedness."[52] The course describes processes for soliciting feedback from exercise participants and for using that feedback to create "improvement plans" that implement that feedback in a "disciplined process for . . . continually improving preparedness."[53] Exercise design, these materials emphasize, is integral to the entire preparedness process; it is a vital component of "a continual cycle of improvement." DHS, in fact, imagines the entire exercise process as a cycle (Figure 4).[54] In this image, the four steps involved in conducting training exercises—exercise design and development, exercise conduct, exercise evaluation, and improvement planning—are depicted as continuous. Not only does exercise design and development lead to conducting the exercise but improvement planning, the "last" step in the process, leads right back into exercise design and development, which leads to conducting exercises, on and on. There is no end to preparedness training, and it continues, as Marty from *A River in Egypt* puts it, "until the end of time."

The temporality of preparedness training is therefore post-apocalyptic rather than apocalyptic. As the statements from DHS about the importance of ongoing training programs referenced earlier show, preparedness training is concerned not with the impending end but rather with the always ongoing aftermath. In Frank Kermode's terms, postapocalyptic narratives, which he calls "fictions of transition," are characterized by "intemporal agony": they "[reflect] our lack of confidence in ends" and are narratives in which "the stage of transition," or the shift from one way of life to another brought on by the apocalypse, "has become *endless*."[55] While pre-

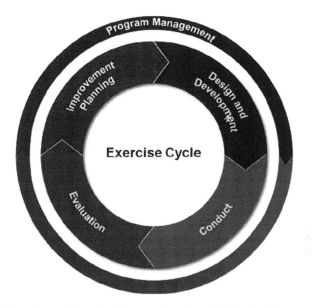

Figure 4. Department of Homeland Security Exercise and Evaluation Program exercise cycle.

paredness materials are not necessarily narrative, they are charac-terized by a similar understanding of the ongoingness of disaster, one in which the catastrophe is understood not as an overturning or an end, as its etymology suggests, but rather as part of a cycle of never-ending training. As Aimee Bahng emphasizes, disaster pre-paredness plans are "tautological" because they "produc[e] the very crisis [they] seek to contain"—they both enact fictional disasters and create an understanding of never-ending, ongoing disaster that calls for "increased securitization," producing yet more disasters, on and on and on.[56]

   We are now in a position to fully understand the strange and para-doxical way preparedness understands fiction. As I argued earlier in this chapter, preparedness materials treat fiction as both unreal and real, as something that has never happened and will never hap-pen and as something from which we can collect data and draw con-clusions based on empirical evidence. I want to add now that this understanding of fiction is what allows preparedness to perpetuate itself. We can critique preparedness all we want for being, for example, ineffective or fantastical. Such critiques are accurate; evidence of the effectiveness of preparedness training is spotty at best, and many preparedness training exercises are ridiculous, awkward, boring, or some combination of the three.[57] But as we will see in the next two chapters, such critiques also do not invalidate or even throw into question the practice of preparedness training itself. When "evaluation and critique" is widely understood to be one of the most important aspects of preparedness training, critiquing training exercises as ineffective misses the point. By basing themselves on fictional events that always "might" happen, and by incorporating criticism as part of the process of continuous training, preparedness exercises protect themselves from critique. Fiction, for preparedness, is always actionable but never consequential.

Realism

Consenting to the Possibilistic
Logic of Preparedness

In 2009 and 2010, junior military officers attending an institute for creating emergency plans and training scenarios at the Joint and Combined Warfighting School created CONPLAN 8888, a "counter-zombie dominance" scenario.[1] It describes a variety of military tactics that could be undertaken "to preserve 'non-zombie' humans from the threats posed by a zombie horde," such as activating "emergency disaster support plans," "shelter[ing] all mission essential personnel in place for at least 40 days," and "conduct[ing] prompt global strike [sic] against initial concentrations of zombies" (4, 12). CONPLAN 8888 also includes detailed descriptions of the different kinds of zombies that might exist—everything from "Pathogenic Zombies (PZ)" to "Radiation Zombies (RZ)" to "Space Zombies (SZ)"—the supplies needed to survive the onslaught, and the challenges the military would face in performing antizombie operations. Such challenges include the facts that "Adequate Zombie defense require sandbags, sand, barbed wire, anti-personnel mines, riot control chemical agents . . . and petroleum (to create flame barriers)" and that "USSTRATCOM forces do not currently hold enough contingency stores (food, water) to support 30 days of barricaded counter-zombie operations" (6, 16). Additionally, the document runs through a series of different "Decisive Points/ Critical Capabilities (CCs)," or "crucial enablers for the strategic and operational centers of gravity to function" (26). These include considerations related to medical infrastructure; law enforcement; the power grid; quarantine procedures; and food, water, and fuel distribution networks. All in all, CONPLAN 8888 assembles a comprehensive inventory of information, strategies, and materials for a military response to a zombie attack.

As is perhaps apparent by now, CONPLAN 8888 is not a "real" training scenario. Rather, it is a pedagogical tool: it was created to teach trainees in military emergency management and planning how to create disaster training scenarios. Planners use such scenarios to form the narrative backbone of preparedness training exercises, as they set the scene of the disaster and provide information that participants need to take part in the exercise. Yet despite the obviously science fictional nature of the scenario, CONPLAN 8888 begins with a disclaimer that it "was not actually designed as a joke" (2). On the contrary, the planners discovered "that the hyperbole involved in writing a 'zombie survival plan' actually provided a very useful and effective training tool" precisely because such a plan was "so ridiculous" and "completely-impossible" (3). The scenario refers to its own impossibility throughout by using fictional sources as evidence for these claims, citing information about the dispositions and behavioral patterns of different kinds of zombies drawn from the game *Plants vs. Zombies*, the film *Signs*, and the books *World War Z*, *The Zombie Survival Guide*, *Zombies vs. Unicorns*, and *The Zombie Combat Manual*. The scenario designers comment on this use of evidence, stating that "the use of science fiction sources does provide a compelling advantage for military planners," especially if such sources are "robust" (21). "The more robust a science fiction scenario related to zombies is," the scenario designers write, "the more useful it is for planning purposes—regardless of how 'outlandish' it might be" (21). "Robust" science fiction scenarios are useful, in other words, because they provide planners with the information they need to create effective training scenarios. They "significantly enhance analyses of courses of actions, facilitate . . . wargaming and adjustment, and provide insight for planners with regards to the development of facts, assumptions, risks and aversions of 'groupthink' or 'cognitive bias'" (21). We should note here that the robustness of "science fiction scenarios" does not necessarily depend on their believability. It doesn't matter how "outlandish" a work of sci-fi is; it is considered robust as long as it provides "facts" that help planners create scenarios in which participants immerse themselves and so challenge their "assumptions." By moving the scenario out of the realm of possibility entirely, the designers of CONPLAN 8888 claim that trainees were better able to learn and practice the intricacies of scenario development because they were not concerned with so-called real-world implications (3). They were freer "to explore the basic concepts of plan and order development" by "suspend[ing] reality" for a few moments (3).

This emphasis on the suspension of reality, however, runs counter to what seems at first glance to be one of the main injunctions of exercise and scenario design: training exercises should be realistic. Preparedness materials generally emphasize that the more "real" a training exercise is, the better it will train people to respond to catastrophe. A handbook by FEMA on exercise design, for example, states that the atmosphere during a training exercise should mimic "the environment of the emergency," meaning it should be "stressful and tense due to real-time action and the realism of the problems"; likewise, emergency planners argue that "scenario-based planning activities" are valuable precisely because "the realism that is brought to the table during these events really makes the planning feel more urgent."[2] According to this logic—and counter to the motivating logic behind CONPLAN 8888—the realism of training exercises is central to their function as exercises meant to train people to respond to disasters. Because they seem real, participants learn to respond to emergencies under these so-called real-world conditions and thus are better prepared to handle actual disasters when they occur. CONPLAN 8888 therefore points us toward a problem for all preparedness training exercises, not only those that are "completely-impossible." While driven by the need to "suspend reality" in order to focus on fictional disasters, training exercises are also, at the same time, supposed to be realistic, both so that participants buy in to them and so that participants are better trained after they complete them. This chapter begins from this contradiction. How can a "completely-impossible" scenario also be "realistic?"

To answer this question, we need to understand what preparedness materials mean by the term *realism*. As we will see, their understanding of realism is surprisingly literary, although not exactly in the way scholars of literature might expect. In general, literary scholars have claimed that the realism of a narrative is related to its plausibility; what is most believable is what "feels real." They have long linked plausibility and probability, often citing Aristotle's well-known maxims that "the poet's job is not relating what actually happened, but rather the kind of thing that *would* happen," and that, in poetry, "probable impossibilities are to be preferred to implausible possibilities."[3] More recently, scholars have sharpened this association by linking the development of the mathematical concept of probability during the seventeenth and eighteenth centuries in Europe to the development of novelistic realism during the same period. As Aristotle's *Poetics* demonstrates, plausible narratives had long been defined as the most convincing ones. The classical understanding of probability emphasized rhetorical, political, or intellectual authority, and a narrative was plausible, therefore, if it was understood as authoritative in some way. However, scholars have emphasized that during the seventeenth and eighteenth centuries, the concept of probability slowly changed, moving away from its classical associations with rhetoric and toward its more modern associations with likelihood. "Reality," not consensus opinion, became the marker of authority.[4] Scholars have also noted that during the same time, the terms *probability* and *verisimilitude* began to converge in the period's aesthetic criticism, associating probability not only with what could likely happen but also with the closely related concept of a representation that is true to nature.[5] Describing a narrative as plausible therefore came to mean that narrative was believable not because it was persuasive or sanctioned by tradition but rather because it seemed true to life and therefore credible.

Scholars have also linked this conception of plausibility to the sophisticated yet logically puzzling "willing suspension of disbelief," to quote Coleridge's famous phrase, required for fiction reading—the idea that readers agree to pretend to believe in the reality of something they know didn't actually happen. These critics have argued that if a narrative is plausible, and therefore probable and true to life, readers are more likely to suspend their disbelief and play along. As Catherine Gallagher puts it, plausible narratives help readers to "extend enough credit to buy into [sic] the game."[6] Indeed, Gallagher has argued that, in eighteenth-century England, the new genre of the novel distinguished itself from other imaginative forms of the period, such as romance, by telling such plausible stories.[7] The form of the novel therefore staged the convergence of the closely associated concepts of plausibility, probability, and verisimilitude, developing its own aesthetic—realism—forged from all three. The historical convergence of a new conception of probability with the growing popularity of novels trained eighteenth-century readers of fiction to understand novelistic realism, in Gallagher's terms, as "fiction's formal sign" rather than as "a way of trying to hide or disguise fictionality."[8] Realism became a self-evident marker of fictionality itself.

This chapter, however, documents how preparedness materials undo these associations between plausibility, probability, and realism. I focus on training exercises, which are designed to develop and test emergency response protocols and plans. Such exercises generally consist of a scenario that provides details about a particular fictional catastrophic event to which participants must then respond through enactment, discussion, or a combination of both. I argue that what such exercises refer to as "real" or "reality" has very little to do with probability or verisimilitude. Instead, these training exercises invite participants to enter into their worlds and to enjoy the experience of immersing themselves in fiction. This experience is what they call "reality."

In this chapter, I detail a movement in preparedness materials away from understanding realism as tied to probability and toward a rhetorical understanding of what counts as "real." The first section examines Herman Kahn's work on disaster scenarios for the RAND Corporation and the Hudson Institute in the 1950s and 1960s. Although Kahn developed a wide range of scenarios for officials to use in preparing for nuclear war and its aftermath, he is not the only figure important to the history of preparedness.[9] However, I turn to Kahn in what follows not to narrate a history of preparedness but rather to emphasize Kahn's contribution to the aesthetic philosophy of preparedness: its possibilistic, rather than probabilistic, logic.[10] The chapter then turns to contemporary preparedness materials to investigate how they have extended this concept. I focus on how preparedness materials create what Tracy Davis has called a

"consensual reality," or a reality that participants, exercise designers, and facilitators agree to treat as realistic, regardless of whether
what it depicts could "actually" happen.[11] Because they are free
from the constraints of probability and verisimilitude, I argue that
preparedness training exercises are designed to bypass questions
of belief or disbelief entirely. Instead, as the previous chapter contends, they train participants to understand fiction and reality as
epistemologically, but not ontologically, the same. This way of understanding the relationship between fiction and reality constitutes
a reversal of Jean Baudrillard's well-known discussion of the role of
science fiction in the "hyperreal era," in which "models of simulation" have "the feeling of the real, of the banal, of lived experience,"
which "reinvent[s] the real as fiction, precisely because it has dis-
appeared from our life."[12] While the fictions preparedness materials produce are indeed banal, preparedness materials do not treat
these fictions as "reinventions" of the real. They posit not that there
is no difference between fiction and reality but rather that fiction
has a reality all its own. Importantly, this reality is not dependent
on the actuality, or even on the probable or plausible actuality, of
the events described in the fiction. Instead, as we will see by the end
of the chapter, this empiricist epistemology of fiction means that
preparedness materials are designed to train participants to agree
to consent to the reality of fiction.

Disciplining the Imagination: Herman Kahn's Possibilistic Logic

We begin with a detour to the mid-twentieth century. Preparedness has a long history in U.S. national security, dating at least as
far back as the development of civil defense programs during the
early Cold War, and preparedness in one form or another has been
a cornerstone of U.S. national security since then. Civil defense,
which was developed as the domestic counterpoint to the military
strategy of nuclear deterrence, sought to prepare American citizens
for the possibility of nuclear war. The forms such preparation took
were many and varied; federal, state, and local governmental agencies, for example, facilitated disaster preparedness courses, carried out emergency drills, built community shelters, and developed

evacuation protocols. What all of these forms of preparation had in common, however, was a concern with how to manage "unthinkable" catastrophe.[13]

Training exercises centered on the "unthinkable" catastrophe of nuclear war were first utilized as a technique of U.S. national security during the heyday of civil defense in the 1950s and early 1960s.[14] Herman Kahn worked as an analyst at the RAND Corporation during this time, and during the 1950s, he began to turn away from his early work on modeling the behavior of particles in nuclear reactors and toward creating nuclear disaster scenarios. These scenarios were situational: they provided details about fictional nuclear attacks, describing where and when the attacks occurred, what they destroyed, and how many casualties they caused. The idea was that officials and planners could use this information to develop response protocols and plans. After the publication of *On Thermonuclear War* in 1960, which contained a number of these scenarios, Kahn became well known both within and outside of the world of strategic analysis for his promotion of scenarios as a way to prepare government officials and the public for nuclear attacks. Kahn is still recognized today among emergency planners, analysts, and academics alike as a pioneer in scenario development, and his influence has spread far beyond the realm of national security to include areas such as environmental science and business. He even popularized the use of the term *scenario* to mean an imagined situation used for planning purposes, borrowing it from Hollywood.[15]

Scenarios of nuclear war were important for Cold War civil defense, Kahn argued, not only because they alerted analysts to current vulnerabilities they may not have previously considered but also because, as Andrew Lakoff writes, they presented officials "with something close to the sense of urgency such a crisis would bring."[16] Scenarios, to Kahn's mind, forced officials to confront the affective as well as the strategic exigencies of future catastrophes. In this aspect, scenarios for Kahn functioned like works of fiction. In fact, Kahn drew explicit connections between scenarios and "the earlier work, or speculation, of individual writers and thinkers" like "H.G. Wells, Aldous Huxley, and George Orwell."[17] In recent years, literary scholars have paid increasing attention to this more literary aspect of Kahn's work, emphasizing the connections between postmodern literature and the national security state during the Cold War.[18] Such discussions of Kahn's scenarios have tended to distinguish between the quantitative and empirical bent of Kahn's earlier work in probabilistic analysis, systems analysis, and game theory, on one hand, and the imaginative and narrative qualities of his scenarios of nuclear war, on the other. Scholars use distinctions between the "rational" and the "imaginative"—or, more broadly, between the empirical and the speculative—as the rubric through which to understand Kahn's scenario thinking and its influence on military strategy and national security policy. In opposition to his earlier quantitative work, Kahn's later work on nuclear prepared-ness is often viewed as "suited to situations recalcitrant to statistical analysis" and as "irrational."[19]

Kahn's scenarios, however, refuse such neat distinctions. Both empirical and speculative, these scenarios grew out of and were influenced by Kahn's earlier experience in probabilistic analysis. During his early career at the RAND Corporation in the late 1940s and early 1950s, he modeled the activity of particles and gamma rays that might penetrate the protective shields of nuclear reactors. In this work, he emphasized what he referred to as the "intuitive" process of designing the model—of deciding what should be mod-eled and how—over the computational processes involved in doing the modeling. As Sharon Ghamari-Tabrizi points out, Kahn spent much of his time during this period writing about how to "con-triv[e] efficiencies that lessened the computational load rather than straining to create a model that faithfully hugged the lineaments of the elemental world."[20] He maintained that a good model need not be directly analogous to reality at all; in fact, since computational resources were limited, the modeler should focus not on precisely modeling the actual phenomenon under investigation but rather on deciding how to limit the size and parameters of the phenomenon so that it could be plausibly yet efficiently modeled. Kahn argued that any refinements to the sampling procedure were "to a certain extent arbitrary" and that they "should be chosen to minimize the total amount of work rather than to be an analogue of the physi-cal situation."[21] In this way, Kahn emphasized the "intuition of the [human] computer" in designing the model over the computation of the model itself.[22] He stressed the importance of cultivating and "training one's own intuition so that one can do a good design job."[23] The probabilistic calculations the model required could never be separated from and even depended on an intuitive sense of artfulness and design.

For Kahn, and as discussed in the previous chapter, modeling brought empirical and speculative epistemologies together. Understood in this way, Kahn's movement in the middle to late 1950s to systems analysis, war gaming, and scenario development is a continuation of his earlier work with modeling rather than a break from it. Ghamari-Tabrizi documents how Kahn's fellow physicists at RAND thought he had "departed from our world" when he turned to nuclear strategy, but for Kahn, the progression from calculating possible movements of particles through a protective shield to writing nuclear war scenarios was straightforward.[24] He viewed both activities as modeling possible realities. For Kahn, both activities involved training one's intuition to properly model highly complex possibilities and contingencies—possibilities and contingencies that, in both cases, had not occurred in reality and would never occur (because they were products of the imagination). Kahn was concerned with creating, through "objective" processes, possible—but not necessarily always probable—worlds.

Although it was not important for Kahn that his possible worlds exactly correspond to reality, it was important that these worlds *seem* like they might correspond to reality—it was important that they feel plausible. Kahn's strategy for lending his scenarios plausibility was to borrow from the language of quantitative analysis. In the 1957 RAND memorandum "Techniques of Systems Analysis," one of Kahn's first forays into military strategy, he and Irwin Mann defend the plausibility of the kinds of calculations they perform. They write, "It is important to note that the approximations we made were not arbitrary, but have been shown to be *intuitively* reasonable by previous calculations. If we had not done these previous calculations we would not now be in a position to intuit which kinds of approximations are reasonable and which are not."[25] In this passage, Kahn and Mann position their intuitive judgments as both the direct results of calculation *and* as the foundation of the probabilistic calculations they detail. It is only through the calculation of possibilities—a process dependent on the modeler's "artful intuition" in the first place—that an analyst can successfully train his intuition to effectively judge the "reasonableness" of any calculation. This recursive logic makes intuition the starting point for calculation while at the same time seeming to subject this intuition to quantitative analysis. In the same report, for example, Kahn and Mann write, "The exciting thing that we have done is to make the above qualitative remarks numerical; that is, we have changed what we called an 'intuitive judgment' into what we called a 'considered opinion.'"[26] Here, in what Kahn and Mann describe as one of the great innovations of systems analysis, the subjective "intuitive judgment" is replaced with the supposedly more objective "considered opinion" to position what Kahn would later call the "'science' of public policy" as a fundamentally empirical enterprise.[27] Even though Kahn and Mann rely on intuitive judgment to perform their calculations, they also efface this method in favor of advancing their approach as scientific. Kahn and Mann advise the analyst to subject their imagination to a seemingly systematic quantitative process, transforming "intuitive judgments" to "considered opinions" so that they can properly assess the validity of their own imagination of the future. In this way, Kahn and Mann take advantage of the cultural prestige of quantification to disguise what are fundamentally speculative and imaginative claims as precise and quantifiable.[28]

This same attention to the systematic imagination of possible futures carried over to Kahn's work in scenario design, specifically in relation to plausibility. Kahn's alignment of plausibility with possibility rather than with probability in this work is particularly important to the rationality of preparedness. Kahn claims that plausibility is "a great virtue in a scenario," and he writes that a plausible scenario must "relate at the outset to some reasonable version of the present, and must throughout relate rationally to the way people could behave."[29] In this statement, Kahn argues that plausibility is established through "reasonable" and "rational" representations of present expectations and behavior. However, for Kahn, what is "reasonable" or "rational" is not necessarily what is most likely to happen. In fact, Kahn cautions against implicitly equating plausibility with probability, writing, "It is important not to limit oneself to the most plausible, conventional or probable situations and behavior," because "to understand the problems of national security and international order we must be sure to analyze improbable and terrible situations."[30] Kahn emphasizes that the possibilities scenarios envision should not be tethered only to what analysts think most likely to happen. This is why Kahn stresses possibility over probability: although it is improbable that things will go badly in the first place, it is also impossible to know how exactly things will go badly if they do, so it is therefore important to analyze in specific detail five or ten of the thousands of equally possible terrible situations to get at least some view, however distorted, of the possibilities. What is plausible is not necessarily what is probable, and vice versa. In the end, for Kahn, the only criterion that establishes a scenario as plausible is that the events it describes are possible. Improbable events, while unlikely to occur, are nevertheless *equally as possible* as probable events.[31] In this way, Kahn relates plausibility to possibility, not probability.[32]

Kahn's separation of plausibility and probability allows him to bypass questions about the specific content of his scenarios and this content's relationship to reality. In response to critics who claimed that his scenarios were essentially fantastic and therefore misleading or dangerous as tools of national security, Kahn writes, "The scenario is usually not used as a predictive device. The analyst is often dealing with the unknown and to some degree unknowable future. In many specific cases it is hard to see how critics can be so certain there is a sure divorce from a reality which does not yet exist and may yet surprise them."[33] The scenario's aim is not to describe what will happen, Kahn claims. Rather, for Kahn, scenarios are narrative simulations of possibilities. Moreover, a scenario will never coincide with reality, no matter how plausible it may seem. Scenarios will always only be fictional. Just like simulations of gamma ray particles, they are models in which the distance between what *could* happen and what *will* happen always remains unbridgeable. Yet Kahn relies on this very chasm to position his scenarios as valuable tools for national security: scenarios are plausible and can therefore produce valuable knowledge about future possibilities precisely because they "rationally" describe "a reality which does not yet exist." They allow analysts and officials to "think the unthinkable," to use Kahn's famous phrase.

Yet, while Kahn relied on the difference between what could happen and what will happen to make the case for scenario development as an important tool of national security, he was also adamant that scenarios were not merely fantastical exercises. He saw scenarios not just as a way to imagine future catastrophes but, more importantly, as a way to "discipline the imagination" through the adoption of standardized protocols for the systematic production of possible futures.[34] He differentiated scenario thinking from storytelling through this emphasis on "objective speculation" or "explicated and detailed calculations of the future done on a priori and analytic bases."[35] For Kahn, scenarios—unlike the fiction of Wells, Huxley, and Orwell he claimed as his inspiration—are the result of a rigorous, disciplined, and systematic training of the scenario designer's imaginative capacities. They are "calculations of the future" produced through training in "objective speculation." This training, rather than the details of the scenarios themselves, establishes the authority of the scenario to project possible futures. In this way, Kahn insisted that the futures scenarios project are in fact the result of objective methods of analysis by borrowing from the language of science. This involved separating the plausibility of these narratives from the probability of their occurrence, while at the same time relying on the implied precision of quantitative analysis to describe imaginative possibility. For Kahn, scenarios are the result of possibilistic, rather than probabilistic, logic.

This disciplining of the imagination culminated for Kahn in the argument for a totally systematic approach to scenario development. Kahn continually emphasized that proper scenario development involved individual training "to learn to do a good design job" as well as "sustained, cooperative, and relatively systematic effort[s]" by groups of analysts to produce, test, and revise scenarios.[36] One of Kahn's main arguments throughout *On Thermonuclear War*, in fact, concerns the need for a systematic program for analyzing future possibilities: "We still need a program, a blueprint, and at least some glimmering of a theory of where we are and where we want to be . . . [and] better mechanisms and organizations than we have had for anticipating technical and political developments and planning to meet them."[37] Kahn's departure from the RAND Corporation and founding of the Hudson Institute in the 1960s was an attempt to provide such a blueprint. The 1966 Hudson Institute report "On Alternative World Futures," for example, is an introductory handbook for building scenarios. In addition to describing the methodology of scenario design, it lays out twenty-one possible themes or contexts for the future "which can . . . be used in generating scenarios or games."[38] These themes, Kahn claims, "are a first step toward the construction of a systematic group of Alternative World Futures" for the next ten to twenty years. With titles like "Containment and Confrontation," "Challenges from Latin America," "New Super Powers," and "Post-nuclear Use International Systems," they consider a wide variety of possible future geopolitical and technological configurations, covering everything from unipolar to multipolar systems, the decline of the West to the rise of Latin America and/or Asia, and the further spread of Communism to its complete containment.[39] Such a "systematic group" of scenarios was created to discipline the imagination of analysts, teaching them to produce possible futures of a specific kind, in a specific way.[40]

Kahn is best remembered today as an early adopter of the scenario for the purposes of national security—and as one of the inspirations for the title character in Stanley Kubrick's 1964 film *Dr. Strangelove*—but perhaps his most important innovation was his possibilistic logic, his severing of plausibility from probability in the context of scenario development. This meant that a scenario could claim to be plausible without also claiming to be probable while, at the same time, borrowing from the language of quantitative analysis to ground its authority to project future disaster in reality. The separation of plausibility from probability also made plausibility a procedural problem, shifting the emphasis from any one scenario's specific contents to the procedures used to create scenarios in general. For Kahn, as for exercise designers today, scenarios are fictional and imaginative, and so what they describe will never happen; yet they are also "objective speculations" about future disaster, the end result of specific systematic methods used to discipline the imagination of the scenario creator. Kahn's disaster scenarios seem to offer authoritative visions of future disaster precisely because they are rooted in this kind of possibilistic logic.

The Realism of the Unthinkable

While Kahn wrote pages and pages on the relationship between plausibility and probability in scenario development, preparedness materials today tend to focus more on the "realism" of training exercises. However, understanding what terms like *realism* and *realistic* mean in the context of post-9/11 national security is difficult because preparedness materials often offer confused definitions of these terms. For example, the Homeland Security Exercise and Evaluation Program (HSEEP), which provides materials members of the general public can use in planning their own emergency management exercises, offers in volume 2 of its policy document this articulation of what constitutes "realism": "the level of detail provided in a scenario should reflect real-world uncertainty," and the future catastrophes that scenarios describe should be "probable" and "credible enough for players to suspend their inherent disbelief in hypothetical situations."[41] Importantly, the document goes on to state that this credibility does not arise from any scenario's description of future events but rather "from an entity's threat/vulnerability analyses."[42] These analyses are used to determine the most plausible threats an area or entity may face:

> For example, in a highly populated, high-profile community, the threat of chemical, biological, or radiological terrorism may be considered more of a risk than in predominately rural areas, where agricultural assets may be more vulnerable to acts of terrorism. Likewise, the threat of hurricanes is far greater in the Southeastern United States, whereas wildfires are a concern in the West.[43]

This definition states that what is most credible, then, is what is "more of a risk" for any particular area or entity. Here the HSEEP document seems to emphasize the familiar association between plausibility and probability that Kahn worked to undo: participants in training exercises will be more willing "to suspend their inherent disbelief in hypothetical situations," the document posits, if those situations seem more likely to happen.

While it's true that hurricanes are more likely to occur in the southeastern United States and wildfires are more likely to occur in the west, beyond these general statements of fact, the HSEEP document, like Kahn's scenarios, borrows the language and logic of probabilistic analysis more than it depends on actual calculation or quantitative analysis. In the preceding quote, for example, certain kinds of disasters are "more of a risk" for certain areas of the country, but all regions, no matter where they are, are potentially disastrous. This rhetoric substitutes possibility—the idea that a terrorist attack could possibly occur anywhere—for probability while nevertheless couching its claims in the language of probabilistic analysis. Likewise, a guide to conducting risk assessments for buildings by FEMA defines the vulnerability assessment as "an indepth [sic] analysis of the building functions, systems, and site characteristics to identify building weaknesses and lack of redundancy, and determine mitigations or corrective actions that can be designed or implemented to reduce vulnerabilities."[44] In practice, the process of conducting a vulnerability assessment involves, as with scenario development, disciplining and quantifying the analyst's imagination through a systematic process. The FEMA risk assessment guide, for example, contains a 47-page checklist analysts can use in identifying building vulnerabilities.[45] After completing the checklist, analysts are supposed to collate the results and use them to rate the building's vulnerability on the "scale for vulnerability," which "is a combination of a 7-level linguistic scale and a 10-point numerical scale (10 being the greater threat)" (Figure 5).[46] The end result of this process is a number that indicates a building's vulnerability to attack. Emergency planners are then supposed to use this information to customize the training scenarios and exercises they create to make them more "realistic."

As with Kahn's scenarios, the FEMA risk assessment guide emphasizes the process of scenario development. This process is actually what makes a scenario "realistic," because it confers the authority of quantitative analysis onto the scenario form as a whole. This conferral of authority positions the scenario as a product of an abstract, impersonal, and objective method. This means that the contents of individual scenarios themselves matter much less in relation to determining what is "realistic." In fact, the HSEEP document describes one of the responsibilities of the exercise planning

Criteria		
Very High	10	Very High—One or more major weaknesses have been identified that make the asset extremely susceptible to an aggressor or hazard. The building lacks redundancies/physical protection and the entire building would be only functional again after a very long period of time after the attack.
High	8–9	High—One or more major weaknesses have been identified that make the asset highly susceptible to an aggressor or hazard. The building has poor redundancies/physical protection and most parts of the building would be only functional again after a long period of time after the attack.
Medium High	7	Medium High—An important weakness has been identified that makes the asset very susceptible to an aggressor or hazard. The building has inadequate redundancies/physical protection and most critical functions would be only operational again after a long period of time after the attack.
Medium	5–6	Medium—A weakness has been identified that makes the asset fairly susceptible to an aggressor or hazard. The building has insufficient redundancies/physical protection and most part of the building would be only functional again after a considerable period of time after the attack.
Medium Low	4	Medium Low—A weakness has been identified that makes the asset somewhat susceptible to an aggressor or hazard. The building has incorporated a fair level of redundancies/physical protection and most critical functions would be only operational again after a considerable period of time after the attack.
Low	2–3	Low—A minor weakness has been identified that slightly increases the susceptibility of the asset to an aggressor or hazard. The building has incorporated a good level of redundancies/physical protection and the building would be operational within a short period of time after an attack.
Very Low	1	Very Low—No weaknesses exist. The building has incorporated excellent redundancies/physical protection and the building would be operational immediately after an attack.

Figure 5. Scale for a building's vulnerability rating, as included in FEMA's risk assessment guide.

team as "ensur[ing] that the design effort is not characterized by a fixation on scenario development," emphasizing that the effective scenario "facilitates achievement of exercise capabilities, tasks, and objectives, which are the foundation of exercise design" and nothing more.[47] The attention here, the HSEEP document states, should be on the procedure or the exercise for which the scenario is being used, not necessarily on the narrative details of the scenario itself. These details are not what make a scenario credible.

Yet, preparedness training scenarios are nevertheless often extremely detailed, and often quite imaginatively so. An example from FEMA's suite of Whole Community training exercises provides a good illustration of this point. FEMA's Whole Community exercises are designed for use by schools and by private-sector organizations in their own emergency preparedness training. The example I want to take up is titled "The Whole Community: Planning for the Unthinkable," a tabletop exercise organized around "an unprecedented catastrophic event."[48] In general, tabletop exercises are a discussion-based form of training centered on a scenario that describes a hypothetical emergency. The "Planning for the Unthinkable" exercise is designed around a worst-case scenario, or what FEMA refers to as a "Maximum of Maximums," featuring a Category 5 hurricane that hits the U.S. eastern seaboard, followed quickly by a 7.8 magnitude earthquake in Puerto Rico, which then triggers an eight- to ten-foot tsunami that rips through the Caribbean.[49] During the exercise, participants discuss as a group how best to respond to the emergency, often receiving video "injects," or "pre-scripted messages that alter the original scenario," to which they must respond as exercise play continues.[50] Participant decisions, in turn, are incorporated into the exercise as it unfolds. The video injects take the form of cable news updates from the fictional network VNN, describing the disasters and the extent of the incredible damage they cause. The injects also feature the heroics of fictional newscaster Rafael Mendoza, who survives both the earthquake and tsunami in Puerto Rico and helps to save the lives of thousands with his volunteer firefighting skills and his timely text messages warning people to move to higher ground.

In what is a hallmark of preparedness training exercises in general, the "Planning for the Unthinkable" scenario simultaneously declares its unreality at the same time that it insists it is realistic. For instance, the scenario's video injects explicitly acknowledge, repeatedly, the unbelievable nature of the situation. The newscasters draw attention to its implausibility by describing events as "surreal," "difficult to imagine," and "unthinkable."[51] The fantastic nature of the exercise is similarly emphasized in the exercise facilitator notes. Because of the "truly catastrophic" and "unusual" nature of this scenario, these notes emphasize that facilitators should urge participants "to be really out of the box" and "innovative" in discussing how they would respond to these disasters, communicate with one another, and "assis[t] our neighbors."[52] Yet, nevertheless, the scenario script also emphasizes again and again that what is happening is real: the newscasters repeatedly reassure participants of the realism of the exercise, stating that even though the events of the exercise are hard to believe, "this is our reality."[53]

What I want to draw our attention to here, however, is the exercise's lack of concern not only with probability—the confluence of a major hurricane, an earthquake, and a tsunami, while possible, seems unlikely—but also with verisimilitude. The scenario video injects, though meant to be presented during the exercise in the style of a newscast, and despite including many details, are not actually invested in setting the scene of the exercise or even in describing it. The injects include very little description of the world of the exercise. Instead, they communicate information: "The storm tore its way up the Eastern seaboard . . . its 20 foot storm surges and 120 mile-per-hour winds wreaking havoc from the Carolinas . . . to Long Island . . . to the New England coast"; "the human toll continues to rise. 8-thousand forty people are confirmed dead . . . with 11-hundred twenty still unaccounted for"; "10 million people are still without power and communications networks."[54] These details do not paint a picture of a rich, complex world, and they are meant only to give the participants the "facts" of the situation. There is nothing particularly vivid about them, nothing to persuade participants that what they are viewing is credible or that it could happen.

This is strange. We might think that such an improbable scenario would invest at least some energy in convincing participants of its verisimilitude, if nothing else. Vivid attention to detail has been a cornerstone of the style of the traditionally "realistic" novel, as

Roland Barthes's familiar formulation of the "reality effect" attests. For Barthes, the "useless details" of a novel—the energy the text invests in describing people and objects, description that may have little to no bearing on the plot or larger themes of the text—create an effect that signifies "the category of the real, and not its various contents."[55] This is what Barthes refers to as "the *referential illusion*" of realism, or the "reality effect" of a text.[56] The realism of a text for Barthes is always an illusion: a novel does not actually constitute or describe so-called objective reality, despite the fact that its useless details attempt to pass themselves off as indications of reality as such.[57] But crucially, even in this critical account of realism, realism is an illusion that rests on the text's attention to descriptive details; the realist novel seems real precisely because it spends so much time describing things. While the "Planning for the Unthinkable" scenario, like all exercise scenarios, provides many details to exercise participants, these details are mainly informative. They are entirely necessary to the exercise because exercise participants use them in making decisions about how to respond. Unlike the descriptive details of a realist novel, these details are not useless—they signify the "various contents" of the real rather than the "category of the real" itself. Given the fact that the "Planning for the Unthinkable" scenario lacks the kinds of details that would provide it with any pretense to the "referential illusion" of realism, we return to the question with which we began this chapter: what does this scenario mean when it purports to be "real"?

Creating a Consensual Reality

Answering this question means turning away from an understanding of realism aligned with verisimilitude and toward one that focuses on the boundary between reader and text or, in the case of preparedness exercises, between participant and exercise. Scholarship on science fiction has most explicitly, although by no means exclusively, discussed this rhetorical understanding of realism.[58] Because science fiction is generally understood as a genre unconcerned with, or even opposed to, realism, this may seem contradictory. However, as many scholars have recently observed, science fiction and realism are intimately connected. Jaak Tomberg, for instance, has argued that under late capitalism, everyday life takes on a science fictional flavor because "high-tech scientific developments" have "become so smoothly and thoroughly integrated into our understanding of the everyday environment."[59] As a result, the generic qualities of science fiction and those of realism have merged: "one and the same text, and all of the motifs therein, feel both plausibly everyday and plausibly cognitively estranging."[60] Seo-Young Chu takes a more formalist approach, arguing that despite depicting "hypothetical if not outright imaginary" things, science fiction does not in fact "operat[e] beyond (or even counter to) mimesis."[61] Instead, she argues that science fiction employs "a high-intensity variety of realism" defined by its dependence on figurative language and poetic tropes.[62] This style utilizes the force of poetic language to make the "cognitively estranging referents" on which the genre generally focuses—things like aliens and advanced technologies—available for representation and thus understanding and experience.[63]

What underlies both of these arguments about science fiction and realism is an implicit understanding of how science fictional texts create a consensual reality. For Tomberg, because everyday life already seems so science fictional, science fiction and realism have started to become indistinguishable; for Chu, it's the lyric force of science fiction—its ability to use figurative language to create new experiences for the reader—that makes it realist. Both arguments, in other words, depend on science fiction's ability to create, and not just to mimic, its own reality.[64] As China Miéville observes, science fiction has long depended on what he calls the *charismatic authority* of the text to do just this.[65] The ability of science fiction to transport its readers to another world—and, importantly, to convince them of the validity or veracity of that world, despite what may be its logical improbability or even impossibility—is, as Miéville describes it, "a *trickery* effected by the author" (238). The reader "surrenders" to or accepts the existence of this world "to the extent that [the reader surrenders] to the authority of the text and its author function" (238). This authority often comes from "an *apparently* cognitively logical and rigorous 'scientific' register" in the text—from appeals to logic or scientific reason, in other words, that are actually, in effect, "*persuasion*" (238).[66] But although Miéville describes the relationship between author and reader as hierarchical and manipulative—the reader surrenders to the author's trickery—he also emphasizes that this relationship is "consensual" (238). Both author and reader, he argues, are aware of its "game-like nature"; indeed, such awareness "is inextricable from enjoyment of the genre" (238, 240).

Despite never once mentioning realism in his essay, the similarity of Miéville's argument about the charismatic authority of the text to Barthes's account of the reality effect is striking. However, there is an important difference. While Barthes ties the ability of texts to produce the referential illusion of realism to their use of descriptive detail, or to their investment in verisimilitude, Miéville is more agnostic about technique. He indicates that authors can persuade readers of their authority using "whatever tools," and that such tools will vary from text to text (238). Moreover, authors can accomplish this act of persuasion despite including things like "preposterous pseudo-science" in their texts (239). For Miéville, then, a text's ability to persuade readers to accept its reality is not tied to any particular aesthetic or content. Rather, what we call realism is better described as an agreement between reader and author, or reader and text, to accept the reality of the text's world *despite* any logical inconsistencies or fantastical elements.

Following from this argument, we might better define "realism" in the context of preparedness training as a consensual reality: it is what happens when readers consent to accept the world of a text as having a reality all its own. This definition of realism is what differentiates Miéville's understanding of the authority of a text from Catherine Gallagher's influential discussion of plausibility, discussed in the introduction to this chapter. For Gallagher, the plausibility of a text, or the willingness of a reader to suspend disbelief and to accept the text as realistic, is ultimately tied to a text's credibility. Plausible narratives are "believable stories that [do] not solicit belief," and they are "credible" in the way that "incredible" tales that "contain talking animals, flying carpets, or human characters who are much better or worse than the norm" are obviously not.[67] While Gallagher's understanding of the authority of the fictional text to project a world is tied to the rise of the realist novel, in other words, Miéville articulates a theory of (science) fictional authority that makes no such claims to verisimilitude. For Miéville, the authority of a text to ask for "buy-in" from readers does not depend on its likeness to reality.

We are now ready to understand what the "Planning for the Unthinkable" exercise means when it refers to its own reality. Instead of creating the illusion of this reality through the use of verisimilitude, the exercise is designed to break down the boundary between itself and participants while still maintaining its status as fiction. It is designed not to convince participants that it is like their reality but rather to invite them into its explicitly fictional reality. Participants are encouraged to suspend their judgments about the exercise's similarity to their world and are instead encouraged to participate in the world of the exercise as such. This has nothing to do with tricking participants into thinking the exercise "really happened" or with convincing them that it might, even if they are convinced. Rather, it has to do with creating a world participants consent to treat as real. The scenario's explicit references to its own fictionality—how the newscasters describe the events of the scenario as "surreal," "difficult to imagine," and "unthinkable" while at the same time repeatedly emphasizing that "this is our reality"—are one way the "Planning for the Unthinkable" exercise creates just such a reality. These moments acknowledge the difference between the world of the participants and the world of the exercise by acknowledging how the world of the exercise seems to participants: "surreal" and "difficult to imagine." But in acknowledging this difference, they also invite participants into the world of the exercise; they invite them, in other words, to play along. Participants are invited to accept the world of the exercise as a reality in and of itself: "this is our reality." It may be a reality that is necessarily different from their own—it is fictional, whereas theirs is actual—but the exercise is the mechanism through which they can enter into it for a while.

Another way the "Planning for the Unthinkable" exercise extends an invitation to enter its world is by casting exercise participants as characters in the fictional world it creates. Most training exercises do this. The point of these exercises, after all, is to involve participants in exercise play directly. Although I will discuss the concept of characterization in relation to preparedness materials in more detail in chapter 4, I want to focus now on how the act of casting participants as characters invites them into the world of the exercise. The "Planning for the Unthinkable" exercise extends this invitation rhetorically by addressing participants directly in the form of newscasts. The exercise newscasts always begin, like actual newscasts, by welcoming participants to the broadcast and situating them in relation to it. "Welcome back to VNN as we continue our coverage of the devastating aftermath of Hurricane Kenley," the first newscast begins. "I'm Jeanne Meserve, live from the VNN headquarters in Washington, D.C."[68] This address is a literal invitation into the world of the exercise; in fact, its opening in medias res ("welcome back") addresses participants as if they were already in it. It also sets up a familiar distinction between the newscaster and her audience—I'm in Washington, D.C., and you are somewhere, anywhere else—while at the same time establishing their shared distance from the scene of disaster happening in "the Outer Banks of North Carolina."[69] Both the newscaster and participants/news audience, in other words, observe the disaster from a distance, just as they would an actual disaster. The temporality of this address is also important: by addressing themselves to exercise participants in the form of live news broadcasts, the video injects enlist participants in the always-unfolding present moment of the disaster. What participants see on the news broadcast, even though they know it is fictional, is happening now, in the everlasting present of fiction that occurs as readers read it (or, in this case, as participants enact it), and the direct address of the broadcast invites them to join that now.

In this way, the video inject newscasts are designed, just like real newscasts, to create what Michael Warner has referred to as the "mass subject of news," or the abstract public created by such forms of address.[70] This mass subjectivity is fictive, but it isn't fictive because it arises from an explicitly fictional preparedness training exercise. Rather, as Warner has argued, all publics are fictive because they "do not exist apart from the discourse that addresses them."[71] By virtue of the fact that public discourse addresses itself to a public, in other words—instead of to an "empirical referent," such as a specific, known person or bureaucratic entity—it addresses itself to an unknown entity that "is always yet to be realized."[72] Warner argues that this mode of address therefore constitutes a form of world building: "all discourse or performance addressed to a public must characterize the world in which it attempts to circulate and it must attempt to realize that world through address."[73] Public address brings into being not only the public to whom it is addressed but also the world in which it circulates as public discourse. Training exercises use this kind of world building, or what Warner describes as the "subjunctive-creative project" of public address, to their advantage.[74] Like actual newscasts, the video injects in the "Planning for the Unthinkable" exercise are addressed to a public created through that address. Just like actual newscasts, they enlist exercise participants as part of the reality they describe and create, and exercise participants become the public to whom the newscast is addressed. It is no matter that this public exists within a fictional world. In this sense, the exercise participants are no different from any other public created through (nonfictional) public discourse. Both are equally fictional—which is not to say that both are equally unreal. Rather, both belong to the same kind of "subjunctive-creative" reality.

The strategies I have outlined here—how the training exercise calls attention to its own outrageous fictionality, how it addresses participants directly and thereby invites them into its world—are specific to just one training exercise, and they are just a few of the strategies available to training exercises for creating a consensual reality. All training exercises depend on this form of realism, however; it is what they mean when they insist on their own reality. But as with any other kind of realism, this realism relies on its ontological difference from (nonfictional) reality to function in the first place. It is only possible to describe training exercises as "realistic" because participants know they are fictional. Therefore, as the "Planning for the Unthinkable" exercise demonstrates, training exercises work by emphasizing their reality at the same time as they insist on their fictionality, and participants agree to play along, consenting to the authority of the text, or exercise in this case, to project a world.

"Very Enjoyable" and "Entertaining"

Planners, like other creators of fiction, know that getting training exercise participants to consent to the reality of an exercise is easier to do if participants are enjoying themselves. Enjoyment, or at least contentment, is therefore important for preparedness training exercises overall, but it becomes especially important when training people to become planners or emergency managers or when training people to train others. Turning back to CONPLAN 8888, the "counter-zombie dominance" disaster scenario with which this chapter began, helps to illustrate this point. CONPLAN 8888 is, by the admission of the scenario designers themselves, "completely-impossible" (3). Yet, as I have discussed, the fact that it could never happen does not detract from its effectiveness as a training scenario. Rather, the disclaimer that begins CONPLAN 8888 states that the scenario works particularly well as a training tool precisely because it is impossible: "Because the plan was so ridiculous, our students not only enjoyed the lessons; they actually were able to explore the basic concepts of plan and order development . . . very effectively" (3). Participants, in other words, find the scenario, in the disclaimer's words, "very enjoyable" and "entertaining" precisely because it is "so ridiculous," not because it's believable (3).

This articulation of the relationship between plausibility and pleasure differs from how Gallagher understands this relationship. She links plausibility and pleasure, claiming that fiction promotes disbelief in "the literal truth of a representation so that one can instead admire its likelihood and extend enough credit to buy into the game."[75] In Gallagher's articulation, the pleasure one gets from reading depends, in fact, on a narrative's plausibility—on "admir[ing] its likelihood." This pleasurable immersion in a fictional world, however, requires readers to pretend, however briefly and for whatever purpose, that there is no line separating the fictional world they read about from their own. When readers knowingly suspend their disbelief in fiction to "extend enough credit to buy into the game," they agree to believe that what they read could actually happen or to ignore the fact that what they are reading is a fictional story.

"CONPLAN 8888," on the other hand, demonstrates that taking pleasure in fiction, what Gallagher calls "the enjoyment of deep immersion in illusion," does not depend on a narrative's credibility.[76] This training scenario shows that pretending to believe a story could happen need not enter into the picture at all. In fact, if participants know that the fictional world they are about to enter is "ridiculous" and "completely-impossible," they may even enjoy immersing themselves in this world more. Ultimately, however, preparedness training exercises do not project future disasters so that participants can read about them or act them out (only) for fun; they project future disasters to train participants to respond in certain ways to these disasters. CONPLAN 8888 demonstrates that preparedness exercises are designed to bypass questions of belief or disbelief entirely and encourage participants to act. Preparedness training scenarios don't require that participants believe a zombie pandemic could occur. They simply enjoin participants to imagine what it would be like if such disasters were already real and to act accordingly, even though they know they are not. They are oriented toward action, not belief. They ask for participants' consent but do not ask them to pretend to believe in the disasters they project. Rather, they ask them to consent to act as if these disasters were real.

Taken together, the materials examined in this chapter demonstrate that questions of belief—and therefore related questions of probability and verisimilitude—are not central to preparedness. You do not need to believe in the possibility of a future disaster "actually happening" to prepare for one. Instead, you just need to follow the protocol outlined in the training exercise. Treating fictional disasters in this way requires your consent, but only your consent to do the training. As we have seen throughout this chapter, giving such consent means agreeing to treat these disasters as having a reality all their own—agreeing to act with the understanding that although such disasters are fictional and therefore not actual, they are just as real as actual events. All you have to do is agree to the reality of these fictional disasters in the present.

3

Thinking Generically

The Professional Management of Disaster

In the last chapter, we saw how preparedness training exercises operate as training tools not by generating belief but rather by garnering the consent of their participants to treat the disasters they project as if they were real. Their science fictional understanding of fictionality means that these exercises tend to abandon verisimilitude and the suspension of disbelief and focus instead on the creation of a consensual reality that participants can inhabit for the duration of the exercise. It doesn't matter, for preparedness, if we find a particular disaster scenario or training exercise particularly unbelievable or poorly crafted (or particularly believable or well crafted, for that matter). It matters simply that we agree to play along. But who exactly is this "we"? To whom are preparedness materials addressed, and why? This chapter examines a key concept in preparedness training, one which provides an answer to these questions: professionalism. Preparedness materials address themselves to the figure of the "professional" and, through this address, create it.

In recent years, governmental officials have called for the professionalization of emergency management. The FEMA Emergency Management Institute (EMI), which offers training and certification in emergency management to people both inside and outside of federal and state governmental organizations, lists "professionalism" as one of the eight core principles of emergency management, and practitioners within the government have called for emergency management to "become [a] profession."[1] According to FEMA, becoming a profession means adopting "a science and knowledge-based approach" to disaster preparedness, drawing on a "specialized body of knowledge" and depending on "professional associations" to define and formalize the profession's "standards and best practices" and to control access to the profession via "board certification."[2] Similarly, emergency management scholars and educators, themselves a product of the growing professionalization of the field, have increasingly focused their work on issues related to "professional certification" in emergency management, especially those concerning "EM-HS [Emergency Management-Homeland Security] program standards, guidelines, and model curriculum that is supported and promulgated by a national professional accreditation body in either EM or HS."[3] These calls for the professionalization of emergency management thereby center on rigorous training—and the standardization and control of this training via official certification and accreditation mechanisms—as the route to professionalization.

This concern with training is not confined to emergency management. The role of training within more general processes of professionalization has also been extensively analyzed by scholars of professionalism, especially those in the sociology of the professions, an interdisciplinary field focused on theories and histories of professionalization and professional systems. Grounded in the foundational work of Karl Marx, Max Weber, Thorstein Veblen, and John Dewey, the sociology of the professions has sought to understand professionalism and its historical development as both an ideology and a set of practices. Scholars in this field continually turn to the issue of training when describing what constitutes professionalism. In Burton J. Bledstein's canonical work on professionalism, for example, he describes a professional as someone who possesses a "trained capacity" and, later, as a "trained person."[4] Similarly, Eliot Freidson, considered one of the founders of the field, claims that what distinguishes professionals from those who have other kinds of occupations that require complex specialized knowledge—auto mechanics, for instance—is their training: "above all else," he writes, "the ideology supporting professional training emphasizes theory and abstract concepts" over "practical training."[5]

These understandings of professionalism all define a professional as someone with specialized training—a professional is, above all else, a "trained person." Usually, undergoing such training involves attending specific schools and receiving specialized certifications or degrees that can take years to complete. Requiring this training thus controls the membership of professions, restricting it by raising the bar for entry. The discussions mentioned above about creating and adhering to "EM-HS program standards, guidelines, and model curriculum," for example, evidence this restrictive understanding of who a professional is and of the role of training in creating the professional. However, as we will see, the concept of professionalism in the context of preparedness is also expansive; a "professional" is also anyone who has undergone preparedness training, no matter what the person's actual job is. Those who receive preparedness training on the job or at school, for instance, also become professionalized. In this understanding, professionalism does not necessarily describe only those relatively few who have completed formal degrees or certificates in emergency management—the experts in disaster preparedness. Rather, it describes a way of thinking about and responding to disaster that theoretically anyone, with the right training, can adopt. It is an understanding of professionalism without expertise.

In this chapter, I examine a range of preparedness materials focused on or geared toward training to argue that we can best understand the professionalization process in preparedness and emergency management as, combining those views articulated in the preceding paragraphs, a kind of practical training in generalization. From emergency management textbooks and preparedness training exercises and courses to congressional reports on the effectiveness of preparedness training materials and political thrillers meant to inform the public about matters of national security, these materials all emphasize that training in professional emergency management means training in how to generalize about disaster—in how to infer broad conclusions from specific instances. Preparedness works by preparing people to respond to any kind of disaster using the same protocols for response; it is concerned with generalizing disaster response to the degree that responding to a hurricane involves the same basic processes as responding to a terrorist attack. As such, it trades in *convention*, a term I use, following Lauren Berlant, in both its normative and aesthetic senses.[6] A genre convention, for example, is a typical or standard trope or element in a work of genre fiction. Moreover, audiences expect to encounter specific genre conventions in works belonging to specific genres, and therefore, because of this expectation, genre conventions make works legible as examples of their genres. They are both ordinary and expected. Genre is therefore a useful concept for understanding how preparedness materials train people to think about disaster because, like the term *generic*, *genre* describes practices of generalization—practices that turn a particular detail into an instance of an overall type.[7]

But however much a genre may trade in convention, genres aren't static, transhistorical categories. *Genre*, as I use the term here, describes a process of accumulation and sedimentation. Genres are living repositories in which particular conventions become deposited, even as such conventions change over time. The conventions that we recognize as particular to one specific genre or another can mutate and shift and still remain recognizable as particular to those genres. Similarly, individual examples of a genre can incorporate new or different elements and conventions and still remain recognizable as part of that genre.[8] The conception of genre I pursue here, then, focuses less on specific formal, historical, or sociological conventions or processes that would serve to define the genre of "preparedness materials" and more on how genres, precisely because they are conventional, work to produce and structure expectations. Such an understanding follows closely from Berlant's definition of genre as "an aesthetic structure of affective expectation," one that "absorbs all kinds of small variations or modifications while promising that the persons transacting with it will experience the pleasure of encountering what they expected, with details varying the theme."[9] In the case of preparedness materials, many of these expectations have to do with what future disasters will be like: what might happen, what the consequences might be, and, perhaps most importantly for this chapter, how they might feel. Such materials, after all, provide a way for participants to enact a specific imagination of the future by constructing a possible world for which they must train and prepare. Furthermore, the preparedness materials

I examine in this chapter all place particular emphasis on instruction in how to recognize and act in accordance with the conventions of their genre. They aim to prepare people to respond to future disaster by instructing them in how to think about these disasters in highly conventional ways. Such instruction in generic expectation, as Mark Jerng puts it, "produce[s] effects of truth and authority through the projection of . . . 'generically specific' worlds."[10]

I term this process of learning to think conventionally about disaster *thinking generically*. In the context of preparedness, thinking generically means thinking about future disaster both as generalizable and in accordance with certain genre conventions. It means learning to recognize only some disasters as "proper" disasters and to treat all those disasters one recognizes as functionally the same, or learning to articulate the conditions of the legibility of disaster itself. As I mentioned earlier, such thinking is tied to the professionalization of emergency planning and response, meaning that it is one mechanism through which people are trained to adopt a professional attitude toward disaster. Training people to think generically—training them to expect some disasters and therefore to regard them as unexceptional and normal, or as conventional, and at the same time, training them to ignore other disasters by learning to exclude these events from the definition of disaster itself—is what constitutes "professional" training in preparedness. This training creates the generic professional of preparedness: someone who is endowed with the skills of generalization.

Preparedness materials ostensibly rely on a fictional universality of address; that is, they rely on the conceit that learning to think generically about disaster and therefore to become a professional is theoretically available to anyone who undergoes preparedness training. However, we will see in this chapter how this free-floating address to "anyone" also remakes the addressee as an implicitly white generic professional. The preparedness materials I discuss address themselves to an abstract and largely implicit audience, one they often only refer to as "you." These materials also incorporate descriptions and images of people of color, men and women, and disabled and able-bodied people to emphasize that this you could "really" be anyone. These descriptions and images thereby signal participation in a liberal multiculturalism that equates representation of "diverse" bodies with an inclusive post-racial society. However, as many have argued, these representational strategies are a form of what Eduardo Bonilla-Silva has termed *color-blind racism*, which operates by "exclud[ing] old-fashioned racist speech" and sentiments and "applying the principles of liberalism to racial matters in an abstract and decontextualized manner."[11] Preparedness materials rarely mention people of color or racialized bodies explicitly; instead, they insist, often implicitly, that race has nothing to do with professionalism while, as the last section of the chapter will argue, using the concept of professionalism to exclude nonwhite people from the supposed protection of the national security state. In what will become visible as a pattern that recurs across the rest of this book, the descriptions and images of people of color that occur throughout preparedness materials constitute attempts to expand the boundaries of whiteness to encompass racialized bodies into an abstract, inclusive whole—the category of the generic preparedness professional. Preparedness materials don't address themselves to white people specifically so much as they address themselves to the general category of whiteness itself, a category that seeks to be generic by making a particular figure—the white professional—stand in for the typical or the general "anyone." Whiteness seeks to encompass everyone while only naming some.[12]

Preparedness discourse manages this complicated form of address through euphemism. In addition to addressing themselves to "you," preparedness materials also tell us they are addressed to "citizens of the homeland." As Donald Pease has argued, the phrase "homeland security" names not a specific place or national territory but rather "a form of governmentality without a recognizable location."[13] Specifically, the homeland is a state of governance "that emerged *through and by way of the people's generalized dislocation from the nation as a shared form of life.*"[14] Pease argues that the events of September 11, 2001, "dislocated the national people" from the geographical boundaries of the nation by shoring up the shared myth that formed their imaginary relationship to the state. This shared myth was that the United States was innocent of any wrongdoing that might have motivated the destruction of the World Trade Center and that the attacks therefore were unprovoked, without cause, and unimaginable.[15] This belief sanctioned the state's extreme response to September 11, including the invasion of Iraq and Afghanistan, the enactment of the USA PATRIOT Act, and the creation of DHS itself. The homeland therefore refers to, as Pease puts it, "the structure through which the state of emergency is realized normally."[16] While I agree with Pease that the homeland names not a place but rather a mode of authoritarian governance, the materials examined in this chapter show how it also names and normalizes a specific group of people. The phrase "citizens of the homeland" names those who felt "dislocated" by the disasters of September 11, 2001, those who, generally speaking, saw the attacks both as unprovoked and as evidence of the need to commit violence elsewhere to secure the "homeland." Most importantly, the phrase names those whose suffering the state has deemed unacceptable, or at least unfortunate, in contrast to those whose suffering the state has deemed acceptable, even necessary. The people of the homeland, in other words, are the implicitly white professionals to whom preparedness materials address themselves. As Deepa Kumar argues, "the 'homeland' . . . tends to be white, even if it is not explicitly articulated as such."[17]

The first part of the chapter focuses on the fictional and nonfictional writing of former national security official Richard Clarke to theorize thinking generically, and therefore professionally, and its implicit racial politics. Next, I expand this discussion to include preparedness training exercise scenarios. As discussed in chapter 2, disaster scenarios are the often narrative portion of a training exercise that provides details about the fictional disaster to which exercise participants must practice responding. As we will see, disaster scenarios rely to a large degree on recognizable genre conventions to manage their audiences' expectations about disaster. The chapter's third section focuses on a popular workplace training exercise developed by FEMA to show how the generic thinking that preparedness training materials instill is designed to extend to subject formation. Preparedness materials encourage trainees to adopt the right attitude about disaster, teaching them to approach disaster with the nonchalance of the (white, male) professional, a coolness that develops from having achieved an exceptional level of competence. Trainees are encouraged to think of themselves as generic "professionals" first and foremost, no matter who they are or what they do, and to act from that capacity if and when disaster strikes.

The final part of the chapter turns back to the congressional hearing reports investigating the federal failure to respond effectively to Hurricane Katrina first discussed in chapter 1, detailing how the language of professionalism functions to cast those who stayed in New Orleans through the storm outside of the homeland, positioning them as undeserving of protection from the national security state. Paradoxically, even when thinking generically ostensibly fails to train people to respond to disaster, this failure can never be a failure of preparedness itself if the generic expectations the training materials set up are met. Instead, those individuals who act "unprofessionally" are to blame.

Thinking Generically

There is perhaps no better emblem of thinking generically than the writing of former national security official Richard Clarke. Clarke's fiction and nonfiction alike demonstrate the extent to which the conventions of preparedness training correspond to the conventions of genre fiction, specifically to those of political thrillers (in chapter 5, I will discuss how the conventions of preparedness also correspond to those of horror). These conventions are related to the genre's management of readerly emotion and to its imagination of its audience. A high-ranking national security official under Presidents George H. W. Bush and Bill Clinton and for the first years of George W. Bush's administration, Clarke resigned in 2003 over the latter's decision to invade Iraq. Since his resignation, Clarke has published several nonfiction books on national security and terrorism, but he has also become something of a self-styled Tom Clancy, publishing four novels about terrorism and the threat it poses to national security.[18] These novels rely on the tried and true conventions of the airport political thriller to stage narratives of future disaster or of what could happen if terrorists attack. They all follow a similar formula: in the near future, terrorists orchestrate some kind of attack, often in one or several Western cities; mayhem ensues; officials from the United States and other Western countries scramble to respond; and further cataclysmic disaster is narrowly avoided by the courageous actions of a few intrepid individuals who aren't afraid to risk their own safety for the lives of millions. The novels are written in a descriptive, plain style that focuses on action, even when no action is taking place: "Ray sat quietly, running his own data analytics program in his head, his eyes darting back and forth as he thought through scenarios."[19] As is usual for this genre, the heroes of Clarke's novels are all professionals. They are highly competent in all matters, from computer hacking to marksmanship to leading conference calls; they have a facility with the argot of professional intelligence agents and law enforcement officers, referring in offhand ways to "thousands of money transfers, from a rat's nest of *hawalas*, Bitcoins, anonymous offshore accounts," "self-evacuation," and "top cover from cyberspace"; and the novels' narrators often refer to them by their last names alone.[20] Unlike the spy thriller, which, as Allan Hepburn has argued, encourages readers to identify with "the fugitive or the agent who hovers on the borders of legality, and who, therefore best expresses the reader's uncertainty about living inside and outside the law at the same time," the protagonists of Clarke's political thrillers are unambiguously heroic.[21] They are the good guys, and the good guys work for the United States, which sanctions their actions. The bad guys, on the other hand, work for corrupt or enemy foreign governments, corporations, or nonstate actors. In the world of the political thriller, there is no ambiguity about operating outside of the law, because there is no "outside of the law" for those who work for the U.S. government. As in Tom Clancy's thrillers, in Clarke's worlds, "the difference between right and wrong is clear and never compromised," William Terdoslavich writes. "The United States is always right."[22]

Clarke's novels advance a conventional understanding of terrorist attacks as events—as sudden and spectacular incidents that arrive without warning, disrupting the fabric of everyday life—and as perpetrated by corrupt corporate or fundamentalist nonstate actors. *The Scorpion's Gate* (2005), *Breakpoint* (2007), and *Pinnacle Event* all open with scenes of small-scale disasters that are connected to the larger attacks around which the novels are structured: a hotel is bombed; a nuclear physicist is murdered; beachhead routers carrying internet traffic explode. These attacks unfold in punctuated, serial form as the novels go on. They are described in short, choppy sentences—for example, "The yellow flame leaped into the air where the ocean hit the land"—and they are contained within short subsections of chapters that comprise only a few pages.[23] *Sting of the Drone*, which is more of a slow burn, tinkers with this formula by portraying several drone attacks by both the United States and terrorist groups. This strategy complicates the more straight-forward narrative of U.S. (and white) victimization at the hands of (brown) terrorists in Clarke's other novels by emphasizing the "col-lateral damage" caused by U.S. drone attacks, as the U.S. characters in the book refer to the people murdered by U.S. drones.[24] But this novel, too, structures each of these attacks as an event. They are de-scribed in short, choppy sentences and contained within short chap-ter subsections.

In these novels, disasters are unexpected and violent, but they are also narratively contained. They are neatly packaged modular units that are nearly interchangeable. A hotel bombing is described and structured the same way as a router explosion and a drone at-tack. This way of organizing the action of his novels connects Clarke on a formal level to the scenario. As I will discuss in more detail in the next section, preparedness exercise scenarios are highly formal-ized, interchangeable chunks of information. Their contents matter much less than this formal codification. Just like the disasters that occur in Clarke's fiction, they are highly generalizable. One can eas-ily stand in for another.

When read in the context of other preparedness training mate-rials, the highly formulaic structure of Clarke's fiction is a method-ology designed to manage readerly interest and engagement. The chapters of Clarke's novels are organized chronologically and pro-ceed linearly, and each one usually covers the events of one day. As suggested earlier, Clarke often further breaks chapters down into smaller sections of no more than ten pages, each one covering a more specific time frame, usually just a matter of minutes in that day, and a specific location where the action is taking place. Such relentless pacing ensures the novels spend most of their energy driving their plots forward. These plots are at once multilayered and intricate—a lot of time is spent describing how characters are connected to one another, even across different novels—and vast and sprawling: the first chapter of *Breakpoint* alone introduces the reader to eighteen named characters and ten different locations. It's difficult to keep it all straight, but the effectiveness of these novels doesn't actually depend on the reader keeping information about the plots or subplots or characters straight. Instead, it depends on the reader's willingness to feel engaged enough to keep reading, to keep turning the page.

Clarke terms this kind of engagement "excitement." He maintains that the best way to teach people about national security issues is to "make it a little exciting" so that "people may enjoy it," something he argues that novels do well: "I think a novel can get the attention of the reader in a way that an analytical, non-fiction book really just doesn't."[25] Like thrillers of all kinds, in other words, Clarke's novels are interested in the aesthetic experience of the thrill. Hepburn defines the thrill as "those tremors of almost-out-of-body attentiveness that seize a reader . . . at moments of crisis," and Clarke's novels certainly rely on crisis to generate "excitement."[26] However, generating excitement isn't all that Clarke's fiction is designed to do. It is also calibrated to carefully manage the excitement it generates so that it doesn't overwhelm the reader. His preferred narrative style makes this clear: he often begins subsections of his novels in medias res, dropping the reader into the middle of an ongoing event or conversation, and ends these subsections once that event or conversation comes to a close. The first subsection of the first chapter of *The Scorpion's Gate*, for example, begins in the middle of a suicide bomber's attack of a Western hotel in Manama, Bahrain, and ends once one of the main characters, a British intelligence agent named Brian Douglas, has made it out alive and has learned that other Western hotels are also under attack.

Many political thrillers utilize cliffhangers, a hallmark of the serial form designed, as Luke Terlaak Poot has argued, to draw the reader's attention to the significance of the rhythm of their reading.[27] Clarke sometimes utilizes cliffhangers in his fiction, but as the previous paragraph indicates, a more common technique for Clarke is something like the inverse of a cliffhanger, what we might call the fall from the cliff. A cliffhanger works by building up excitement and then refusing to discharge it; Emily Nussbaum describes it as "a climax cracked in half."[28] Clarke's technique, however, discharges the excitement generated by its cold open. If the cliffhanger is all potential energy, Clarke's fall from the cliff is all kinetic. Yet this energy is not frenetic; it is always well managed: a controlled descent rather than a free fall. After the initial burst of energy that opens *The Scorpion's Gate*—after the hotel lobby has blown up and "the waiter [has flown] through the lobby café" and Douglas and his bodyguard have run "through the smoldering debris" of the lobby, "out the door to the pool deck," and down "the service stairwell" into an alley, shooting and kicking down locked doors and avoiding "pools of blood" and "pieces of pink and white and gray that had so recently been living flesh"—the narrative action starts to slow.[29] Douglas reaches the safety of his team, and instead of ceaseless movement, readers are confronted with several pages of dialogue and paragraph-length exposition where he learns the details of the attack from his "number-two" and holds a conference call with the director of the British Secret Intelligence Service in London.[30] In marked contrast to its beginning, the subsection ends with understatement: "A long, low rumble shook the bubble room in Bahrain. The exhaust fans seemed to cough."[31] This "cough," we learn in the next, final paragraph of the section, is "the sound of the Crowne Plaza, down the street from the Diplomat, pancaking."[32] Like the Crowne Plaza, readers land at the end of the subsection with a thud.

The formulaic nature of Clarke's novels means this pattern repeats. Each of the subsections in his novels usually comprises only one small piece of the action, a few minutes out of the days or months that will eventually make up the entirety of each novel's strictly linear timeline. As such, none of these subsections can stand on their own; they constitute only a small part of the vast, interlocking system of these novels' plots. Reaching the end of one subsection therefore encourages you to read more, but not necessarily because you're hooked. As Poot argues, the cliffhanger uses narrative delay to generate reader interest by "turning narrative momentum against itself, marshaling the reader's desire to know what happens next as a means of reflecting on what has happened before."[33] The fall from the cliff, however, doesn't rely on stopping narrative time. Rather, it barrels on ahead, using the expectation of narrative satisfaction—the sense that every event will be expertly handled by both the novel's characters and its author, that every crisis will be resolved—to generate reader engagement. Instead of leaving readers in a state of uncertainty about what will happen next, the fall from the cliff generates the satisfaction and reassurance of knowing everything will turn out right in the end, no matter how hard things may get. The novels' subsections are energetic and action packed, but they are also easily digestible and defined by a clear narrative arc, packaged and distributed to resolve themselves and so reward readerly attention. What's more, the experience repeats across the entirety of each novel. You get the feeling you are reading a finely calibrated machine for producing, if nothing else, the repeated experience of resolution.

Clarke's approach to narrating future disaster, in other words, is highly professional. This approach seeks to manage readerly excitement at all times: there can never be too much or too little, and the goal is to keep the reader moving forward in a calm, cool, and collected manner. Unlike spy thrillers, which, Hepburn argues, generate thrills by playing on the pleasures associated with the interplay of fear and catharsis, Clarke's novels manage thrills through the achievement of affective neutrality.[34] They drop readers and characters into already existing moments of crisis, supplying a ready-made thrill from which they must then bring readers down. Fear is not the dominant sensation associated with reading Clarke's fiction; the satisfaction of a known ending is. There is no crisis too dangerous, no situation too complex, for the professional heroes of Clarke's fiction to handle.

There is nothing particularly remarkable about the genre conventions, or the novels, described earlier, as they are variations on what is more or less expected from airport political thrillers. But this is precisely what makes them powerful. Indeed, as Berlant's definition of *genre* suggests—genre is "an aesthetic structure of affective expectation"—this is what keeps readers coming back for more. They know that to read Clarke's fiction is to "experience the pleasure of encountering what they expected."[35] Taken as an example of preparedness training materials, the conventionality of Clarke's fiction becomes legible as an articulation of these materials' abiding concern with how to manage future disaster.[36] The future disasters Clarke's fiction stages, in other words, all have a highly recognizable and formulaic shape: that of the airport political thriller, where disasters are spectacular, where individual competence or "just doing my job" is a kind of heroism in and of itself, and where all of the important action happens in short sections of easily digestible narrative prose. This is part of what thinking generically entails. It involves the imprinting of a conventional structure of affective expectation onto experience. In the case of preparedness training materials, this experience is called a disaster.

Thinking generically is also itself a process of generalization. To think generically is to expect to see and understand specific events according to certain genre conventions. We can better understand this process by examining the nonfiction Clarke claims inspires him in tandem with his own nonfictional work. Clarke emphasizes that he models his writing style on a specific work of nonfiction: on "the way the 9/11 Commission wrote prose."[37] By focusing on how national security issues affect day-to-day life, he says that he strives to "bring it home" and "make it real."[38] Clarke's mention of *The 9/11 Commission Report,* for which he provided testimony, reveals the extent to which he sees the distinctions between fiction and nonfiction as rather blurry. As a work of nonfiction, the report's self-described "mandate" is also pedagogical. "The law directed us to investigate 'facts and circumstances relating to the terrorist attacks of September 11, 2001,'" the report states, and it emphasizes that "we have been committed to share as much of our investigation as we can with the American people."[39] Yet, curiously, the report nevertheless often reads like a work of fiction, and specifically like a work from the same mold as Clarke's fiction. For instance, in one section, the report narrates the events of the morning of September 11, 2001, from the perspectives of those on board each of the four hijacked planes and of those on the ground in New York City and Washington, D.C. The report describes in detail the "19 men . . . aboard four transcontinental flights" who "were planning to hijack these planes and turn them into large guided missiles, loaded with up to 11,400 gallons of jet fuel" and who "had defeated all the security layers that America's civil aviation security system then had in place to prevent a hijacking."[40] The report moves quickly from one event to the next, focusing on what happened aboard each hijacked plane and on the ground in air traffic control centers, even incorporating bits of (actual recorded) dialogue:

FAA: Hi. Boston Center TMU [Traffic Management Unit], we have a problem here. We have a hijacked aircraft headed towards New York, and we need you guys to, we need someone to scramble some F-16s or something up there, help us out.

NEADS: Is this real-world or exercise?

FAA: No, this is not an exercise, not a test.[41]

Structurally, *The 9/11 Commission Report*, like Clarke's fiction, continually employs the inverse cliffhanger or the fall from the cliff. It, too, is broken up into chapters composed of short subsections, many of which begin in medias res and end with the expenditure of the energy built up by their cold open. Each subsection describing the hijacking of a plane, for instance, begins with the plane taking off and ends with a line like this: "All on board, along with an unknown number of people in the tower, were killed instantly."[42] Clarke's claim that he has modeled the style of his fiction on *The 9/11 Commission Report* so that it feels more "real" thus turns out to be strangely circular: he has modeled his writing style on a work of nonfiction that appears to have modeled its style on the kind of genre fiction Clarke writes.

Clarke's nonfiction continues this pattern. His 2004 best seller *Against All Enemies*—part memoir of his career in intelligence and national security, part critique of the Bush administration's decision to invade Iraq after 9/11—often reads like a work of fiction (or like a page out of *The 9/11 Commission Report*). For instance, the first-person narrator sometimes has seemingly omniscient access to other people's states of mind—"Condi [Condoleezza Rice] knew it looked odd, but she also had enough self-confidence to feel no need to be in the chair. She did not want to waste time"—and the dialogue, like the dialogue in Clarke's novels, tends to read as snappy: "'You shouldn't still be here, Gare,' I tried. 'You want this fuckin' video to work, don't you?' 'Okay, well if you're staying . . .'"[43] The book's first chapter is a description of the events of September 11, 2001, from Clarke's perspective, and, like his fiction, it begins by dropping the reader in the middle of things: "I ran through the West Wing to the Vice President's office, oblivious to the stares and concern that brought."[44] The first chapter also utilizes Clarke's fall from the cliff technique, discharging the energy of its action-packed beginning by ending with a description of the funeral of one of Clarke's friends, who died in the World Trade Center, and Clarke's self-reflection: "There was so much to grieve about. How did this all happen? Why couldn't we stop it? How do we prevent it from happening again and rid the world of the horror? Someday I would find the time to think through it all and answer those questions. Now is that time."[45]

The similarity of this style of writing to that of Clarke's fictional prose is no surprise, given that Clarke is the author of all these books, but it is nevertheless revealing. Clarke's novels and non-fiction share the same goals. His novels are marketed as "instructive," as full of "an insider's expertise in geopolitics," and even as "prophetic," and he has said that he wrote *Against All Enemies* to "stimulat[e] public debate" on the Iraq War.[46] Clarke sees his role as an author of both fiction and nonfiction as "help[ing] people understand complex security issues" so that we can "aver[t] the really bad scenarios if we think about them in advance."[47] The word "scenarios" here is especially telling. Clarke uses the word to refer not to fictional events but to supposedly impending actual events. This description of reality in fictional terms underlines the convergence of Clarke's fictional and nonfictional writing. Both kinds of writing, in other words, use the techniques available to fiction writers—and specifically to writers of political thrillers—to animate disaster scenarios, whether potential or actual, and to help readers understand their impact. They both strive to "bring it home" and "make it real." The scenario form, as a favorite technique of preparedness, therefore links genre fiction to the professional management of disaster. Clarke's statement that he hopes his writing helps people avoid "the really bad scenarios if we think about them in advance" signals that he views all of his writing, both fictional and nonfictional, as training in preparedness.

But who is the putative audience for this training? Who does Clarke imagine as his readers? We can infer answers to these questions by looking to the characters in his novels. The majority of these characters are white men, or racially unmarked, which is the same thing. A few are white or racially unmarked women, and very few are not white. As in the actual world, professionals in Richard Clarke's novels are much more likely to belong to particular racial and gender groups. Furthermore, when nonmale, nonwhite professionals do appear in these novels, this generally comes as a surprise to characters in the novel. For example, Mbali Hlanganani, a supporting character in Clarke's 2015 novel *Pinnacle Event*, is the South African president's director of the Special Security Services Office and a Black South African woman. Before Ray Bowman, a white ex–intelligence officer for the U.S. government who also appears in Clarke's 2014 novel *Sting of the Drone*, even meets Hlanganani, he assumes she is a man, telling his coworker to "tell him I accept his invitation [to go to South Africa]."[48] The chapter ends with "a good belly laugh" from the coworker, who replies, "but Raymond, make no mistake, Mbali Hlanganani is definitely not a him."[49] As the last line of the chapter, this sentence reads like this subversion of expectation—a subversion of both Bowman's and the reader's expectations—is supposed to amuse the reader. When Bowman meets Hlanganani, the narrator draws attention to Bowman's impression of her physical appearance, as he "shak[es] his head at the striking, tall woman in the chair" and "star[es] at her long legs."[50] Despite, or perhaps because of, her deviation from the norm, Hlanganani clearly impresses Bowman, who describes her as "a no-nonsense professional" after a brief chat.[51] In contrast to how the narrator lingers on Hlanganani's body, the narrator never draws attention to Bowman's appearance. As a white man, he does not depart from the expected norm of the "no-nonsense professional," and so there is nothing amusing or contradictory about his professionalism. Later, Bowman notes that the men from Hlanganani's security team are white, not Black, as he had expected. He is surprised that "Mbali's security team was multiracial," and he wonders "how often she had used white agents when blacks would stand out too much."[52] Bowman sees the integrated security team, in other words, as a sign of Hlanganani's competence because it is evidence of her ability to strategize. His surprise at the subversion of his—and, again, through him, the reader's—expectations is therefore once again recoded as admiration for Hlanganani's professionalism. She is "different" in the way that Bowman is different: they both excel at their jobs. In other words, the novel posits, she and Bowman are exactly alike.

The simultaneous marking and erasure of difference the descriptions of Mbali Hlanganani perform clues us in to whom Clarke's writing imagines as its target audience. This target audience is everywhere assumed, consciously or not, yet nowhere named. His books, like preparedness materials produced by the state, address the abstract category of the "professional," a general type of person rather than a group of specific people. This type of person is abstract, generic, and racially unmarked. However, as the descriptions of Hlanganani show, the absence of racial markers connotes whiteness; whiteness, in other words, is a condition of generalizability itself. As a Black South African woman, Hlanganani cannot be assimilated into the category of the professional until she is explicitly marked as different from it. Once this happens, her difference can be subsumed under the banner of admiration for her extreme professionalism, and she can become just like Bowman. She can become an example of the generic professional.

This kind of assimilation is also, therefore, what I mean when I claim that preparedness materials train people to think about disaster according to certain conventions, or to think generically. Thinking generically not only involves learning to generalize about disaster. It also involves learning to make individuals general, to think about individuals according to a logic of type and kind, one in which professionalism, and therefore whiteness, is the assumed and implied baseline. To be white is not necessarily to be generic, but to be generic, to stand in for "anyone," the people in Clarke's fiction must be white or exist in some relation to whiteness. Clarke's body of work thus draws our attention to how a supposed universality of address—his books are, after all, addressed to "anyone" who wants to read them—masks the implied whiteness at the core of the conception of "anyone" in the contemporary United States. Whiteness, Howard Winant argues, has no "discrete, 'positive' content" of its own but rather exists only in relation to nonwhiteness.[53] Richard Clarke's novels, however, quite literally give whiteness content by filling themselves with white characters or with nonwhite characters who are effectively whitewashed through their own professionalism. Like whiteness, "anyone" is a category devoid of specific content that exists only in relation to what it is not: a specific person. And yet, also like whiteness, anyone is also meant to refer specifically to you.

The Generalization of Disaster

While Clarke's writing provides a case study in what thinking generically looks like outside of "official" national security contexts, contemporary exercise scenarios also encourage thinking generically. They encourage this capacity through their formal arrangement and through this form's standardization. Many of the training exercises in use across both governmental and nongovernmental contexts today have been developed by FEMA's Homeland Security Exercise and Evaluation Program (HSEEP). This program provides materials that officials across various public and private sectors can use in planning their own emergency management exercises, including sample scenarios, training exercises, and documents about how to design and facilitate training events. These materials constitute a set of "guiding principles" for these exercise programs, providing a standardized and "consistent approach to exercises" across all "mission areas" and sectors.[54] The HSEEP defines scenarios as "an outline or a model of the simulated sequence of events for the exercise" that "can be written as a narrative or depicted by an event timeline," providing a standard definition for the form that other preparedness agencies and organizations are supposed to use as a guiding principle when constructing their own preparedness training exercise scenarios.[55]

Like Clarke's writing, which contains disasters within short, easily digestible sections, HSEEP scenarios, while less narrative, also perform this containment using a standardized format. In 2006, DHS published "National Planning Scenarios," a document containing fifteen different scenario types for use in federal, state, and local preparedness exercises. These scenarios "provide a basic set of common homeland security events and their related impacts" in order to establish "a common foundation for exercise development" across different agencies and organizations.[56] Each scenario contains a general description, detailed information about the disaster, a discussion of elements to consider when planning the exercise, and possible implications of the event. Scenario 1 is "Nuclear Detonation—10-kiloton Improvised Nuclear Device," which describes how a group of terrorists "plan to assemble a gun-type nuclear device using Highly Enriched Uranium (HEU) stolen from a nuclear facility located in Pakistan," smuggle the device into the United States, and detonate the device in the business district of a large metropolitan area (1-1). This scenario describes a detailed range of possible implications of this disaster, including fire and blast damage at ground zero; the effects of an electromagnetic pulse on communication networks; damage to "public support infrastructure" like "transportation lines and nodes (e.g., air, water, rail, highway), power generation and distribution systems, communications systems, food distribution, and fuel storage and distribution"; and psychological effects that "would forever change the American psyche, as well as its politics and worldview" (1-8). It also includes nearly thirty pages of maps, charts, and graphs—using Washington, D.C., as an example—that show estimates for day- and nighttime populations in specific areas of the city; projected infrastructural damage; and possible casualties due to the blast, thermal, and radioactive effects of a nuclear detonation.

All of the scenarios in "National Planning Scenarios" adopt this formulaic structure. Like scenario 1, each contains a combination of description and "planning considerations" like calculations of expected fatalities, infrastructural damage, and economic cost. Each scenario also includes multiple summary tables of important information and calculations (Table 1) (1-39). The shared characteristics of these scenarios are designed to improve and expedite training, as is the HSEEP's similarly formulaic guidance on how to construct scenarios. The HSEEP states that all scenarios should contain three basic elements: "(1) the general context or comprehensive story; (2) the required conditions that will allow players to demonstrate proficiency and competency in conducting critical tasks, demonstrating core capabilities, and meeting objectives; and (3) the technical details necessary to accurately depict scenario conditions and events" (3-12). Scenarios should also "be divided up into distinct, chronologically sequenced modules," with each module representing "a specific time segment of the overall scenario, based on exercise objectives and scenario requirements" (3-14). This is generic thinking in action: following this procedure will produce a properly designed scenario that can be used as a springboard for training exercises.

Table 1. Summary table of estimated results for scenario 1 from 2006 "National Planning Scenarios" document.

	Zone 1 (0.76 km)	Zone 2 (0.82 km)	Zone 3 (1.0 km)	Zone 4 (1.2 km)	Zone 5 (380 REM)	Zone 6 (280 REM)	Zone 7 (210 REM)	Zone 8 (150 REM)	Zone 9 (1 REM)
A Possible Set of "Realistic" Estimated Results for a 10-kiloton Nuclear Device									
Numbers of People in Thousands (k)									
Total Population	14.6	16.9	31.7	46.6	203	236	270	303	439
Total fatalities	13	17	19	21	82	91	94	97	99
Instant (within minutes)	7.7	8.5	8.6	8.6	8.6	8.6	8.6	8.6	8.6
Within 24 hours	9.8	11	13	15	45	45	45	45	45
Within 96 hours	10	13	15	16	61	62	62	62	62
Within 8 weeks	11	14	15	17	66	71	79	83	85
Injuries (initially alive)	4.1	7.9	9.1	18.7	106	123	128	136	138
Blunt trauma plus other effects	.6	.9	1.0	1.1	1.1	1.1	1.1	1.1	1.1
Burns	.8	1.4	1.6	1.7	1.7	1.7	1.7	1.7	1.7
Prompt radiation	.5	.6	.7	.7	.7	.7	.7	.7	.7
Multiple (excluding fallout)	2.3	2.6	2.9	3.2	3.2	3.2	3.2	3.2	3.2
Able to walk	1.5	4	7	15	101	123	128	136	138

(continued on next page)

Table 1. Summary table of estimated results for scenario 1 from 2006 "National Planning Scenarios" document. *(continued)*

A Possible Set of "Realistic" Estimated Results for a 10-kiloton Nuclear Device									
	Numbers of People in Thousands (k)								
	Zone 1 (0.76 km)	Zone 2 (0.82 km)	Zone 3 (1.0 km)	Zone 4 (1.2 km)	Zone 5 (380 REM)	Zone 6 (280 REM)	Zone 7 (210 REM)	Zone 8 (150 REM)	Zone 9 (1 REM)
Requiring special care	3.9	7.5	8.5	17	80	84	89	91	95
Injuries from Fallout	.1	.3	3.6	12	99	116	121	129	131
Eye Damage	6.9	8.4	23.1	38	194	227	261	294	430
Flash Blindness	.2	.7	1.6	1.8	2.2	2.3	2.4	2.4	2.5
Retinal Burns	.1	.3	.5	.7	.9	.9	1.0	1.0	1.1
Evacuation needed	6.9	8.4	23.1	38	194	227	261	294	430
Critical to evacuate	Extreme?	Extreme?	Extreme	Extreme	Very	Yes	Yes	Yes	Less so
Needing shelter	6.9	8.3	17	28	150	170	200	225	310
Requiring decontamination	6.9	8	20	32	75	82	91	101	110
Major fires (not in thousands)	200	220	235	245	247	250	250	250	250

(continued on next page)

Table 1. Summary table of estimated results for scenario 1 from 2006 "National Planning Scenarios" document. *(continued)*

A Possible Set of "Realistic" Estimated Results for a 10-kiloton Nuclear Device									
	Numbers of People in Thousands (k)								
	Zone 1 (0.76 km)	Zone 2 (0.82 km)	Zone 3 (1.0 km)	Zone 4 (1.2 km)	Zone 5 (380 REM)	Zone 6 (280 REM)	Zone 7 (210 REM)	Zone 8 (150 REM)	Zone 9 (1 REM)
Electrical Power									
Out for more than 1 week	Yes	Yes	Yes	Yes	Yes	Likely	Maybe	Maybe	Maybe
Out for more than 4 weeks	Yes	Yes	Yes	Likely	Maybe	No	No	No	No
City Water System									
Contamination with radiation	Unlikely	No	No	No	No	No	No	No	No
Contaminated with "dirt"	Yes	Maybe	No	No	No	No	No	No	No
Telecommunication									
Out for more than 1 weeks	Yes	Yes	Yes	Yes	Yes	Yes	Likely	Likely	Likely
Out for more than 4 weeks	Yes	Yes	Yes	Yes	Likely	Maybe	Maybe	No	No
EMP damage	Yes	Yes	Likely	Maybe	No	No	No	No	No

This table indicates a *possible* set of consequences for people in a given zone at the time of the detonation. The numbers are accumulative with respect to the zones (e.g., Zone 2 includes the values for Zone 1). *Note that these results depend strongly on the assumptions used and the methods used to apply those assumptions. The values are estimates and are not supported by computer calculations.*

The codification described in the preceding paragraphs marks the scenario not only as a highly conventional genre but also as a highly professional approach to future disaster. Preparedness training exercise scenarios are invested in training their audiences to understand the future in conventional terms, according to the strictures of their genre; as such, these scenarios provide practical training in abstraction and generalization. As one book on emergency management puts it, "scenarios are thus a valuable tool in creating the necessary mental reorientation" trainees need to "appl[y] theoretical knowledge to practical problems under emergency conditions."[57] They are also a product of this kind of generic thinking, an encapsulation of what professional training in preparedness, or practical training in the generalization of future disaster, can produce. Finally, they are an indication, as we will see in the next section, of how the ideology of professionalism in the context of disaster preparedness is disseminated beyond those professionals working in emergency management. Scenarios are portable, and they help preparedness travel beyond the confines of the government or of state agencies into the wider world.

Like the writing of Richard Clarke, the preparedness training exercise scenario makes visible the power of generic expectation. As Diana Taylor writes of scenarios in a different context, the scenario's "portable framework bears the weight of accumulative repeats."[58] When it comes to scenarios, "we've seen it all before"; the scenario is not so much a "copy"—even with preparedness training exercise scenarios, the details of any one scenario will vary—as it is "a once-againness."[59] We can understand the weight of these accumulative repeats as an index of the expectations the scenario form carries with it. Scenarios are not so much authored as they are automated. Whereas the details of any one scenario may be significantly different from those of another, officials can easily adapt the procedure for developing a scenario for a nuclear attack to a hurricane or an earthquake. The specific details of any given scenario ultimately matter less than the procedure through which a scenario is produced, a procedure that determines the scenario form itself. Input information on a particular threat, output future disaster. Unlike a political thriller, then, preparedness training exercise scenarios do not so much tell a story as they produce a highly codified and generalizable situation. The next section turns to this situation itself to understand how thinking generically affects not only trainees' conceptions of disaster but also their conceptions of themselves in relation to disaster. It focuses on what a professional attitude toward future disaster entails.

Attitude Adjustment

Just as Richard Clarke manages readerly experience by keeping readers engaged enough to keep reading and educating themselves about national security threats without overwhelming them with excitement, training exercises are designed to manage participants' experiences of the conventional disasters they encounter. FEMA's EMI produces free online and in-person courses designed to train "Federal, State, local, tribal, volunteer, public, and private sector officials" in emergency management procedures.[60] One of its more popular recent courses is Active Shooter: What You Can Do, which provides training for "non–law enforcement employees" in how to respond to an active shooter situation both before and after law enforcement arrives.[61] Designed specifically for use in the work-place, it has the instantly recognizable feel of the corporate train-ing seminar, complete with a PowerPoint presentation filled with stock images depicting a diverse cast of attractive professionals at work (Figures 6–8).[62] This kind of training acknowledges that such disasters are ordinary, in the same way that, for example, work-place sexual harassment training acknowledges such harassment as ordinary—so ordinary, in fact, that official policies and mechanisms exist for how to formally deal with it. As discussed in chapter 1, we can thus understand preparedness training as one example of what Berlant has referred to as "neutralizing affect management," a kind of "ordinary compartmentalization" that allows one to continue on in the face of "being overwhelmed by knowledge and life."[63]

But exercises like the Active Shooter exercise also contribute to and help to construct the ordinariness of disaster by making some-thing overwhelming feel conventional. In terms of preparedness, this has the effect not only of making everyday life seem especially disastrous but also of making disasters seem particularly banal.[64] Participants must repeat their training over and over again to gain

Figures 6 and 7. Example visuals from FEMA's Active Shooter training course materials.

proficiency, a process that FEMA's exercise design materials simply call "practice." "Practice is an important aspect of the preparation process," exercise design materials suggest, not only because it "reveal[s] planning weaknesses" but also because it allows participants "to practice their roles and gain experience in those roles" and "to improve individual performance."[65] Practice is purposive in that it is geared toward continual improvement. Officials should use the "lessons learned from exercises" not only to "revise operational plans" but also to provide more training so participants can "improve proficiency in executing those [revised] plans."[66] Training begets more training, more practice. But this form of repetition also involves the continual adjustment of expectations. Through practice, you "gain experience" and become "proficient." As you master a skill, you learn to expect that your body will do certain things, that you will think and feel certain ways. These things become normal, and you get used to them.[67]

When trainees undergo active shooter training, they are not only preparing for an active shooter situation; they are also learning to expect it, to get used to it as just something that happens all

Figure 8. Example visual from FEMA's
Active Shooter training course materials.

the time (even if it doesn't; even if it hasn't happened to them). The
exercise materials DHS distributes online and that course materials encourage participants to download after they have completed
the course are also invested in this kind of normalization. These
materials include a thirteen-page booklet, a two-page pamphlet, a
poster, and a pocket card, all of which provide instruction in how to
respond if there is an active shooter situation (Figure 9).[68] They are
examples of what John Guillory refers to as "information genres,"
genres that exist *primarily* to transmit information" and that are
"the humblest yet perhaps the most ubiquitous genre of writing in
the modern world."[69] Meant to be placed on your desk, hung on
your cubicle wall, and carried around in your wallet, they are as banal as the many other flyers, memos, and employee ID cards that
form the backdrop to professionals' day-to-day working lives. They
not only transmit information about what to do during an active
shooter situation; they also, when taken together, communicate the
assumption that the disasters, like mass shootings, for which preparedness asks us to prepare are as normal, as expected, as copier
jams and performance evaluations. They also communicate the

assumption that there is little anyone can do to stop such disasters—that, as Patrick Blanchfield has put it, "the intrusion of rampaging killers with assault rifles [is] a random force of nature analogous to a fire or an earthquake."[70] To carry an active shooter preparedness pocket card around in your wallet or to hang the poster on your office wall is to live this future disaster as your present, everyday reality, not necessarily because you are experiencing mass shootings every day, or even the specter of mass shootings every day, but rather because the expectation of such events is part of your everyday life, an expectation that is affirmed and reaffirmed with every training course, poster, or pocket card.

Exercises like Active Shooter that are designed for "non–law enforcement employees" for use in their workplace therefore evidence the extent to which professionalism, understood as practical training in abstraction, is itself generalizable, indifferent to the specificities of any one profession as compared to another. The exercise

HOW TO RESPOND
WHEN AN ACTIVE SHOOTER IS IN YOUR VICINITY

1. Evacuate
• Have an escape route and plan in mind
• Leave your belongings behind
• Keep your hands visible

2. Hide Out
• Hide in an area out of the shooter's view
• Block entry to your hiding place and lock the doors
• Silence your cell phone and/or pager

3. Take Action
• As a last resort and only when your life is in imminent danger
• Attempt to incapacitate the shooter
• Act with physical aggression and throw items at the active shooter

CALL 911 WHEN IT IS SAFE TO DO SO

HOW TO RESPOND
WHEN LAW ENFORCEMENT ARRIVES

• Remain calm and follow instructions
• Put down any items in your hands (i.e., bags, jackets)
• Raise hands and spread fingers
• Keep hands visible at all times
• Avoid quick movements toward officers such as holding on to them for safety
• Avoid pointing, screaming or yelling
• Do not stop to ask officers for help or direction when evacuating

INFORMATION
YOU SHOULD PROVIDE TO LAW ENFORCEMENT OR 911 OPERATOR

• Location of the active shooter
• Number of shooters
• Physical description of shooters
• Number and type of weapons held by shooters
• Number of potential victims at the location

Figure 9. One side of the pocket card associated with FEMA's Active Shooter training exercise.

provides an abbreviated experience of other kinds of accreditation and certification processes, designed to be completed in an afternoon. An "instructor" leads the training exercise while "students" participate, participants are meant to complete several worksheets throughout the session and an online exam at the end, and participants receive a "completion certificate" when they pass the exam. This makes both the training and the techniques and skills the training is meant to teach feel "official," providing participants with evidence of their passage from "student" to "graduate" and hence their attainment of a specialized body of knowledge. No matter where they are employed or what their jobs are, once participants complete the training exercise, they have achieved a level of official or professional competence in active shooter preparedness.

Emergency management training materials often define professionalism in emergency management as something like "a commitment to emergency management as a profession."[71] This tautology—professionalism constitutes a commitment to one's job as a profession—should alert us to the fact that "professional training" consists, regardless of its content, of what Mark Seltzer calls "worldview exercises."[72] It means learning the skills and techniques proper to one's occupation, of course, familiarizing yourself, for example, with the "specialized body of knowledge" and "best practices" in emergency management.[73] But it also means learning to see and experience the world in particular ways. Exercise design materials, after all, claim that training exercises are "aimed at . . . achieving changes in perceptions."[74] Understood in this way, the ethos of professional emergency management becomes almost indistinguishable from the training exercises professionals design and in which they participate. Professionalism becomes a form of self-relation, a way of living your life, and professional training involves learning to adjust yourself to this worldview, to see yourself and your work in a particular way, regardless of what that work is.[75]

The professional self-conception encouraged by exercises like the Active Shooter exercise, however, is also devoid of individuality. Exercise materials instruct participants in the proper protocol to follow in the event of an active shooter situation—things like "evacuate," "hide out," "take action" by "disrupt[ing] and/or incapacitat[ing] the shooter" and "call 911 when it is safe to do so."[76]

This protocol is not very specific; indeed, it is designed, like any protocol, to apply to any number of violent situations. This lack of specificity is mirrored, and even increased, by the stereotypically corporate aesthetics of the exercise materials. In addition to the stock images referenced previously (Figures 6–8), the cover of the Active Shooter booklet features shadowy, featureless human figures (Figure 10).[77] Meant to represent everyone, they stand in for no one in particular: they are anyone. The booklet also contains a series of instructions that are addressed to "you" and that tell "you" what to do:

Good practices for coping with an active shooter situation

Be aware of your environment and any possible dangers

Take note of the two nearest exits in any facility you visit

If you are in an office, stay there and secure the door

If you are in a hallway, get into a room and secure the door

As a last resort, attempt to take the active shooter down. When the shooter is at close range and you cannot flee, your chance of survival is much greater if you try to incapacitate him/her.

CALL 911 WHEN IT IS SAFE TO DO SO![78]

This "you" is anyone—simultaneously everyone undergoing the training and no one in particular. Additionally, images from the exercise PowerPoint presentation of anonymous white hands holding guns pointed at the viewer seem to call out to you—specifically to the "you" who is viewing the PowerPoint presentation and is undergoing training, the "you" the title of the exercise itself addresses (Figure 11). You are meant to understand your position as both the target of a shooting and the target of address. As such, you are the type of person for whom the training materials are designed. The vulnerability of your position as a target fuels your desire to learn to respond to active shooter situations in the right way. This mode of address has the effect not necessarily of collectivizing the individual, or of atomizing the collective, but rather of making "you" generic. You become a type: the type of person who is both targeted by and who knows how to professionally handle just such a situation.

The Active Shooter exercise materials not only tell you what to do

Figure 10. Cover of FEMA's Active Shooter training exercise booklet.

in the event of an active shooter situation; they also focus on adopting the right disposition toward the potentiality of such an event.
The course materials offer training not only in active shooter preparedness but also in general professional comportment. Employees and managers alike should try to "foster a respectful workplace"
while also working to be "intuitive" so that they can "notice characteristics of potentially violent behavior in an employee" and thereby

Figure 11. A white hand points a gun at the participant in a visual from FEMA's Active Shooter training course materials.

prevent an active shooter situation.[79] They should "remain calm, professional, and prepared to lead" at all times, but they should also be ready to "[adopt] a survival mindset during times of crisis."[80]

The recommendation that trainees should be taught to remain calm while also preparing themselves to adopt "a survival mind-set" demonstrates the importance exercise materials place on mood management. Jonathan Flatley writes that the concept of mood "names a collective affective atmosphere."[81] Working from Martin Heidegger's comparison of a mood to a melody, Flatley emphasizes that moods are aesthetic—they constitute a way or style of being in the world and with other people. Training exercises are designed to create particular "styles of response to crisis," in Berlant's words, and to attune participants collectively to these styles.[82] Indeed, this kind of calibration is a large part of the training in professionalism that exercise participants receive. But as a style of being, moods are nebulous and unspecific; unlike affects or emotions, which tend to be directed toward something specific, a mood is "usually about everything in general" and "can color everything we encounter."[83] Different kinds of moods suffuse and create different kinds of affective atmospheres, but these atmospheres, Dora Zhang reminds us, are "difficult to pinpoint or localize, and thus always verg[e] on fiction."[84] A mood always exceeds the aesthetic experiences crafted to create it. It suffuses, permeates, seeps, and infects, but these metaphors of leakage and permeability themselves signal what is so difficult to describe about moods: where they come from in the first place.[85]

We can, however, get a sense of what moods training exercises like the Active Shooter exercise imply they are trying to manage by looking to documents aimed at exercise designers and facilitators. For example, one FEMA handbook on exercise design encourages exercise facilitators to create an atmosphere during training exercises that is both tense and calm. This handbook recommends that, since the exercise scenario "sets the mood" and "captures [participants'] attention and makes them want to go on," it should be "written in short sentences that lend immediacy and tension," and it should "devote more detail to the environment of the emergency . . . to create intensity of feeling."[86] If the exercise designers have done their job well, the atmosphere during a training exercise should mimic "the environment of the emergency" in that it should be "stressful and tense due to real-time action and the realism of the problems."[87] This viewpoint echoes that articulated by the authors of an emergency management textbook, who encourage the use of hypothetical scenarios and training exercises because of the excitement they generate. Such training techniques "create an atmosphere closely mimicking an actual disaster," where participants must act as they would "during a real event."[88] As another textbook puts it, during training exercises, participants must "appl[y] theoretical knowledge to practical problems under emergency conditions," using "quick judgment" to develop "rapid answers to immediate problems."[89] The creation of an atmosphere of intensity during the exercise aims to help participants acknowledge their own vulnerability and lack of preparedness. Exercises should produce, as Grégoire Mallard and Andrew Lakoff emphasize, "an 'experiential' knowledge of vulnerability" or "a visceral sense of [participants'] own incapacity to deal with this type of event."[90] The idea is that this experience of vulnerability will lead to more successful training exercises because participants will be better able to recognize and acknowledge their own failures and the failures of the preparedness plan.

But the FEMA handbook on exercise design also stresses that facilitators and participants should not allow themselves to be carried away by this emotional intensity. The exercise facilitator, for example, should seek to avoid conflicts that can arise when participants are pushed out of their comfort zones. "People may come with fragile egos and little exercise experience," the handbook warns. "If you see mounting frustration or conflict, stop the exercise. Reach into your experience as a discussion leader to help the players resolve conflicts and feel comfortable." Despite the intensity of the exercise, then, those participating should also feel "at ease" at all times.[91] This kind of mood management, one book on emergency management asserts, will produce "well trained disaster manager[s]" who "will be able calmly but rapidly to analyze complex situations, make decisions firmly, and manage people and resources under pressure."[92]

FEMA's exercise design handbook encourages exercise facilitators to employ a variety of strategies to modulate participants' feelings between the two poles of excitement and boredom, never allowing them to remain for too long at either end of the spectrum. One way facilitators can maintain this balance is by controlling when participants receive messages that provide them with "real-time" information about the disaster to which they are responding: "The controller can control the pace of the exercise by adjusting the message flow—slowing things down when the pace is too frantic or speeding it up when the exercise drags."[93] Facilitators should make such adjustments to avoid both frenzied frustration and distracting

boredom among participants.[94] Such techniques of attention distribution are meant to, as one planner has put it, "wake [participants]
up a bit."[95] The paradoxical exhortations to both excite exercise
participants and to put them at ease—to wake them up a bit, but
only a bit—suggest that the efficacy of these exercises is tied less to
either emotional intensity or to the suppression of emotions than it
is to something like their median: an attitude of detached neutrality. This detached neutrality does not depend on the ironic distancing of the participant from the exercise, as there is nothing ironic
about the Active Shooter materials. Rather, it depends on the calm
cultivation of competence. Additionally, both FEMA and scholars
of emergency management alike emphasize that emergency managers should follow a "code of ethics" that emphasizes "respect" and
"commitment"; they should be "proactive," "collaborative," and
"flexible"; and they should receive and design formalized training
that "synchronize[s]" "individual practitioners' goals and idiosyncrasies" so as to "promote group status and social mobility" and "ac-
quir[e] respectability from the outside world."[96]

This attitude of committed respectability—this willingness to
be flexible, to get the job done and to do it well, to "synchronize"
your personal idiosyncrasies in service to the team—is a nice encapsulation of the kind of affective detachment we also often term
professionalism. Alan Liu has identified this attitude as "cool," the
"remoteness, distantiation, [and] impersonality" characteristic of
white-collar jobs that represents "the *cultural* face . . . of knowledge
work."[97] Like Richard Clarke's writing, the Active Shooter materials
address themselves to the professional, the kind of person who regards disaster with a cool, competent eye. Like the stock images and
the mode of address aimed at a generalized "you," the mood management that exercise design materials emphasize as an integral part of
a training exercise encourages a form of self-conceptualization that
aims to make you, the participant, think of yourself as generically
professional, no matter who you are. Training exercise participants,
the Active Shooter materials reveal, should strive not only to act
professionally at all times and to think about disaster in a professional manner but also to think of themselves as an example of that
most generic of people: the professional.

As we also saw in relation to Richard Clarke's writing, the generic professional created and addressed by the Active Shooter exercise is implicitly white. The attention to the optics of diversity throughout the Active Shooter materials makes this addressee clear (Figures 6–8). The generic workplaces the campaign's images depict are precisely calibrated to read as inclusive. As discussed in the introduction to this chapter, this is in keeping with liberal ideologies of diversity that equate representation of people from nonwhite or nondominant groups with the absence of racism. By representing people from a wide variety of identity groups, these materials—and preparedness as a whole—can always deny the claim that they are for and about whiteness.[98] The optics of diversity in the Active Shooter materials "safeguar[d] racial privilege," as Bonilla-Silva puts it, by absorbing representations of "diverse" bodies into the supposedly inclusive whole of the category of the professional. In this way, color-blind racism shores up white supremacy by allowing it to become "covert, institutional, and apparently nonracial."[99]

The Active Shooter materials also show us, however, how this method of covert racism, beyond denying or obscuring race in any form, actually denies and obscures nonwhite people in the interest of asserting white identity as the only specific racial formation. As discussed earlier, white hands hold the guns pointed at participants in the exercise materials (Figure 11). The targets of this violence, meanwhile, the "diverse" professionals depicted elsewhere in the materials (Figures 6–8), smile and go about their work. This not only aligns whiteness with the supposed universality of the address to "anyone," as described previously; it is also perhaps the most realistic aspect of the Active Shooter exercise in that it depicts the structural violence of whiteness. As Inderpal Grewal has argued, the figure of the active shooter is explicitly racialized as white. The active shooter is "an exceptional US citizen who belongs to the past and a future of the racial, imperial state," one whose "violence [is] derived from the sovereignty endowed to white males."[100] Using Dylann Roof, who killed nine Black people in the Emanuel African Methodist Episcopal Church in Charleston, South Carolina, in 2015, as a case study, Grewal shows how the government and the news media rhetorically separate "shooters" from terrorists. She explains that despite the fact that the USA PATRIOT Act defines terrorism specifically as a political act of violence, and despite the fact that Roof undoubtedly acted with political goals in mind, the FBI refused to classify Roof's acts as terrorism, and the media referred to him not as a terrorist but as a "shooter" or a "gunman." Grewal argues that, unlike *terrorist,* the term *shooter* "euphemistically disavow[s] the violence of the exceptional citizen's [i.e., the white male's] sovereignty."[101] However, the Active Shooter materials demonstrate that such euphemistic disavowal is also a process of subject formation. If the figure of the terrorist, as I will discuss more fully in chapter 5, is implicitly nonwhite, the figure of the shooter is often explicitly white, as it is in the Active Shooter exercise materials. If, as we will see in that chapter, the violence of the terrorist is intolerable to the national security state—because it comes from elsewhere and is performed by "other" people—the violence of the shooter remains tolerable because it mirrors and upholds the violence the national security state itself perpetrates. Why is an "active shooter event" the only kind of terrorism for which FEMA has designed a general workplace training exercise for nongovernmental employees? The figure of the shooter doesn't disavow the violence of white supremacy so much as it provides a figure for its representation and a vehicle for identification with it.

By depicting shooters as exclusively white and their potential victims as often nonwhite, while also presuming whiteness as the universal target of address, the Active Shooter exercise locates whiteness—the whiteness of the professional, the whiteness of the shooter—at the center of preparedness. Whiteness in these materials is both a generalized condition and a specific subject position; it is both what makes the figure of the professional generic and what endows the shooter with his specific form of power (the power to commit, within the context of national security, tolerable violence). Only whiteness is afforded the flexibility to be both general and specific in this way, to address no one in particular and also everyone— including you, no matter who you are—all at once.

We Are Not Prepared, but Preparedness Cannot Fail to Prepare Us

Preparedness materials claim that what I have called thinking generically throughout this chapter is an effective method of teaching people to respond to disaster because, in making responses to disaster and disasters themselves generalizable, people learn how to respond not just to discrete events but also, theoretically, to almost any disaster. Various agencies and emergency management scholars have attempted to prove this by studying the effectiveness of preparedness exercises. FEMA's EMI measures the effectiveness of its training exercises using participant self-assessment; likewise, scholarship in emergency planning on the efficacy of preparedness training exercises generally focuses on what exercise participants claim they have learned after undergoing training.[102] While not a direct measure of exercise effectiveness, this scholarship emphasizes that focusing on participant self-assessment is much more straightforward than attempting to evaluate the effectiveness of training exercises, which, as one study puts it, is "difficult, if not impossible, to measure."[103] However, we can examine what happens when the kind of training described above seems, by any measure, to fail outright by turning back to the Hurricane Pam exercise discussed in chapter 1. I argued there that the Hurricane Pam exercise is evidence of preparedness's empiricist epistemology of fiction, or how it treats fiction as both an imagined, unreal thing and as something from which we can collect data and draw sound conclusions based on empirical evidence. In chapter 2, I argued that this empiricist epistemology of fiction relieves preparedness training exercises of the burden of plausibility and verisimilitude. I want to emphasize now how this understanding of fiction also ensures that preparedness training is always "effective," even when it's not.

After FEMA's failure to adequately manage the response to Hurricane Katrina, the Senate Committee on Homeland Security and Governmental Affairs launched a months-long investigation to determine the reasons behind this failure. The committee held a series of hearings in early 2006 and produced a report, titled *A Failure of Initiative*, released in February 2006. Like *The 9/11 Commission Report*, *A Failure of Initiative* was meant to describe "facts about the preparation for and response to Katrina" to establish "what [we have] learned" from the disaster.[104] Part of the investigation involved a discussion of the Hurricane Pam exercise, a hurricane preparedness exercise held in southeastern Louisiana in July 2004, one year before Katrina. The exercise involved local, state, and federal emergency response officials in a scenario-based training exercise designed to assist in the development of comprehensive hurricane response plans at the state and local levels. According to Innovative Emergency Management Inc., the private firm that designed and ran the exercise for FEMA, the response plan developed during the Hurricane Pam exercise was meant to be "a 'bridging document' designed to serve as a guide and roadmap to be used by emergency operational officials at the state and local level" (83).

Despite the existence of this response plan—and although the Hurricane Pam exercise, as the chairman of the Committee on Homeland Security and Governmental Affairs Susan Collins put it, "predict[ed] with eerie accuracy the all-too-real problems of Katrina"—the hearing transcript indicates that the general consensus of the congressional committee is that "we were not prepared" when Katrina hit.[105] The hearing transcript also indicates that those at the hearing argued that this failure should be conceived as a failure to take appropriate action, not as a failure of the preparedness exercise itself. The Hurricane Pam exercise is described as "Cassandra, the mythical prophet who warned of disasters but whom no one really believed" (2). The exercise, in other words, was not to blame. This is in keeping with the logic of preparedness. As Andrew Lakoff writes of the results of the government's investigation into the response to Hurricane Katrina, "from the vantage of preparedness experts, [the failure to properly manage Hurricane Katrina] pointed to problems of implementation and coordination, of command and control," not of "the normative rationality of preparedness."[106] The logic to which Lakoff draws our attention here claims that while we can certainly fail to be prepared—Lakoff also emphasizes that the "shared lesson" of Hurricane Katrina and its aftermath for emergency managers and government officials alike was *"we are not prepared"*—preparedness training exercises *themselves* cannot fail to prepare us.[107] This seeming contradiction—preparedness training cannot fail even when it obviously does, and miserably—is evidence of the power of thinking generically.

The hearing transcript reveals that, like other training exercises, the Hurricane Pam exercise followed certain conventions that marked it as generic or as belonging to its genre. For example, it contained practical ideas about concrete measures and tactics first responders could utilize to improve their response to a large hurricane like Hurricane Pam. These included things like "the idea of a 'lily-pad' type of search and rescue operation" and "the concept of a Temporary Medical Operations Staging Area" (64). They also included much more vague concepts, such as the idea that because Hurricane Pam projected that more than sixty thousand people would die, officials took Hurricane Katrina more seriously, meaning that "Hurricane Pam helped save lives and reduce suffering after the massive catastrophe of Hurricane Katrina" (65).

However, this "evidence" of Hurricane Pam's effectiveness, such as it is, is ultimately not that important to those participating in the hearing. What seems to be more important is simply the fact that the Hurricane Pam exercise existed in the first place. Several hearing participants highlight the idea that the Hurricane Pam exercise "was really a success story" simply because it was used as a theoretical or conceptual touchstone during the response to Hurricane Katrina (14). The actual response protocol developed during the Hurricane Pam exercise was less important to these hearing participants than the "knowledge of inter-jurisdictional relationships and capabilities, identification of issues, and rudimentary concepts for handling the consequences" that the Hurricane Pam exercise provided. Such concepts, these participants claim, were "quite beneficial to all involved in the hurricane response" (9). The effectiveness of the Hurricane Pam exercise, then, rests not on its ability to concretely prepare people to respond to catastrophe but rather on its ability to meet the most basic expectations of its genre as a training exercise—to provide "knowledge of . . . capabilities" and to help participants "identif[y] . . . issues" and "rudimentary concepts" in preparedness. If it meets these expectations, then, by the logic of preparedness as a national security paradigm, it hasn't failed to prepare participants.

While this logic claims that training exercises, as long as they are designed and conducted properly, can't ever fail to train participants, it also claims that individual people can certainly fail to be trainable. Usually, the failure of individuals is described in terms of a failure to act more efficiently or flexibly—in other words, as a failure to act professionally. The hearing transcript, for example, emphasizes that if emergency management officials had only implemented the recommendations of the exercise more swiftly, efficiently, and competently, the response to Hurricane Katrina would have been better. *A Failure of Initiative* comes to a similar conclusion when it argues that the failure to respond to Katrina was primarily one of "initiative," "agility," "flexibility," and "adaptability" (1). Although the report also focuses in detail on the structural failures of New Orleans's levee system, this, too, is often construed as a failure on the part of city officials and engineers or the professionals in charge of infrastructure maintenance. The failure to be prepared for Katrina was, in the report's terms, a failure of professionalism, not of preparedness itself. Emergency managers, government officials, and levee inspectors all failed to act "professionally."

Most often, however, this report uses the language of professionalism as a cudgel against individual citizens who found themselves in the way of the storm. The report claims, for instance, that those individuals who "chose" to stay behind and "play 'hurricane roulette'" "share some of the blame" for the response failure, while the people who "cooperated" with officials by "evacuat[ing] early on their own" and "mak[ing] their own informed choices" acted properly (114, 113). The people who remained, the report argues, ignored "the advice of the authorities" to leave because of "hurricane fatigue," or because they were "just 'set in their ways,'" or because they "procrastinated" (114, 115). Though the report acknowledges the possibility that some "people did not have money for gas to evacuate," it nevertheless condemns those who remained by describing the conditions they had to face as the consequence of their actions:

> Many of these people paid for their poor choices with their lives—as rising floodwaters drown them in their homes. Others who stayed, but could have left, suffered the less severe consequences of walking through floodwaters to crowded shelters or other high ground. These individuals suffered in horrible conditions—some with shelter and food and water and some without any of these—while they awaited evacuation, which they could have done for themselves earlier. (114)

This passage contrasts activities like "procrastination" and "gambling" to "cooperation," "making informed choices," and doing things for yourself, which are things professionals do. Such language effectively excuses the failure of the federal government to meaningfully respond for days after the storm and lays the blame on individuals. By this logic, the horrors people faced in the aftermath of the storm were, if not entirely of their own making, then at least entirely avoidable, if only they had acted in an informed way instead of gambling or procrastinating away their lives. This is in keeping with the logic of professionalism, which demands individual responsibility. Professionals must be responsible for their actions; they must adhere, in the words of FEMA quoted at the beginning of this chapter, to the "standards and best practices" created by the "professional associations" that control the profession's "board certification." People who act unprofessionally, the report implies, act without thinking of their responsibilities, and they do so because they are stubborn, recalcitrant, or reckless. The report dismisses them as untrained, despite any training they might have received.

But of course, as opposed to the emergency managers, officials, and infrastructure inspectors who the report also claims didn't do their jobs, residents of New Orleans who were caught in the storm didn't necessarily have any kind of (actual, official) professional responsibility or relationship to storm preparedness or response. They didn't "share some of the blame" for the failed response. What's more, the strange slippage into the present tense in the block quote cited above—"as rising floodwaters drown them in their homes"—positions this quality of unprofessionalism as just "how some people are." The people who made the poor choice to stay behind, the report suggests, drowned in their homes then, and they are drowning still. This language implies that, despite the best efforts of officials and emergency responders, such outcomes are unavoidable for "some people." It implies not only that these people are untrained but also that they are effectively untrainable. When the report uses this language of professional responsibility against those who actually bore no professional responsibility, we can see how the language of unprofessionalism in the context of preparedness serves to mark some people as undeserving of protection.

As I have argued throughout this chapter, talking about professionalism is a way of implicitly talking about and addressing whiteness. In this case, whiteness is represented by the people who "had the means to evacuate" or who listened to authorities and made "informed decisions" (114). *A Failure of Initiative* visually contrasts this abstract category of people to those who "chose" to stay behind. The report includes many images of Black people wading through flood-waters, of Black people enduring what the report describes as the "unbearable" conditions at the Superdome, and one image of a dead Black body (117). Images of Black suffering, in other words, "illustrate" the report, providing evidence of the report's titular "failure of initiative" and its consequences. But they also work to differentiate the report's audience, the implicitly white professional, from the victims of the storm. Those who stayed behind, those who suffered and died, those whose images fill the "Evacuation" portion of the report—the report emphasizes that these people all failed to act professionally. Look what they did to themselves, it almost seems to say. Yes, the report admits, "planning was not what it should be at DHS," but these people are also to blame (123).[108]

For all that training exercises focus on training people how to act when disaster strikes, they are far more effective at training people how to think generically. As the investigation into the failed response to Hurricane Katrina demonstrates, thinking generically protects preparedness as a national security paradigm by ensuring that preparedness training is always effective, no matter what, even when disasters very much like the specific (fictional) disasters depicted in specific preparedness training exercises actually happen and people fail to respond. This has profound political consequences: it's what allows emergency managers and government officials to view the Hurricane Pam exercise as "a success story" despite the many catastrophic failures of the response to Hurricane Katrina. These many failures—the failure to provide buses to evacuate people; the failure to provide anything approaching adequate shelter, food, and water for those who weren't evacuated; the failure to provide medical care to those who needed it; the failure to remove dead bodies from the streets—are, due to the remarkable flexibility thinking generically affords, not failures of preparedness per se. Thinking generically means that it becomes possible for members of Congress to agree that emergency managers and government officials weren't prepared for Hurricane Katrina because their preparedness plans were not properly and professionally implemented, not because preparedness itself is a problem.

One of the most pernicious problems associated with preparedness training is thus not that it creates unthinking robots who are trained to respond automatically to catastrophe. Rather, it is that the cognitive and affective management techniques preparedness inculcates—the practical training in abstraction it imparts, or how it teaches people to think generically—is impervious to failure. The failure to respond appropriately or adequately can always be excused as a failure of "professionalism," or as part of the process of preparedness training itself, not as evidence of the inadequacy of preparedness to address catastrophe. Preparedness training, by its own logic, can never fail to prepare people to respond adequately to future catastrophe, even when it clearly does. This means that if we focus our critiques of preparedness on its ineffectiveness, we are missing the point. What we can do instead, however, is probe the rationality of preparedness to discover where it stretches itself too thin, contradicts itself, breaks down. The last two chapters of this book shift from theorizing how preparedness works to investigating the fictions it produces. I focus in each on a key concept for preparedness—resilience and plot, respectively—and I emphasize how preparedness materials engage with these key concepts in contradictory and often conflicting ways. While the concepts of resilience and plot may seem apolitical or neutral, chapters 4 and 5 will demonstrate how these concepts, in the context of preparedness, inform both the aesthetics and the politics of preparedness. What does it mean to be the most resilient character in preparedness narratives? What does it mean to learn to read everyday situations and events as "plots"? These are the questions to which we now turn.

4

Character

The Resilience of the Hero

Preparedness training materials tout resilience as a cardinal virtue, one that all people of the homeland should strive to adopt. The origins of the concept of resilience, however, are in nonhuman properties. The term was originally used in engineering to refer to the elasticity or flexibility of an object; from the Latin *resilientia*, it refers to the ability of matter to recoil or bounce back. Most scholars now trace its contemporary popularization to the work of C. S. Holling, an environmental scientist who, in 1973, adapted the term for ecological contexts by defining *resilience* as "a measure of the persistence of [ecological] systems and of their ability to absorb change and disturbance and still maintain the same relationships between populations."[1] From there, the concept quickly spread to the arenas of economics and public policy, where it has become a foundational concept of predominant crisis management frameworks, including preparedness.[2] In the context of national security, *resilience* refers to the ability to adapt to and recover from disaster. This is the self-avowed ultimate goal of preparedness training: to make our buildings, our infrastructure, our communities, even the nation as a whole, resilient. The 2011 document "International Strategy for Cyberspace," for example, states that U.S. computer networks should not only be "secure and reliable" but also "resilient to arbitrary or malicious disruption"; likewise, the first line of the 2013 "National Infrastructure Protection Plan" states that "our national well-being relies upon secure and resilient critical infrastructure."[3] The 2015 "National Preparedness Goal," which articulates DHS's overall approach to preparedness, describes the goal of preparedness as building "a secure and resilient Nation," and the twenty-four-page document uses the words "resilient" or "resilience" thirty-six times.[4] DHS also defines part of its mission as being committed to "relentless resilience."[5]

Individuals should also be resilient. As DHS puts it, resilience is "the shared responsibility of all levels of government, the private and nonprofit sectors, and individual citizens."[6] To that end, DHS has sponsored a variety of programs aimed at cultivating resilience in individuals: the Alabama Be Ready Camp, for instance, "provide[d] Alabama youth with skills and knowledge to be prepared and more resilient when a disaster strikes," and the mission of the Do 1 Thing campaign in Michigan was "to move individuals, families, businesses, and communities to . . . become disaster resilient" by teaching individuals to "take small steps that make a big difference."[7] As we can see from these examples, DHS views teaching individuals to be resilient as one of the key goals of preparedness training.[8] In these formulations, resilience is not only a virtue of well-designed systems; it is also an individual, moral virtue, one that speaks to a person's character. The understanding of resilience common in preparedness discourse, therefore, has a synecdochal logic: individuals stand in for communities, for critical infrastructure systems, and even for nations as a whole, and vice versa. The DHS statement on resilience quoted earlier—it is "the shared responsibility of all levels of government, the private and nonprivate sectors, and individual citizens"—illustrates this idea. It's not clear if each individual has a responsibility to be resilient or if national resilience is a collective responsibility—but it also doesn't really matter. When discussing resilience, individuals stand in for nations, and vice versa. This logic brings the nonhuman, object-oriented origins of the term into contact with its moral connotations. Resilient individuals are like flexible objects—nonhuman in their ability to bounce back.

Security studies scholars have also emphasized the importance of the individual in discussions about resilience within preparedness discourse. Many have argued that preparedness discourse fetishizes individual responsibility and flexibility—or resilience—as a moral good, and they tie this emphasis on the individual to the connections between neoliberal economic policies and the rise of preparedness in the United States. For instance, Jonathan Joseph contends that resilience discourse in the context of national security "is consistent with neoliberal practices of governance" in that it "emphasi[zes] individual responsibility, adaptability, and preparedness."[9] Jeremy Walker and Melinda Cooper also highlight that preparedness demands "a 'culture' of resilience that turns crisis response into a strategy of permanent, open-ended responsiveness, integrating emergency preparedness into the infrastructures of everyday life and the psychology of citizens."[10] Additionally, in his discussion of resiliency training in the military, Pat O'Malley writes that such training is designed to produce a "resilient subject" that is "more responsible and more communicative, more innovative and enterprising, and thus also more able both to withstand the shocks *and* grasp the opportunities presented in the risk society," just as Kevin Grove states that "resilience approaches . . . fashion subjects proper to contemporary neoliberal order: resilient subjects capable of withstanding catastrophic shocks."[11]

The critiques of resilience by security studies scholars tend to focus on what these scholars sometimes call the *resilient subject*, an ideal subject imagined by preparedness discourse who enacts the quality of resilience by taking individual responsibility for adapting herself and her local community to disaster. These scholars argue that the resilient subject, endlessly flexible and adaptive, is trained to regard the future as fundamentally uncertain and to accept and even embrace this uncertainty as an opportunity for self-fulfillment.[12] The critiques of resilience in these accounts thus often rest on emphasizing the brutal social and political consequences of neoliberalism.[13]

These arguments are convincing. However, by focusing their critiques on the ideal subject of preparedness—the resilient subject—the aforementioned accounts gloss over the range of attitudes preparedness materials themselves take toward this resilient subject. Preparedness materials extoll resilience as a virtue in the abstract, but they also, as we will see throughout this chapter, exhibit ambivalence, sorrow, and, as Kaiama Glover has pointed out, "repugnance" toward those individuals they call resilient.[14] This affective range results, I argue, from the uncomfortably close relationship between resilience and death. This relationship is uncomfortable not because death is the opposite of resilience, nor because resilience implies confronting the fact that not everyone will bounce back and not everyone will survive. On the contrary, preparedness materials are pretty comfortable with this uneven distribution of death. As the justification for an endless war on terror, preparedness in fact relies on the idea that the people of the homeland are exceptional and therefore that exceptional measures should be taken to protect them. Preparedness relies on the idea, in other words, that the people of the homeland are only safe if those outside the homeland are not. Part of the point of preparedness is that not everyone will, or should, survive.

Rather, as will become gradually clear throughout this chapter, the relationship between resilience and death is discomfiting for preparedness materials because it foregrounds the state of being an object, a thing. Resilient individuals, again, are almost nonhuman, even nonliving, in their flexibility. Their inhuman ability to survive brings them to the brink of objecthood. This closeness to thingness illuminates the bio- and necropolitical foundations of the contemporary national security state, or what Jasbir K. Puar has termed its "bio-necro collaboration."[15] For Michel Foucault, biopower is a "power that exerts a positive influence on life" and that "endeavours to administer, optimize and multiply it."[16] This power is what the term *resilience* invokes—the ability to optimize and multiply life in the face of disaster. Achille Mbembe's concept of necropower turns our attention from an understanding of politics as the administration of life to an understanding of politics as the dealing out of death. Mbembe argues that Foucault's concept of biopower does not sufficiently attend to how the forces of modern governmentality are also organized around "the capacity to define who matters and who does not, who is *disposable* and who is not."[17] In Mbembe's formulation, far from ignoring or denying death, as Foucault argues, governmentality makes some people, in some places—for Mbembe, the colony is the most emblematic site—killable. Though at first it seems only to deny it, the concept of resilience within preparedness discourse also invokes this death-dealing power. Not only do resilient individuals come close to the brink of death, of ceasing to be a person, but the most resilient individuals are often those who have been deemed disposable. The repugnance at the heart of resilience, to echo Glover, is a repugnance at the continued survival of those who have been made killable or those who, following Mbembe, have been relegated "to the status of *living dead*."[18]

The status of living dead will assume physical form in the chapter's third section when zombies appear as both the limit case of the concept of resilience for preparedness and its most paradigmatic example. As lively corpses, zombies straddle the line separating person from thing, a distinction the concept of resilience simultaneously blurs and defends. Zombies are also explicitly racialized figures; as Glover has argued, even when "the contemporary zombie makes no explicit reference to blackness, it nonetheless taps into racial fantasies that lead us right back to Haiti and to Africa—to Haiti as Africa in America's backyard."[19] And as many scholars have powerfully argued, the long history of white violence against Black people in the United States has turned on defending divisions between people and things.[20] Zombies are therefore evidence of how the national security state uses resilience to talk about and figure Blackness indirectly, without ever addressing Blackness or Black people. Unlike the figure of the professional discussed in the previous chapter, who is both the target of address and a vehicle for identification with whiteness, the zombie is neither a target of address nor a vehicle for identification. It is a method of comparison and differentiation—never who "we" are supposed to be, only what "we" are not. Inspiring a range of attitudes, resilience stands for both what preparedness materials most want from trainees and what they cannot, in the end, abide.

To understand this full affective range, I turn in this chapter from resilient *subjects* to resilient *characters*. In moralizing about resilience, preparedness materials often rely on fictional characters to embody the quality of resilience they want people to adopt. Embodying resilience in the form of a character mirrors the synecdochal logic embedded in the concept of resilience in national security contexts, in which an individual—a citizen of the homeland—comes to stand in for the nation as a whole, and vice versa. The concept of character therefore draws our attention to the tension between person and thing suggested by the concept of resilience.

A character, like the generic professional discussed in the previous chapter, is both an individual and a type, both a person and a thing. As J. Hillis Miller observes, characters are "both peculiar, particular, distinctive, and at the same time . . . repeatable, generalizable, able to be used and reused in a variety of circumstances."[21] Like a letter in the alphabet—a different kind of character—a character in a work of fiction represents a specific individual while also exemplifying a more general type that recurs across a variety of works of fiction (the hero, the villain, etc.).[22] Focusing on resilient characters instead of resilient subjects thus means turning from the psychological depth implied by *subject* to the iterative and synecdochal logic of *character.*[23]

I make my argument about the role of characterization in preparedness materials by focusing throughout on that most resilient of characters: the hero. The hero of a story is the one who survives, who bounces back, who lives to fight another day. As any action film reminds us, the most important characteristic the hero possesses is this bounce-back. Heroes endure the trials and obstacles the plot places in their way and emerge alive on the other side.[24] I trace the figure of the hero as it appears in three different examples of public-facing preparedness materials: in online games that teach children how to prepare for natural disasters designed by or in consultation with FEMA and DHS; in speeches by presidents on the anniversaries of the September 11, 2001, terrorist attacks; and in a graphic narrative published by the Centers for Disease Control and Prevention (CDC) as part of its popular 2011 zombie pandemic public awareness campaign. These materials all valorize their heroes as resilient, but they also, at the same time, empty out the figure of the hero, emphasizing the conceptual and sometimes literal disintegration and death of the individual person under preparedness. They make heroes killable by focusing on the hero as a resilient character instead of as a resilient subject. Everyone becomes a character type—the hero—defined simply by his ability to survive, especially when "survival" means something very close to or indistinguishable from death.

The chapter ends with a coda that rereads the CDC graphic narrative—and the value of resilience—in the wake of Audre Lorde's 1978 poem "A Litany for Survival."[25] Lorde's poem makes visible the conceptual and moral poverty of preparedness's understanding of resilience by emphasizing the lived, affective experience of resilient people. Like the preparedness materials discussed in this chapter, Lorde's poem is about survival. However, the poem has no characters, and through its specific first-person plural address—the poem is by a Black woman, for a Black audience—"A Litany for Survival" assumes the personhood of those it addresses. Instead of depicting a character type, it describes how it feels to survive for people who "were never meant to survive" in the first place.[26]

The Failure to Fail

We turn first to heroes who cannot die. These heroes appear in two free online games designed to teach natural disaster preparedness to children, both released in 2013: *Disaster Hero*, which was designed by the American College of Emergency Management and the game development firm Legacy Interactive and funded by a grant from DHS, and *Disaster Master*, part of the Be a Hero! Ready.gov educational campaign designed by FEMA to be taught in K–12 schools.[27] The cyberpunk premise of *Disaster Hero* is that the player is a "challenger" competing for the chance to join an "elite disaster specialist team" put together by "internationally famous disaster specialist" Dante Shields. The player competes against members of this Disaster Hero team—Tectonic, Tempest, Whirlwind, and Dr. Deluge, each of whom is a "specialist" in a different natural disaster—in a series of challenges in Dante Shield's Disaster Arena, a "high-tech holographic simulation" arena (Figure 12). The challenges are designed to teach the player "how to pull off the Big Three of Disaster Preparation . . . making a plan, getting a kit, and being informed," and they are organized into "Before," "During," and "After" disaster stages, with each stage focusing on teaching the user skills relevant to each aspect of disaster preparedness and response. Completing all of the challenges and earning more points than her opponent, Dante Shields relates in the game's introductory animated sequence, will teach the player how to survive a disaster and earn her a spot on his team.[28]

Disaster Master, in contrast, involves the player in its world through second-person address. As part of Ready.gov's Be a Hero! campaign, *Disaster Master* is designed to provide students "with the knowledge, awareness, and life-protecting skills needed to prepare for a variety of emergencies and disasters."[29] Centered on a narrative about a group of five friends from different regions of the United States who

Figure 12. *Disaster Hero* opponents. Copyright 2011–16, American College of Emergency Physicians. Reprinted with permission.

meet at summer camp, the Be a Hero! campaign enjoins students to "become 'heroes'" by completing the entire program and developing the skills to prepare for and survive a disaster (the choice to put the word "heroes" in quotation marks indicates that we are dealing here with a logic of type and kind).[30] *Disaster Master*, a centerpiece of the campaign, takes the player, who is addressed as "you" throughout the game, through a variety of emergency situations faced by each of the five hero friends, quizzing the player along the way about the emergencies the characters face and what they should do next. As the game's home screen shows, each level of the game centers on a different kind of natural disaster (Figure 13).[31] The object of the game is simply to survive. If the player makes the right choices and correctly answers the questions about what the characters should do next, he sees characters survive the disasters with which they are faced, and the player makes it to the next level (Figure 14). If the player makes too many wrong choices, he must start the level over again (although the characters do not explicitly die).[32]

Figure 13. *Disaster Master* home screen.

Figure 14. *Disaster Master* level survival screen.

As discussed in chapter 2, when people participate in training exercises, they are asked to play a part, to act as if they are responding to a disaster. *Disaster Hero* and *Disaster Master* make this invitation explicit by turning the player into an actual character within the game (the player's avatar in *Disaster Hero* and the "you" in *Disaster Master*). I argued in chapter 2 that such strategies induce players to consent to the reality of the world of the exercise—or in this case, of the game— even though they know this world is fictional. As John Frow writes of the function of the avatar in gaming, "it is . . . the mechanism by which the player is inscribed, both functionally and affectively, into the game and by which the gameworld, in turn, is made to seem intuitively obvious."[33] Similarly, critics have focused on the "simulated immediacy" that second-person address imparts to players of interactive fiction.[34] Both games, then, use familiar gaming conventions to invite players into the world of the game. These games also invite player involvement by offering up their characters as models of what a hero is. Like the Active Shooter exercise materials discussed in the previous chapter, the games participate in a liberal politics of multiculturalism by depicting these heroes as "diverse"; each game's cast includes characters who belong to visibly different identity groups, ostensibly inviting "anyone" to see herself as a hero. As I argued in the previous chapter, an address to whiteness often lies at the center of the national security state's address to "anyone," and these games are no exception. However, in these games, this address also arrives in the form of a demand. As the title of the Be a Hero! public awareness campaign indicates, the object of these games is for the player to undergo a process of training that makes him into a hero. The *Disaster Hero* home screen, for instance, invites potential players to "compete against the members of [the] elite disaster specialist team" and assures them, "If you can prove victorious then you could become the next Disaster Hero!"[35] Similarly, the *Disaster Master* home screen reads, in part, "Help the Heroes! . . . Survive all 7 levels plus a turn in the hot seat and become a Disaster Master!"[36] Both games, that is, emphasize a process of becoming-hero that is often couched as an imperative to do something: players need to "help the heroes," "become" a hero, and "be a hero."

This mode of characterization is typical of video games. As many critics have argued, a character within a game—unlike a character within a novel—acts as a vehicle for player engagement and action rather than as a vehicle for player sympathy or empathy. Ken Perlin, for example, points out that games traditionally consist of a series of challenges the player must master, and "a 'character' in a game is traditionally merely a convenient vehicle for framing and embodying these challenges"; similarly, Marie-Laure Ryan claims that, as opposed to dramatic narratives, which tend to "feature the mind of their characters," a character in a game is "a rather flat character whose contribution to the plot is . . . a matter of exploring a world, performing actions, solving problems, competing against enemies, and, above all, dealing with interesting objects in a visually stimulating environment."[37] The distinction between centering on the inner life or psychology of a character and centering on the character as a vehicle for player action is therefore key to understanding the differences between characters in (realist) narratives and characters in games.[38] In both *Disaster Hero* and *Disaster Master*, the player must master challenges that, through her completion, turns the player into a hero. The games therefore don't so much ask their players to identify with their characters by seeking to understand aspects of their personalities as they ask them to identify with their characters by acting as them. Instead of empathizing or sympathizing with characters, players are asked to perform tasks while acting as the games' characters. The slogan "Be a Hero!" is therefore less of a statement about *being* than it is about *acting*: do this to step into the role of hero.

However, this understanding of the role of characterization in games in general ultimately fails to account for what the character of the hero means for these games in particular. Taking a closer look at what the players of each game are actually asked to do when they play the game reveals an overall lack of action. In *Disaster Hero*, for example, although the player nominally competes against his chosen opponent in each challenge he undertakes, the player doesn't actually see his opponent or compete directly against her. For instance, the "Find the Difference" challenge involves comparing two images of a room or the outside of a house—one before a disaster, one after—and finding the differences between them (usually things like downed power lines, cracks in walls, the presence or absence of a first-aid kit or a first responder). If the player finds the requisite number of differences between the images, the player completes the challenge. Pointing out a difference between the images means the player scores points and must also then read tips or further information about each item (Figure 15). Meanwhile, the opponent who the player supposedly competes against, one of the Disaster Heroes, doesn't actually participate "directly" in the challenge; instead, she is awarded points based on the player's performance and how long the player takes to complete the challenge (although the rubric for this point allocation is never clear). Those points are then tallied at the end of the game and compared to the player's points to determine who "won" the challenge. The narrative of competition on which the entire premise of the game is based—that the player, a challenger, is competing against Disaster Heroes to become a hero himself—turns out to be a setup. It simply provides the occasion for challenges the player must complete to undergo preparedness training. While this is arguably true of any game in which the player competes against the computer, the fact that the player's "heroism" is narratively tied in the game to his ability to beat his chosen opponent is significant. Players are supposed to become heroes by beating the members of Dante Shields's squad. If the player only ever competes against himself, whom is he "beating" in order to become a hero? The player in *Disaster Hero* is *doing* something all the time, but what meaning does this action have?

Disaster Master is slower and more stilted in its game play than *Disaster Hero*. At first, the game seems akin to a work of interactive fiction, ostensibly placing you, the player, in the position to act in the world of the game. However, you soon discover that your actions have no effect on this world. You are repeatedly asked to "Help the Heroes!" by answering questions about the emergencies they face or making decisions about what they should do, but your decisions do not alter the narrative of the game itself, which continues on unchanged regardless of what you choose. While the game repeatedly enjoins players to become a hero by playing the game, the player's actual role is of a reader. "Playing" the game means reading about heroes in action, with brief interruptions to answer questions. And when you read the game, you realize that the five hero friends are already heroes; they do not need to become them. They already know what to do in emergency situations—they are,

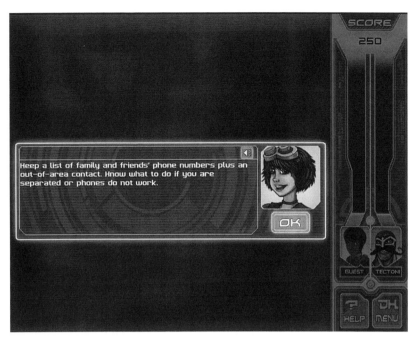

Figure 15. *Disaster Hero* "Find the Difference" tip screen. It reads: "Keep a list of family and friends' phone numbers plus an out-of-area contact. Know what to do if you are separated or phones do not work." Copyright 2011–16, American College of Emergency Physicians. Reprinted with permission.

after all, the protagonists, or heroes, of the campaign—and you, the reader, are just supposed to stick around long enough to read about how they do it. Your role as a reader rather than a player of the game becomes especially clear after you complete a level of the game. After "surviving" the level, you have the opportunity to "print out" that chapter of "your graphic novel." Upon completion, each level of the game therefore transforms into a print artifact that you can read again later (or at least a PDF, a potentially printable artifact). At the end of the game, you can download a cover for your graphic narrative, with the implication that you have now created a book that contains all of the facts and information you need to prepare for disasters (Figure 14). *Disaster Master* therefore demands the player-reader become a hero like the five hero friends—"Be a Hero!"—but actually offers very little for the player-reader to do to become one.

The failure on the part of *Disaster Hero* and *Disaster Master* to engage the player suggests that, as games, they are simply unsuccessful or bad. However, as examples of preparedness materials, the games' procedural weaknesses are revealing. For example, as we have seen in this book, preparedness materials often profess the importance of failure; they argue that it is important to create a space for failure through training exercises, so that exercise participants can discover the weaknesses in their response plans and address them. After all, preparedness training exercises are supposed to encourage and cultivate resilience in their participants. Similarly, Jesper Juul has argued that the experience of failure is integral to the enjoyment of games: "games have an undisputable ability to motivate players to meet challenges and learn in order to overcome failure," a learning process that provides "pleasure spiked with pain."[39] We might therefore think that *Disaster Hero* and *Disaster Master* would encourage player failure to some degree so that players can learn from their mistakes, become more expertly trained in preparedness, and enjoy themselves in the process.

But part of the reason these games are so uninspiring is because they are very difficult to fail. And they're not just easy to win—they are actually hard to fail, meaning they are designed to make it difficult for players *not* to win. For example, apart from *Disaster Hero*'s general low level of difficulty, even for a game aimed at children, it's difficult to fail while playing it because, as discussed, the player doesn't actually compete in a direct way against the opponent she chooses. And even if the player loses the challenge because she scores fewer points than her opponent, she still must eventually finish the challenge—meaning stick it out to the end, not win—to move on to the next one. After completing the game's challenges, the player's points are tallied up and compared to the opponent's points. If the player has scored more points than the opponent, the player wins, and, as Dante Shields says in the game's animated closing sequence, the player will "from this day forward . . . be known to all as a Disaster Hero!" If, on the other hand, the opponent has more points than the player, the opponent wins, and the player doesn't make the team. But while it is possible to fail to win the game, it is not possible to fail to complete the game without quitting. No matter how many challenges the player loses, she will always advance to the next round if she simply finishes each challenge. There is no way to receive a game over. And this is the point: because the game is designed as a preparedness training mechanism, it is not possible to complete it without undergoing some kind of preparedness training, however nominal. All of the challenges are designed to teach the player something about disaster preparedness, whether through the game play itself—the "Quick Care" challenge, for instance, involves applying bandages and slings to simulated wounds—or through the tips and quizzes the player must read or answer as part of the challenge (Figure 15). And because the player can't fail to complete a challenge without quitting the game, even if the player ends up scoring fewer points than her opponent, she will still have completed training in disaster preparedness. As Dante Shields says in the game's closing sequence before the points are tallied, "No matter what the results, we all know that two heroes met today in Disaster Arena." To complete the game is to be a hero, regardless of the outcome. The game doesn't create a safe space for failure; it makes failure impossible.

Disaster Master is similarly concerned with mitigating the effects of failure on the player's preparedness training. Unlike in *Disaster Hero*, however, it is possible to fail a level in *Disaster Master* by failing to answer a certain number of the game's quiz questions about preparedness correctly (this number decreases as the player progresses through the game's levels). If a player receives a game over, he must start that level over again. However, as mentioned, until the player receives a game over, the narrative of the game continues on unchanged after each quiz question, regardless of whether the player answers the question correctly. And the narrative is designed to teach the player—or, if he gets the quiz question right, to reiterate—the correct answer to the question. For example, the first quiz question in level 1, "Wildfire," occurs after the player has read through a part of the narrative in which a counselor at summer camp tells the five hero friends that they can't have a campfire. The multiple-choice question following this sequence asks the player what the five hero friends "might . . . see and smell that would prevent them from having a campfire" and gives the player three options from which to choose: "lake breezes," "smoke," and "farm animals." The correct answer is "smoke," and regardless of whether the player chooses that option, the panels the player reads after the quiz feature a discussion between one of the hero friends, Sonny, and the camp counselor about the fact that "there are wildfires in the distance" (Figure 16). By making the correct answers to the quiz questions part of the narrative the player reads, *Disaster Master*, like *Disaster Hero*, ensures that all players, even if they answer some questions wrong, will receive preparedness training. The game also mitigates potential player failure by making it impossible to fail the first level, no matter how many questions you answer wrong, and, as discussed earlier, by turning each level into a chapter of a graphic novel once the player completes it (Figure 14). This means that the player, after "surviving" each level, walks away with what amounts to an instructional narrative about preparedness to which he is supposed to refer in the future. Because it's possible to make it through the first level without answering any of the questions correctly, no player has to complete the game, or even answer any questions correctly, to receive preparedness training, "survive," and become a hero.

Disaster Hero and *Disaster Master* do as much as they can to nullify the possibility and effects of player failure while still nominally maintaining their status as games. While this may make for unin-

Figure 16. Panels from *Disaster Master* level 1, "Wildfire."

teresting and boring games, it does ensure that all players will receive some form of preparedness training by engaging with these
fictions. These games thus point us toward a strange issue with the
"gamification" of preparedness training, one that centers on the
role of characterization. In video games, the player, through his avatar, is supposed to have an actual causal role in a game's outcome.
As discussed, game avatars allow players to explore, confront, and,
ideally, overcome the challenges of a game's world. But the insistence on player success in *Disaster Master* and *Disaster Hero*—games
that were created with preparedness training, not gaming, as their
first and foremost goal—means that a player's actions have seriously diminished consequences in the worlds of these games. In effect, this makes the character of the hero, whom the player is trying
to become, the default player position, regardless of how the player
performs in the game. The player doesn't actually have to do anything to become a hero, and therefore any player can be a hero simply by playing the game. This is especially odd for a game meant to
train players in preparedness. As discussed in chapters 1 and 2, preparedness training centers on action rather than belief; training exercises do not ask participants to believe the disasters for which they
are training will happen, only to act as if they will. These games,
however, show us that actually taking action is even less important
for preparedness training than is simply receiving training about
what actions you might take. They privilege the communication of
training over its rehearsal. This is also why much of preparedness
training, not just these games specifically, has a gamelike quality or
structure. For preparedness, imaginatively enacting or inhabiting
your response to disaster is more valuable than practicing what you
would "actually" do.

Disaster Hero and *Disaster Master* therefore reveal that, for some
preparedness materials, heroism, and its corresponding quality of
resilience, is a protected status. The people of the homeland are continually enjoined to be resilient, but for these games, resilience is
assumed from the get-go. It is built into these games, something
the people of the homeland, in some sense, already are just by playing the game. The heroes of these games are therefore resilient in
both the most important (for preparedness) and the most technical senses: they are still there at the end of the game. Beyond being

difficult to fail, the games are designed so that they do not deal with or mention death. The player can lose a challenge or fail to complete a level—but the player's avatar can't ever die. *Disaster Hero* and *Disaster Master* therefore handle failure differently than many games, which often, as Amanda Phillips has pointed out, rely on the fun of death and dying to encourage player engagement.[40] As we saw earlier, the language or structure of "survival" is built into each game. In *Disaster Hero*, you must beat the disaster heroes to become one yourself, and in *Disaster Master*, you must make it to the end of each level. But these games are not actually interested in survival, or bouncing back from the brink of destruction. Instead, they are interested in everlasting life, or in how, as Lauren Berlant has written of biopolitics more generally, preparedness "*force*[s] living not just to happen but to endure and appear in particular ways."[41] Players, the heroes of the games, always live on, the form of resilience without any content.

Exemplars of Resilience

While the heroes of *Disaster Hero* and *Disaster Master* can't die, the next heroes to which we turn our attention are both living and dead. They are fixtures of 9/11 anniversary speeches by presidents: the victims and survivors of the September 11, 2001, attacks, or those George W. Bush described in one of his speeches as the "heroes of September the 11th."[42] These speeches invert the temporality of other preparedness materials. Instead of projecting forward to discuss how to prepare for or respond to a future disaster, they project backward to tell a story about how the nation has responded to disaster—in particular, the disaster that has become emblematic for national preparedness. Usually given at nationally important sites or sites with some specific significance in relation to 9/11—locations have included Ground Zero, the Pentagon, the White House, and Ellis Island—these speeches are often televised as "addresses to the nation." They are generally brief, with survivors, first responders, members of the military, and/or various public officials featured as "honored guests." These speeches turn individuals into characters in morality plays about resilience. They all tell stories about Americans' "resolve," "courage," "optimism," and "strength," about the "sacrifices" the people of the United States have made, and will continue to make, in the unending war on terror. In telling and retelling these stories, these speeches often focus on individual people who are supposed to serve as examples of what it means to be a hero. This mode of characterization has at least two seemingly competing functions, each of which centers on a different aspect of the concept of resilience. On one hand, the speeches hold up survivors of the attacks as examples of the importance of staying strong and continuing on. On the other, they also memorialize those who died as a result of the attacks and try to make their memory last. Both kinds of characters, the living and the dead, are heroes.

What's perhaps most remarkable about 9/11 anniversary speeches given by presidents is that, despite the differences in rhetorical style between the three post-9/11 U.S. presidents to date, the speeches never deviate from their pro forma emphasis on resilience. From George W. Bush's speech on the first anniversary of 9/11 in 2002 to Donald Trump's speech on the sixteenth anniversary in 2017, 9/11 anniversary speeches all valorize the resilience of individuals and of the nation as a whole as one and the same, even if they don't explicitly use the term "resilience." In other words, they all use the concept of character to name the qualities of living on associated with resilience. In 2002, Bush put it this way: "yet, in the events that have challenged us, we have also seen the character that will deliver us," a character that is "patient and steadfast" and that reflects "the greatness of America."[43] In 2011, Barack Obama described "our belief in America . . . [which] through tests and trials, has been only strengthened" as a cornerstone of "our character as a nation."[44] And in 2017, Trump described "the incredible character" of the "dedicated civil servants" who died on September 11, 2001, as emblematic of "our resolve" as a nation.[45] In these examples, the word "character" is used in a moral sense to describe the qualities of the people of the United States, and resilience becomes the sum of these qualities, defining the character of the nation's citizens.

Presidential 9/11 anniversary speeches also, however, commonly turn the people of character they discuss into characters in a more literary sense. Bush's 2005 anniversary speech, for example, mentions a few of the "heroes of September the 11th" who died that day, including "Firefighter Donny Regan," "Firefighter Ronnie Gies,"

"Senior Court Officer Thomas Jurgens," and "New York City Police Officer Moira Smith." The speech also describes some of these people's most distinguishing characteristics: Regan "was cited six times for bravery"; Gies is noted for his "determination"; Jurgens is praised for his "refus[al] to leave his post" and Smith for "her fearless spirit on and off the job," "her steady blue eyes," and "her even voice."[46] Similarly, Obama's 2011 speech tells the story of "a woman named Suzanne Swaine," who "lost her husband and brother in the Twin Towers." The speech quotes from a letter she sent to Obama, incorporating Susan Swaine's words to explain how she feels she has been "robbed of 'so many would-be proud moments where a father watches their child graduate, or tend a goal in a lacrosse game, or succeed academically,'" but that she is also proud of her daughters for their "strength and resilience." Like the others, her story is one of resilience; she and her family have succeeded despite the hardships they have faced: "it has been 10 years of raising these girls on my own," she writes, but, as Obama notes, despite this, "her daughters are in college, the other doing well in high school."[47] Trump also follows this formula, telling the story of "Pentagon Police Officer Isaac Ho'opi'i," "a special person"—a hero—who saved almost thirty people from "the burning rubble" and "smoldering darkness" of the Pentagon after it was hit by a plane.[48]

In emphasizing the resilience of ordinary or typical individuals, the speeches characterize these individuals. By "characterize," I don't necessarily mean that the speeches give these people specific qualities, although the quality they all share is resilience. Rather, I mean that the speeches transform these people into specific instances of a general type; they turn them into characters. The resilient people on whom the speeches focus—the "heroes of September the 11th"—are positioned as characters other citizens of the United States should strive to be. Another way of saying this is to say that the speeches present these people, as John Frow puts it in his discussion of fictional character more generally, as "a resource for moral analysis"; they become moral exemplars.[49] The speeches emphasize the resilience of these characters so that they might inspire resilience in the American people, so that they might use them to construct "moral selves or good personal character."[50] In these speeches, to be an example of resilience is to be a resilient character, the kind of person who is resilient. The literary sense of the term carries the moral with it, and vice versa; to be a character is to have character worth emulating.

This dovetailing of the moral and literary senses of character should indicate that, as with the games *Disaster Hero* and *Disaster Master*, when we are discussing character in the context of preparedness, we are not discussing the conception of character most commonly associated with realism (or with the novel, for that matter). We are not discussing, to use E. M. Forster's well-known terminology, round characters.[51] Instead, the characters we encounter in preparedness materials are quite flat. Indeed, as the previous paragraph attests, this is the point: the one-dimensionality of these characters means they can easily exemplify something else, such as the quality of resilience. These speeches use the figure of the hero—the individual who displays the quality of resilience—to tell morality tales and thereby create, in their audience, people of resilient character.

We can see how this works in the 9/11 anniversary speeches as Donny Regan, Ronnie Gies, Thomas Jurgens, Moira Smith, Suzanne Swaine, and Isaac Ho'opi'i all come to act as models of the ideals of resilience the rest of the speech details. Obama closes his description of "a woman named Suzanne Swaine," for example, by stating that her resilient "spirit typifies our American family."[52] And Bush and Trump introduce the characters they discuss according to type—"Firefighter Donny Regan," "New York City Police Officer Moira Smith," "Pentagon Police Officer Isaac Ho'opi'I," and so on—the capital letters announcing each occupation as a category of person.[53] As Aaron Kunin has stated, one way of understanding character is as "a formal device that collects every example of a kind of person."[54] In these speeches, individuals become collected as examples of resilience; they come to "typify" the collective of the hero.[55] So while it may be the case that the proper name "Suzanne Swaine" in Obama's speech, for example, refers to an actual person, this name becomes generalized through the speech to the point of exemplification. "Suzanne Swaine" comes to typify resilience—a quality, the speech wants to emphasize, that is also typical of "our American family." Suzanne Swaine the character, in Kunin's terms, "posits an ideal."[56] She not only becomes collected—along with Firefighter Donny Regan, New York City Police Officer Moira Smith, Pentagon Police Officer Isaac Ho'opi'i, and the rest—as an example of resilience but also acts as a model of resilience itself in the speech. She exemplifies it.

It's obvious in the speeches that resilience is supposed to be a good thing. Resilient people are heroes, and resilience is a desired national characteristic, something people should praise themselves for exhibiting and strive to emulate when they see it in others. Characters like Suzanne Swaine are held up as moral exemplars precisely because they are resilient—precisely because they bounce back, they keep on going. But it is also possible to read bouncing back as something less optimistic: simply continuing to live. From this perspective, the 9/11 anniversary speeches are not so much about bouncing back as they are about the fact of being alive. In this reading, a hero is a hero simply because, like the "final girl" of a horror movie, she lives to tell the tale.[57] In this reading, Suzanne Swaine and her daughters are also resilient because they are the ones left alive.

However, it's also true that most of the "heroes of September the 11th" invoked in these speeches haven't survived. The speeches often acknowledge this by spending time discussing those (U.S. citizens, importantly) who died on September 11, 2001, and in the years since in the wars in Iraq and Afghanistan. For example, here's Bush on the first responders who died on September 11: "We lost brave rescue workers who gave their lives so that others could live. We lost many other citizens who assisted in the rescue efforts, and whose courage and sacrifice that day made them extraordinary."[58] Similarly, Obama mentions that "two million Americans have gone to war since 9/11" and that "too many will never come home," and, speaking of those who died at the Pentagon on September 11, Trump also notes those who have died since 2001: "since 9/11, nearly 7,000 service members have given their lives fighting terrorists around the globe."[59]

These repeated invocations of the dead emphasize how closely related life and death are to one another in these speeches. Like the living, the dead are also counted as heroes. They are the "heroes of September the 11th," "those brave Americans" who "died as they had lived: as heroes doing their duty and protecting us and our country."[60] Similarly, when Obama discusses those "two million Americans" who "have gone to war since 9/11," he links those who "will never come home" with those who will, stating that "those that do [come home] carry dark memories from distant places and the legacy of fallen friends."[61] To survive—to be a hero, in the logic of the speeches—is to be like those who have died, who are also heroes. Indeed, one of the effects of the speeches from this perspective is to flatten, through their equivalent characterization as heroes, the differences between the living and the dead. This is yet another meaning of resilience for preparedness. The online games discussed in the previous section make the hero the default player position by making it impossible for the player to fail; this is resilience as the forced endurance of life. Presidential 9/11 anniversary speeches make survival rhetorically the same as death by characterizing both the living and the dead as heroes; this is resilience as the equivalence of life and death. What's more, both the living and the dead live on through their invocations in these speeches. The speeches thus tie resilience and heroism to the condition of characterization itself. Regardless of whether the heroes of these speeches have survived, to be characterized at all is also to be resilient. Both the living and the dead live on, even if they don't, through the figure of the "hero of September the 11th."

Horde of Heroes

We are now in a position to understand the third resilient character in this chapter's pantheon: the zombie. The zombie takes the figurative equivalence of the living and the dead embodied in the figure of the hero of September 11 literally. A zombie is an example of what happens when there is no difference between living and dying. A zombie is also an example of the limit of the kind of exemplification characterization performs itself. There is nothing more generic, more typological, than a zombie. As Mark McGurl puts it, zombies are "monstrously generic" "anti-characters," "a pure negation of the concept of character at the heart of realism."[62] Zombies don't have qualities or characteristics so much as they have generic conventions; furthermore, an individual zombie isn't so much a specific example or instance of a type so much as zombies *are* the type itself. It doesn't make sense to speak of zombies as individuals, only as a collective. The negation of character, and even of exemplarity itself, that zombies perform highlights how they threaten to undo the synecdochal logic that undergirds the use of characterization in preparedness materials. Instead of standing in for a resilient nation, zombies detach the concept of resilience from personhood altogether. The zombie is, as Glover puts it, "depersonalized," "a non-person."[63] Zombies are the most resilient characters precisely because of their inhuman qualities, their ability to keep on going despite everything. They are figures of the state of objecthood at the heart of resilience.

The comic *Preparedness 101: Zombie Pandemic* was produced by the CDC in 2011 as part of a campaign to increase public awareness about emergency preparedness. The zombie-themed campaign is the CDC's most popular campaign to date, spawning educational and promotional materials, social media badges and buttons, and its own dedicated blog. The initial blog post that kicked off the campaign in 2011 attracted 3.6 billion impressions in less than a year, with 10,000 of those coming in the first ten minutes it was up on the CDC website. Within three days, the CDC's zombie preparedness page was experiencing more than sixty thousand page views per hour.[64] *Preparedness 101* tells the story of Todd, the male protagonist, his female partner, Julie, and their dog, Max, who, late one night, hear reports of "a strange virus" on the nightly news.[65] The narrative includes all of the most recognizable conventions of the zombie disaster genre: a once-familiar friend turns zombie and tries to attack the protagonists; these protagonists then gather their emergency supplies and hole up in their basement for several days until they are forced out; they flee to a government-run emergency shelter, barely making it through a gauntlet of the undead on the way; scientists scramble to create a vaccine while the military guards the perimeter of the shelter; the scientists succeed in making a vaccine, but the zombies defeat the military and overrun the shelter anyway (Figure 17).

But then the narrative takes a sharp turn away from the familiar contours of the zombie disaster genre. With the zombies closing in on Todd, the next frame jumps to an image of Todd waking up alone on his floor with Max. The readers learn, along with Todd, that "it was all just a *dream. . . ?*"; there had been no zombies after

Figure 17. Zombies overrun the shelter in *Preparedness 101.*

all, not really (32). Instead, Todd learns that a severe thunderstorm is on the way, and he goes down to his basement to look for a radio to use during the storm. After looking around, he realizes he should have all of his emergency supplies gathered in one place "in case something happen[s]." Todd's dream therefore inspires him to plan to create an emergency preparedness kit. The inside back cover of the comic also lists items the reader can include in her own "All-Hazards Emergency Kit." And its back cover includes a statement from the CDC, reminding the reader that the story she has just read is "fictional" and "meant to be both educational and entertaining" and enjoining the reader to make her own kit. "Now that you've seen the importance of being prepared," it reads, "take the time to put together an emergency kit with the items included in the checklist on the inside of the back cover" (35, 36).

The comic therefore works as an allegory of the rationality of preparedness itself. An imagined scenario, Todd's dream about a zombie pandemic, teaches Todd not only that he needs to be prepared for anything but also how to prepare for anything. The zombie pandemic of Todd's dream is echoed by another disaster when Todd wakes up: a severe thunderstorm that, like the zombie pandemic in his dream, demonstrates to Todd his own fundamental unpreparedness. The substitution here—a thunderstorm replaces a zombie pandemic as the disaster that spurs Todd on to preparedness—implies not only that a zombie pandemic and a thunderstorm are in some way equivalent but also that preparing for a zombie pandemic is functionally the same as preparing for any other disaster. If you're prepared for zombies, you're prepared for anything. Furthermore, the comic itself is of course yet another fiction—one about a character who uses the fiction of his dream to prepare for actual disasters—that readers are supposed to use, in turn, to learn about preparedness. Todd therefore functions as a model for the reader, who should use the fiction *Preparedness 101: Zombie Pandemic* to motivate her own preparedness actions.[66]

While the graphic narrative ostensibly sets Todd up as the hero because he is the protagonist and the character that models "good" behavior for the reader, he also makes for an odd and ultimately unconvincing hero. Like the other characters this chapter has explored, Todd is a character type, a form empty of content save a few general characteristics. In fact, Todd is just about as generic as it gets (without being a zombie): he is a white male protagonist, the quintessential "everyman" character. The narrative invests no energy in specifying him any further. Todd is meant to be the hero of the narrative, we are left to assume, simply by default, simply because of his subject position. However, the one thing he needs to be a hero, survival, is complicated by the retrospective narrative framing of the zombie pandemic as a dream sequence. Yes, just as the zombies close in on him, Todd wakes up on his floor and realizes it was all a dream. But within the world of the dream—which is also what readers presume is the world of the comic until Todd wakes up—he does not survive. In fact, his failure to survive in his dream is what motivates him to create an emergency preparedness kit of his own. This failure to survive, in other words, is integral to the pedagogical purpose of the graphic narrative itself. And while Todd is important to the narrative because he is a vector for teaching readers about emergency preparedness, he was definitely not the reason the CDC's zombie preparedness campaign garnered so much attention. The zombies were. The zombies, after all, are what make the comic, as the back cover puts it, "entertaining." As in CONPLAN 8888, the zombie pandemic disaster scenario designed to teach military officers how to create disaster scenarios discussed in chapter 2, the zombies are meant to make learning about preparedness fun. From this perspective, the zombies are really the heroes of this story, even as they also, because the term "zombie" only ever names a collective, negate the very concept of the "hero of the story."

Of course, in many ways, it's no surprise that the CDC chose to create a preparedness parable about zombies. A zombie plague is a perfect allegory for the logic of twenty-first-century national security in the United States.[67] This logic emphasizes that the threats for which people must prepare always intrude from without, from outside the homeland—terrorists from the Middle East, hackers from Russia, hurricanes from the Caribbean. Such threats compromise the security of the citizen of the homeland while, this logic insists, having no relation to the supposed homeland itself. The zombies in *Preparedness 101* make the racial distinctions at the heart of this logic clear. Although the zombies in this particular graphic narrative aren't explicitly racialized, Kaiama Glover has argued, as discussed in the beginning of this chapter, that the contemporary zombie is always linked "to 'Haiti' . . . as stand-in for the wider, browner, poorer Third World."[68] In Glover's reading, zombies are thinly disguised allegories for "our fears of what the Third World wants"—our resources, our capital, our way of life, us.[69] Gerry Canavan has emphasized the "racial panic" this allegory represents and enacts:

> Because zombies mark the demarcation between life (that is worth living) and unlife (that needs killing), the evocation of the zombie conjures not solidarity but racial panic. . . . One of the ways the State apparatus builds the sorts of "preaccomplished" subjects it needs is precisely through the construction of a racial binary in which the (white) citizen-subject is opposed against nonwhite life, bare life, *zombie* life—that anti-life which is always inimically and hopelessly Other, which must always be kept quarantined, if not actively eradicated and destroyed.[70]

The zombie is therefore an exemplary figure not just of the violence of white supremacy and colonialism, violence that continues to undergird the project of national security in the United States today, but also, from the perspective of the national security state, of the supposed consequences of such oppression and violence. The people of the homeland, this logic goes, must remain vigilant against these consequences at all times. Zombies are the return of the repressed—the nightmares of imperialism, colonialism, and enslavement come home to roost.

Preparedness 101, like most zombie narratives, repeats this logic. The narrative's plot is structured around Todd and Julie's movements from one enclosed, safe space to the next: from their basement to their car to the emergency shelter. Eventually, all of these enclosed spaces are breached, and the zombie hordes intrude. This is how zombie plots usually proceed: by enacting the failures of securitization over and over and over again. The visual aesthetics of *Preparedness 101* make the implied racial consequences of this failure to secure even more explicit. Despite the graphic narrative's gloomy overall look, the living are drawn throughout with light, bright skin, while the dead are dark and shadowy. We can see this contrast most clearly when the zombie hordes break into the emergency shelter (Figure 17). In the bottom row of panels on the page, the bright faces of the living are easily distinguishable from the gray flesh of the undead. But the top panel of this page also suggests the scandalous intermixing of light and dark skin as the dead overrun the living. Toward the bottom of the middle part of the panel, one man's hand seems to become zombified—monstrously oversized, clawlike, and grayish in color—before our eyes as a zombie latches on to his back;

skull-like faces, impossible to distinguish as either living or undead, arise from the middle of the horde and seem to cry in anguish; the face of a woman in the lower right seems to take on the grayish hue of the zombie that is taking her down; a black shadow that belongs to no one in particular runs away from a shambling zombie in the far left of the panel. This panel, in other words, depicts the moment the living become undead, a literal darkening of light skin.

Because the figure of the zombie remains attached to and calls upon its historical specificity regardless of the context in which it occurs, the zombie, paradoxically, is the most general form of disaster in the context of U.S. national security. Zombification, like all modes of characterization, is a process of generalization—to become a zombie is to become general, a type rather than an individual. Additionally, zombies are the most general form of disaster because they describe the general condition of the contemporary security state. They function as allegories of its thinly veiled racial and xenophobic logic, that of protecting the (white) people of the homeland against (Black and brown) "outsiders." From the perspective of the national security state, zombies express the potential horrors of generalization. In zombie narratives, one zombie becomes many; formerly safe spaces, such as one's home or neighborhood, become unsafe; distinctions once considered inviolable—white and Black, us and them—become meaningless as the contagion spreads (or, as Glover argues, the figure of the zombie showcases the fact that there were really not many irreducible differences between us and them after all).[71] Zombies, that is, threaten to make the people of the homeland generalizable, to gloss over their particularities and, more importantly, the distinctions between them and others. As Canavan puts it, "to become a zombie would be to obliterate the line dividing 'us' from 'them.'"[72] This is what *Preparedness 101* cannot abide, the nightmare it must enact to immediately disavow. Although preparedness materials everywhere enjoin the people of the homeland to be more resilient, resilience itself, when pushed to its limit, becomes horrific for preparedness. As Glover wonders, what, after all, is more resilient than a zombie?[73]

Yet *Preparedness 101* does not only depict the zombie pandemic as horrific; it's also meant to be funny. The comedic aspects of the graphic narrative point us toward another reading of the zombies as the heroes of *Preparedness 101*, one suggested by the fact that Todd is an ultimately unconvincing hero for this story. In this reading, the zombies stand in for only themselves—zombies—and in so doing, they are meant to promote the national security state. To read *Preparedness 101* as funny—as a comic—is to focus on the quintessentially comedic nature of the zombie as a character. Henri Bergson famously described the comic as "something mechanical encrusted on the living," which is also a great description of a zombie.[74] Furthermore, Alenka Zupančič's understanding of comedy as the "concrete labor or work of the universal itself" emphasizes another important capacity of the zombified.[75] As discussed, to become a zombie is to become general, even abstract. Zombies present as a swarm, a horde. As such, they are monstrously collective, both the quintessential and one of the most extreme examples of a character type.[76] Yet, to become a zombie is also to become absurdly concrete: a walking corpse and nothing more. Zombies are walking objects, animated dead matter. Zupančič observes that the concreteness of the comic character lies in its resilience as well. As she puts it, "regardless of all accidents and catastrophes . . . that befall comic characters, they always rise from the chaos perfectly intact, and relentlessly go on pursuing their goals."[77] Think of Wile E. Coyote chasing the Road Runner. No matter how far Wile E. falls or how many times he is flattened by a train or how often he blows himself up, he always bounces back. He is indestructible. Zombies, too, just keep on coming.[78]

Preparedness 101: Zombie Pandemic also plays up the comedic side of its narrative through its cartoonish visual aesthetic and its highly theatrical writing. For example, Todd's first encounter with a zombie, his neighbor Mrs. Clements, passes over from conventional to parodic (Figure 18). Todd hears a "racket" outside, and he opens the door to find zombified Mrs. Clements. After telling her she doesn't "look so good," Todd suggests she go "lie down." Mrs. Clements grabs Todd, to which he replies, "Aah!! Okay, maybe not . . . !" and shoves her off the front stoop with a "Later, Mrs. Clements!" All the while, Mrs. Clements moans and groans—"Urrr!" "Aaargh!" "Urrk!"—echoing the growls and yowls of her cat, Snowball, and Todd's dog, Max (10).[79] This sort of zany energy infuses many of the comic's scenes, especially those involving zombies, reinforcing its comedic effect. Indeed, the preponderance of exclamation points throughout the narrative; the pliability of characters' bodies and faces reinforced by the slapstick humor of many scenes involving zombies; and Todd's tendency toward hammy, chipper dialogue all contribute to the zaniness of *Preparedness 101*. As Sianne Ngai notes, zaniness is an "aesthetic of nonstop acting or doing" "pushed to strenuous and even precarious extremes."[80] The desperation of the characters' battles with zombies therefore heightens the comic's affective impact, but this never spins out of control. As we saw in chapter 1 in relation to the comic *A River in Egypt*, *Preparedness 101* uses a regular panel structure to contain and control disaster; even when the zombies break in to the emergency shelter, in arguably the most chaotic moment of the narrative, they are contained within the panel structure (Figure 17). And like I argued in chapter 3 in relation to Richard Clarke's writing, *Preparedness 101* uses this simultaneous generation and control of excitement to promote an even affective keel in the reader. By modulating between the terror of a zombie apocalypse and the zany antics of battles with the undead, and by relying on the visual structure of the comic form to control the expressions of both, the comic seeks to make preparedness "both educational and entertaining," to echo the back cover of the comic. The narrative's ending drives the importance of affective resolution home: the dystopian nightmare of Todd's dream gives way to the banal domesticity of a TV sitcom, complete with a sassy punchline ending (Figure 19).

From this perspective, the zombies are "heroic" because they are what make this narrative fun, what draw attention to it as a public awareness campaign, and what make it endure as perhaps the most popular preparedness public awareness campaign to date.[81] Without the zombies, *Preparedness 101* is a boring story about a boring guy who has a bad dream and then creates an emergency preparedness kit. The ability of the zombies to make the campaign last is evidenced by the CDC's investment in preserving the campaign's materials for the public. Although it ended in 2012, unlike many defunct public awareness campaigns, the CDC's zombie pandemic preparedness materials have been archived on the CDC's website. As the website asks, "Wonder why zombies, zombie apocalypse, and zombie preparedness continue to live or walk dead on a CDC web

Figure 18. Todd's encounter with Mrs. Clements in *Preparedness 101*.

site? As it turns out what first began as a tongue-in-cheek campaign to engage new audiences with preparedness messages has proven to be a very effective platform."[82] The zombies have helped this campaign endure. To read the zombies in this way is to recognize that they are there "simply" to be zombies, meaning they are there to help the CDC and preparedness benefit from the popularity of zom-

Figure 19. The last page of *Preparedness 101*.

bies by drawing attention to the public awareness campaign. This is their function. By making the zombies the heroes of the narrative, which subsequently makes the narrative and the public awareness campaign a little bit funny, a little bit unexpected, a little bit self-aware, the CDC hopes to encourage people not only to read its materials but also to spread the word about the publicity campaign online. The zombies are there to make the CDC's preparedness campaign go viral. What is resilient, in this reading, is preparedness itself. The zombie pandemic public awareness campaign enacts the dream of preparedness as policy: to be unending.

I want to make one final point about how *Preparedness 101* regards the heroes of its story. The alternately horrific and comedic attitudes it takes toward the zombies exemplify what, as discussed in the introduction to this chapter, Glover has referred to as "the repugnance embedded so sneakily in the notion of resilience."[83] Repugnance implies disgust and revulsion; as a now-obsolete synonym for resilience, it captures the sense of affective recoil from something. But repugnance also carries with it its older, now nearly obsolete meaning of contradiction or incompatibility.[84] A zombie is just such a revolting contradiction: someone who is dead, decomposing even, but walks. Someone whose survival is unnatural. This survival is horrific—but it's also meant to be funny, in the way that disgusting things often are.

When we think of the repugnance *Preparedness 101* displays toward the heroes of its story, then, we should think not only of the terror the flesh-eating zombie is supposed to inspire but also of the laughter evoked by the figures on the stage of a minstrel show. Viewed from this perspective, the depiction of the zombies overrunning the emergency shelter in *Preparedness 101* is also a depiction of blackface, as formerly white faces take on a dark hue for laughs (Figure 17).[85] As Eric Lott's influential account of antebellum American minstrelsy emphasizes, much of the humor of minstrel shows was related not only to their vulgarity but also to the feelings of disgust they were supposed to generate by connecting this vulgarity to Blackness itself.[86] Minstrelsy, in other words, was humorous precisely because a white person "dressing up" as Black was meant to be repugnant. This repugnance resulted from the central contradiction minstrel shows saw themselves as repeatedly staging: the liveliness of objects, or the denial of the personhood of the figures depicted on stage. As Fred Moten has argued, "Blackness . . . is a strain that pressures the assumption of the equivalence of personhood and subjectivity."[87] In this reading, the zombies shambling through the pages of *Preparedness 101* are comically alive things.

This is why they are supposed to be funny. Yet this humor—the humor of the minstrel show—arises from the abjection of disgust. Saidiya Hartman has called this form of humor "the violence that undergirded the comic moment in minstrelsy" or "the terror of pleasure."[88] No matter how "cool" the CDC thinks zombies are, *Preparedness 101* doesn't intend for readers to identify or even sympathize with the zombies. Repugnance is a way of distancing yourself from something, not encouraging identification with it. The zombies are there to be feared, loathed, and laughed at.[89]

This chapter has shown how preparedness materials make use of the concept of character, how they take advantage of the fact that a character is never only an individual person but also an instance of a general type, to tell stories about resilience or the state of being just more than, or just less than, human. It is this flickering between the specific and the typological, and between personhood and objecthood, that the materials investigated in this chapter exploit. They want both participants and readers to see themselves in the hero—to become "heroes" in their own right by becoming prepared for disaster, by "surviving"—and to make it easy for anyone, or, in the case of the CDC's *Preparedness 101: Zombie Pandemic*, no one, to be a hero. They flatten distinctions between the hero and other characters, even while they also valorize the hero for her most characteristic trait: her resilience or survival.

The zombies in *Preparedness 101* push this ambivalence into contradiction by suggesting the detachment of resilience from personhood altogether. This troubles the lesson about resilience the CDC narrative ostensibly wants to teach. The purpose of *Preparedness 101* is to teach its readers how to prepare for and thus survive any disaster by using a fictional disaster to inspire the reader's own preparedness efforts. But it only ends up communicating the futility of learning such survival skills. In his dream, after all, Todd dies anyway, no matter what he does. The zombie horde overruns him. Of course, the comic's insistence on the unreality of Todd's death reveals its investment in upholding and protecting the whiteness of the homeland by providing fodder for various nightmare scenarios of a white homeland invaded by blackened hordes from without. Nevertheless, Todd's implied death also makes room for a momentary glimpse of something else, of an understanding of survival without the repugnance of resilience. It is to this understanding of survival that I now turn.

Coda: On Survival

The understanding of resilience promulgated by preparedness materials, and therefore the one discussed in this chapter, is conceptually and morally deficient. The preparedness materials I have discussed interpret the concept of resilience quite literally. Resilience means survival in these materials, especially when survival looks like something very close to or even exceeding death. As Andrew Lakoff writes, "from the vantage of preparedness, the conditions of existence of members of the population are not a political problem."[90] It is only important from the perspective of preparedness, as a mode of bio- and necropolitical governance, that members of certain populations continue to exist while others are made killable. This dual operation is distilled into the concept of resilience. But shifting our gaze ever so slightly from *resilience* to *survival* opens up new conceptual and affective terrain, foregrounding personhood and the endurance of community. Audre Lorde's 1978 poem "A Litany for Survival," which I reproduce in full, provides us with just such a shift:

> For those of us who live at the shoreline
> standing upon the constant edges of decision
> crucial and alone
> for those of us who cannot indulge
> the passing dreams of choice
> who love in doorways coming and going
> in the hours between dawns
> looking inward and outward
> at once before and after
> seeking a now that can breed
> futures
> like bread in our children's mouths
> so their dreams will not reflect
> the death of ours;

For those of us
who were imprinted with fear
like a faint line in the center of our foreheads
learning to be afraid with our mother's milk
for by this weapon
this illusion of some safety to be found
the heavy-footed hoped to silence us
For all of us
this instant and this triumph
We were never meant to survive.

And when the sun rises we are afraid
it might not remain
when the sun sets we are afraid
it might not rise in the morning
when our stomachs are full we are afraid
of indigestion
when our stomachs are empty we are afraid
we may never eat again
when we are loved we are afraid
love will vanish
when we are alone we are afraid
love will never return
and when we speak we are afraid
our words will not be heard
nor welcomed
but when we are silent
we are still afraid

So it is better to speak
remembering
we were never meant to survive.[91]

Perhaps Lorde's best-known poem, "A Litany for Survival" is a hymn to Black survival in the United States. Its refrain, "we were never meant to survive," is a statement of defiance in the face of the myriad acts of everyday violence against Black speech, writing, bodies, and personhood. Critics have read the poem as a work of speculative fiction that imagines Black life and hope into existence. For Alexis Pauline Gumbs, Lorde's poetry describes the possibilities of a "queer Black feminist futurity," and it "draws on the generic traditions of both horror and utopia," traditions that equally invoke the experience of Black life in the United States.[92] Similarly, Alexis Lothian reads "A Litany for Survival" as Afro-futurist, arguing that although "Lorde uses the language of procreation to describe how possible futures emerge from the present when she hopes for 'a now that can breed / futures,'" Lorde also "transforms the term "'breeding' . . . from a term antithetical to queerness and offensive to blackness into a nexus of hope and possibility for the black, queer, feminist subjectivity she articulates."[93] In these accounts, Lorde's vision of Black survival is one of proliferation (of hope, of children, of love) cast in the future tense, something readers must continually imagine into existence because of its radical departure from the here and now.

The poem's temporal slipperiness bolsters these readings. As the title suggests, it is composed of a litany of qualifiers and phrases that describe the addressees of the poem—a community to which the speaker also belongs, as evidenced by the poem's use of the first-person plural ("those of us" and "we"). There are no characters per se in this poem; there is only the collective "we" and "us." The phrases that qualify these pronouns are often associated with liminality, fear, and anxiety, making it difficult to place the speaker of the poem and the people the speaker addresses temporally. For example, the speaker addresses the poem to "those of us who cannot indulge / the passing dreams of choice / who love in doorways coming and going / in the hours between dawns" and to those who elide the present moment with fears about the future: "And when the sun rises we are afraid / it might not remain / when the sun sets we are afraid / it might not rise in the morning." In the long lists of qualifying phrases that accumulate throughout most of stanzas 1–3, all of which begin with the repeated words "who" or "when" and describe the poem's audience and speaker, the present moment of the speaker's enunciation slips and slides away under the pressure of the not-now. The poem is "for those of us who" are "seeking a now that can breed / futures" and for those of us who "when we are loved we are afraid / love will vanish." The liminal figures to whom the poem is addressed, in other words, are never fully present. They exist in what Berlant has called "survival time" or "the time of struggling, drowning, holding onto the ledge, treading water—the time of *not-stopping*."[94]

However, the poem also focuses the reader's attention on the present moment. Its refrain—the line "we were never meant to survive" that occurs at the end of the second and fourth stanzas—breaks up the litany of these not-nows. The first time the refrain occurs, it interrupts yet another descriptive phrase, leaving the last "For all of us" incomplete and focusing the reader's attention instead on "this instant and this triumph." The second time it happens, at the end of the poem, it is with the speaker's full assurance that "it is better to speak" now. The force of this refrain is temporal: each time it occurs, it breaks the poem's anxious temporality by insisting on the present. The refrain's insistent presentism is complicated by the fact that it is written in the past tense. However, precisely because it is written in the past tense, the phrase "we were never meant to survive" functions as something like the opposite of the future anterior, or the "what will have been." The future anterior describes not simply what will happen in the future but that which *will have happened*. To speak in the future anterior tense is to "look back" on a "past" that is still the future at the moment of enunciation—to make the future already past. This is the temporality of preparedness. Lorde's "we were never meant to survive," in contrast, describes a present moment or situation that was not predicted or intended by a past moment or situation. It describes how the past always fails to fully predict the present, even though that past also survives into the present. It also describes someone else's intention, someone else who didn't intend for the "we" of the poem to survive. "We were never meant to survive" thus describes survival in the present against all odds, despite hundreds of years of economic oppression, political repression, and state-sanctioned violence against Black people in the United States, as much as it describes the intentions of the past.

Lorde's poem, then, provides a different take on the value of survival than the preparedness materials discussed in this chapter, one without the repugnance of resilience evidenced in the CDC's zombie pandemic preparedness comic. Lorde's poem is "A Litany for Survival," a collective prayer for the strength to keep going in the face of "the heavy-footed" who "hoped to silence us," who "imprinted [us] with fear." It is also, however, a litany *of* survival, cataloging what survival feels like for those who "were never meant to survive" in the first place. It is a poem for the wayward, as Hartman has put it; it describes "a *beautiful experiment* in how-to-live," "the untiring practice of trying to live when you were never meant to survive."[95] Survival in this poem is an ongoing, lived practice of defiance that occurs in the present. In the face of the repugnance *Preparedness 101* shows for the continued existence of those who were never meant to survive, the poem performs what Christina Sharpe has called "wake work"; it makes it possible to "continue to imagine new ways to live in the wake of slavery, in slavery's afterlives, to survive (and more) the afterlife of property."[96] There is nothing "mere" about survival as Lorde presents it. To have survived—to have persisted through time despite one's dislocation from the present—and to insist on the present tense of one's survival, "this instant and this triumph," is an achievement. Lorde's articulation of survival therefore focuses not only on the durational aspects of the concept, on what it means to last through time while subject to haunting by it, but also on how this specific kind of survival defies all expectations. It was never meant to happen in the first place. To survive, in this formulation, is to resist the genre of disaster.[97]

What would it mean to turn back to *Preparedness 101: Zombie Pandemic* now, to read it in the wake of "A Litany for Survival"? In doing so, I am not suggesting that *Preparedness 101* performs the same kind of wake work as Lorde's poem—far from it. But "A Litany for Survival" does provide us with a method, a mechanism through which we can place pressure on the CDC's graphic narrative and reveal its fissures, if only momentarily. To see how this works, we need to think again about one moment in particular from *Preparedness 101*: the moment when the zombies break in to the emergency shelter and overrun it, or when *Preparedness 101* breaks from its generic expectations by (almost) killing Todd (Figure 17).

Although the narrative doesn't quite depict Todd's demise, and although it quickly disavows this almost-event by claiming it was all

a dream, Todd's (near) death is surprising. Lorde's poem's refrain—
"we were never meant to survive"—in all its defiance of expectation,
applies in this moment to the zombies that are about to dismember
Todd. Despite the fact that they were also never meant to survive,
they do; even though they are dead, they walk. What *Preparedness
101* presents as both a nightmare (the blackened hordes overrun the
emergency shelter, the last bastion of civilization) and as good, clean
fun (zombies make learning about emergency preparedness cool!)
is, in this moment, a true statement about those to whom preparedness is not addressed, those who are not included in the putative
homeland and whose lives have been deemed not only expendable
but also killable. Reading "we were never meant to survive" as a
zombie refrain therefore turns the zombies, despite the intentions
of the comic itself, into vehicles for identification by enfolding them
into the poem's community of survivors.

This move also disrupts the future anterior tense of *Preparedness
101*, in which a projection of future fictional disaster (a zombie pandemic) spurs on preparedness in the present and thereby positions
the future as already having happened. The zombies briefly disrupt
this temporality, not because they, as in Lorde's poem, insist on the
present tense of survival, but rather because they lay bare the fact that
preparedness does little to address the problems for which disasters
are only symptoms. The narrative begins, after all, on the night the
zombie pandemic begins; by then, as the fact that the zombies ultimately prevail in Todd's dream makes apparent, it is already too
late. No amount of preparedness can save Todd from this disaster.
In fact, as discussed earlier, what is perhaps most unexpected about
Preparedness 101 is that Todd dies *despite* the fact that he follows all
of the proper preparedness protocols and guidelines. He doesn't do
anything wrong, but the zombies still prevail. In this moment, the
zombie refrain "we were never meant to survive" registers defiance
of one more expectation. Todd, as the white everyman protagonist,
the putative hero of the story, is meant to survive; he is a person to
whom preparedness is addressed and someone who is included in
the homeland. Yet, briefly, this is not enough to save him. In this
moment, *Preparedness 101* undoes itself, however incompletely. This
moment shows us how, because preparedness is premised on the

survival of some at the expense of others, it does nothing to address the problems it is designed to mitigate. It cannot protect anyone, even those resilient people of good moral character—heroes—it is supposed to protect. Instead, as we will see in the next chapter, it tries to convince those to whom it is addressed—the white people of the homeland, the Todds—that although the world is burning around them, they need only follow the protocol and everything will be fine.

Looking for the Plot

Counterterrorism and the Hermeneutics of Suspicion

The preceding chapter centered on what the concept of character does for preparedness materials, or on how citizens become (or don't become) heroes. This chapter focuses on another role for the citizen of the homeland, a role that, in the context of counterterrorism materials, is hermeneutic. Good citizens of the homeland, the materials I will discuss emphasize, must learn to detect and thus to thwart terrorist attacks. The temporality of this detection is significant; instead of training people to respond to a terrorist attack after it happens, the documents, posters, and videos I discuss in this chapter all emphasize learning to stop a terrorist attack before it fully materializes. Even though preparedness, as I have stated throughout this book, emphasizes institutional readiness and emergency management rather than prevention, as of this writing, the latest version of the five "mission areas" that DHS defines as constituting preparedness does include prevention (the others are protection, mitigation, response, and recovery).[1] Interestingly, the prevention mission area is the only mission area specifically focused on terrorism. "The Prevention mission area," FEMA states, "is composed of the capabilities necessary to avoid, prevent or stop a threatened or actual act of terrorism" and "is focused on ensuring we are optimally prepared to prevent an imminent terrorist attack within the United States."[2] The idea is that unlike natural disasters, terrorist attacks can be avoided; more precisely, in the words of DHS, people can "prepare to prevent" them. The "capabilities" associated with this area of preparedness—the actions people should be trained to do to prepare to prevent, such as "planning," "intelligence and information sharing," and "screening, search, and detection"—therefore center on trying to stop terrorist attacks before they occur.[3] This is what DHS means by the strange phrase "prepared to prevent." In the context of counterterrorism, preparedness training should center on teaching people to anticipate and thus to prevent an attack.

Preparing to prevent terrorist attacks is most often described in these materials as "disrupting terrorist plots." Indeed, disrupting terrorist plots is one of the most common rhetorical formulations in contemporary U.S. national security discourse; discussion of disrupting, busting, stopping, thwarting, countering, and foiling terrorist plots is so ubiquitous both within the national security community and without that it's practically unremarkable. For instance, the House Homeland Security Committee releases monthly "Terror Threat Snapshot" reports documenting the number of "jihadist plots" that "have been thwarted" each month, and it holds hearings about "Working with Communities to Disrupt Terrorist Plots"; DHS includes "disrupting terrorist plots" as part of its "founding mission" and emphasizes in reports that "counterterrorism and law enforcement efforts to disrupt plots are a continuing priority"; and news headlines trumpet one "foiled terror plot" after another.[4] While a successful terrorist incident is usually described in these same materials as an "attack," a potential incident is a "plot" that needs disrupting. In this chapter, we will think through why preparedness materials are so invested in understanding terrorism as a plot. What is at stake in this imaginative formulation?

My first claim is that when counterterrorism materials talk about "disrupting plots," they use the word *plot* to mean not only a secret plan or scheme but also a narrative plot. In fact, this chapter will show how, in the context of preparedness and terrorism prevention, these two meanings overlap.[5] This claim may seem strange, given that the counterterrorism materials I discuss are not narrative. What's more, the House Homeland Security Committee explicitly defines the word *plot* in one of its reports as "schemes, either executed or disrupted, by an individual or group to commit violent terrorist acts."[6] This meaning of the word doesn't, at first, appear to have much relation to the meaning of plot more common in narrative contexts, which, in its most general sense, refers not only to a sequence of events but also to a sequence of events connected to one another via causation.[7] The documents, posters, and public service announcements associated with the counterterrorism campaigns I discuss in this chapter do not really have plots in this way.

Yet, despite their nonnarrative structure, these materials nevertheless rely on the narrative meaning of the word when they refer to "terrorist plots." They encourage their audience to regard such events as if they were narratives, as if they were part of sequences of events connected to one another via cause and effect. They encourage their audience to make causal connections between disconnected actions and events and to assume that these actions and events will lead—inevitably, unless they intervene—to a terrorist attack. This mode of interpretation is what Peter Brooks defines as plot itself, identifying "the *anticipation of retrospection*" as the "master trope" of the strange logic of plot. As we read a narrative, Brooks emphasizes, we know the end of this narrative is already in place, and even though we may not yet know what that end is, we do know "that what remains to be read will restructure the provisional meanings of the already read."[8] For Brooks, the plot of a narrative refers less to the structure or order of its events and more to "the interpretive activity" any reader must perform when they read a narrative.[9] This definition of plot presupposes the equivalence of a "plot" and of what Brooks calls "reading for the plot." The preparedness materials I discuss in this chapter advance precisely this understanding. The "plots" they train people to detect reside not in what they teach people to read—everyday situations instead of stories, in this case—but rather in the imaginations of the people they seek to train. Plotting, or hatching a plot, is therefore indistinguishable from detecting plots; they are one and the same interpretive activity, one and the same responsibility deflected onto the subjects of preparedness. This understanding of a plot also suggests that, because they encourage people to arrange objects and events into coherent structures, plots, plotting, and detecting plots are a way of exerting control over these events and objects. They are a way for subjects to structure and arrange their lives.

In what follows, I track the role of plot in three examples of counterterrorism materials: the influential 2007 "radicalization model" created by the New York Police Department (NYPD), meant to describe the "homegrown threat" of radicalization in the West, including the "trajectory" along which a Muslim person travels on his way toward committing a terrorist act; DHS's well-known "If You See Something, Say Something" public awareness campaign; and the Department of State's failed "Think Again Turn Away" public awareness campaign. These materials vary in their target audiences, styles, and approaches, but they are all marked by their encouragement of interpretive practices designed to detect terrorist attacks—or, in one case, by the absence of encouragement of such practices. The 2007 NYPD radicalization model and the "If You See Something, Say Something" campaign are addressed to people preparedness materials imagine as the people of the homeland, a group, as this book has detailed, that is not coterminous with people living in the United States or with citizens of the United States. For these materials, this interpretive practice involves reading for the plot or training their audience to "recognize" nascent terrorist attacks in progress. It involves encouraging people to see certain objects and behaviors—backpacks or packages left behind in public places, "unauthorized" people showing up where they shouldn't be, people behaving "suspiciously"—as part of ongoing terrorist plots. Regardless of how harmless or unrelated such objects and actions may seem to be, these materials suggest, they should nevertheless be understood as part of a plot whose end point is a terrorist attack on U.S. soil.

The "Think Again Turn Away" public awareness campaign, on the other hand, was addressed to people outside the homeland who might have been considering joining an Islamic terrorist organization. I focus on a video from the campaign that circulated widely on social media in 2014, titled *Welcome to the Islamic State Land*. Rather than teaching its audience to read for the plot using even the smallest of seemingly innocuous details, or to read for a plot without events, this video emphasizes the effects of terrorist plots by depicting the violence caused by terrorists. It doesn't need to try to teach anyone to see potential harm in everyday objects and actions, because the world it depicts is already obviously, gratuitously terrible. Rather than teaching people to recognize something in nothing, it merely "documents" this world as it is.

Taken together, the preparedness materials I discuss in this chapter show how the mechanisms of plotting subtend a Janus-faced conception of homeland security. The people of the homeland, these materials avow, must remain vigilant against plots, striving to keep the homeland plotless and areas outside the homeland eventful. Yet, because detecting plots and plotting are the same thing, to "recognize" terrorist plots in progress, people of the homeland must learn to plot themselves, mimicking the practices of the plotters they oppose. This circularity is further evidence of Jasbir K. Puar's claim that the figures of the patriot and the terrorist depend on one another for their meaning and legibility in counterterrorism discourses.[10] However, paying attention to plots and plotting also attunes us to how the objects in and of plots—the "somethings" counterterrorism campaigns enjoin people of the homeland to watch out for—come to stand in for the plotters. Objects and behaviors like backpacks, hoodies, and researching certain things on the internet become metonyms for the terrorist, detached from this figure yet nonetheless bearing its trace. This detachment means counterterrorism preparedness materials ultimately focus on objects and actions associated with terrorism rather than on the figure of the terrorist, a structure of disavowal that allows them to deny charges of discrimination or racism while at the same time relying on these objects and actions as implied racial markers.[11]

Like the figuration of Blackness discussed in chapter 4, this disavowal is another way of indirectly representing nonwhiteness. As many scholars have argued, counterterrorist discourse racializes the terrorist as an implicitly Black or brown outsider come to destroy the homeland, even if they are American or living in the United States.[12] And as Alexander G. Weheliye emphasizes, although such processes of racialization are often displaced in contemporary political and national security discourse onto religion or nationality—"Islamic" terrorism is the issue, these materials claim—they are nevertheless implicitly racial because they are dependent on and "translated to visual phenomena."[13] The counterterrorism materials I discuss in this chapter, including the entreaty to "see something," all rely on appearance or visual mediation to train people to distinguish the harmless objects of "everyday life" from the potentially harmful objects of terrorism—in other words, to look for the plot.[14] In the terms of Charles Sanders Peirce's philosophy of signs, counterterrorism preparedness materials train people to treat *symbols* of terrorism like backpacks as *indexes* of terrorism. They teach people to interpret these objects, which have, as Peirce puts it, no "actual connection" to terrorism, as somehow directly or materially related to it, reinforcing and naturalizing the seeming inevitability of this symbolic system.[15]

The chapter's coda positions the 2017 film *Get Out* (dir. Jordan Peele) as another kind of counterterrorism material, one that subverts the subject–object relationship suggested by counterterrorism materials produced by the state. One of the tag lines for the film during its promotional campaigns was "Say Something," and one of its characters, the protagonist Chris's friend Rod, is, in his own words, a "TS-motherfucking-A" agent (Transportation Security Administration), the governmental agency perhaps most directly associated with the "If You See Something, Say Something" campaign. These references to the counterterrorism campaign reveal the close association between the "If You See Something, Say Something" campaign and horror film in general: both rely on suspicion to train people to look for the plot. Moreover, *Get Out* specifically connects the post-9/11 U.S. national security state's obsession with (nonraced but implicitly racialized) Islamic terrorism to the long history of anti-Black terrorism in the United States. As Christina Sharpe has argued, "in much of what passes for public discourse *about* terror . . . Black people . . . become the *carriers* of terror, terror's embodiment, and not the primary objects of terror's multiple enactments."[16] *Get Out*, however, reverses this dynamic, using the horror genre to make visceral, following Sharpe, "the quotidian experiences of terror in black lives lived in an anti-black world."[17] In critiquing the fantasy of control presented by "If You See Something, Say Something," the film instead offers a fantasy in which agents of the national security state are engaged in thwarting the true homegrown threat: white supremacy.

Looking for the Plot

Counterterrorism materials about how to detect and disrupt terrorist plots—and by "terrorist plots," such materials almost always mean so-called Islamic terrorist plots—often spend a lot of time describing the "radicalization process" people supposedly undergo on their way to becoming terrorists. Perhaps the account of such a process cited the most often is the 2007 NYPD report titled *Radicalization in the West: The Homegrown Threat*. This report focuses on identifying and describing the "radicalization process in the West," or the process through which "the potential terrorist or group of terrorists begin and progress through a process of radicalization," the "culmination" of which "is a terrorist attack."[18] The four phases of radicalization it describes are "pre-radicalization," "self-identification," "indoctrination," and "jihadization," phases the authors of the report created by researching "five prominent homegrown groups/plots around the world which resulted in either terrorist attacks or thwarted plots" and then "identify[ing] common pathways and characteristics" among the groups and plots (15). The report is therefore meant to work as a tool for identification that other law enforcement officers can use in detecting the plots of "potential terrorists" (5).

The methods and findings of this report have been widely discredited by the American Civil Liberties Union (ACLU), which succeeded in pressuring the NYPD to remove the report from its website in 2016.[19] The NYPD itself issued a statement in 2009 claiming that "this report was not intended to be policy prescriptive for law enforcement" (even though the report's preface states that its aim is "to assist policymakers and law enforcement officials" in "developing effective counter-strategies" [2]).[20] Nevertheless, the NYPD report has had a large impact on counterterrorism policy and discourse at the federal level. A 2013 report by a researcher in the Congressional Research Service, for example, uses the NYPD radicalization model to describe the "radicalization process"; both the Federal Bureau of Investigation and the Senate Committee on Homeland Security and Governmental Affairs have embraced the model; and federal agencies and organizations, including DHS and the National Institute of Justice, use the model as a touchstone in creating "counter-radicalization" policies.[21] The effects of this influence have been well documented by the ACLU, which has shown how both local and federal law enforcement agencies have used the NYPD report to justify warrantless surveillance of Muslim American and Muslim communities in the United States.[22]

The four phases described in the NYPD report constitute a linear model of radicalization—one phase leads to the next, and each successive phase builds on the last. In other words, although the model is not narrative, it encourages officials to understand the reality it supposedly maps onto as a plot. A person begins in the "pre-radicalization" phase and makes choices and experiences events in such a way that the person progresses incrementally through the phases on her way toward the end (in this case, perpetrating a terrorist attack). Unlike a narrative, however, the NYPD radicalization model doesn't concern itself with causality. Or, better put, it doesn't concern itself with explaining the causal connections between its four phases or what might drive a person to progress along such a trajectory. While it speculates that individuals "most vulnerable" to the process of radicalization "are often those who are at a crossroad in life," it also emphasizes that "the majority of these individuals [who carry out terrorist attacks] began as 'unremarkable'" (2).[23] Instead of focusing on causal connections between events or actions, the report focuses on behavioral "indicators" that suggest "progression along the radicalization continuum," for whatever reason—things like "regular attendance at a Salafi mosque," "withdrawal from the mosque," "politicization of new beliefs," "researching on the internet," and "acquiring material/developing the device" (31, 36, 45). These "indicators" of terrorism substitute in the report for causal explanations, becoming indices of actions and events that haven't yet happened but through which law enforcement officials can see the contours of a plot.

This arrangement of such "indicators" into a linear sequence has the effect of inevitability. One event in the model leads to the next, which leads to the next, and so on. As Seymour Chatman argues of plots in general, "the working out of the plot (or at least some plots) is a process of declining or narrowing possibility. The choices become more and more limited, and the final choice seems not a choice at all, but an inevitability."[24] The seeming inevitability of the

NYPD radicalization model is an artifact of its fundamentally retrospective design: the end result of the "radicalization process"—a terrorist attack, whether successful or attempted—determines the constitution of the entire model (Figure 20). The retrospective orientation of the model becomes even more obvious when we consider the fact that the report authors use actual people convicted of terrorist charges to provide descriptive details about the facets of each supposed phase. That is, at the time of its writing, the report's authors and researchers knew how the story of each individual they discuss in the report would end: with an attempted or successful terrorist attack. This known ending makes it possible for them to retrospectively create a trajectory toward radicalization—a plot—by working backward.

For instance, the first phase of the NYPD model is "pre-radicalization," which, in the words of the report, "describes an individual's world—his or her pedigree, religion, social status, neighborhood, and education—just prior to the start of their journey down the path of radicalization" (22). Such a phase, which

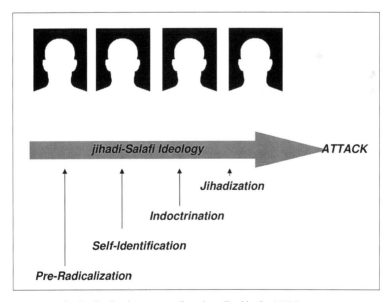

Figure 20. The "radicalization process," as described in the NYPD report *Radicalization in the West*.

describes nothing more particular than the "world" within which an individual exists, only makes sense as a legible phase along a so-called journey toward radicalization if the end of this process is already known. While claiming that there is no "psychological profile of a likely candidate for radicalization," the report nevertheless builds a profile of just such a supposed candidate by identifying "commonalities" among the people who later became radicalized: things like "male Muslims," "under the age of 35," "educated; at least high school graduates, if not university students," and "do not begin as radical or even devout Muslims" (23). Obviously, these characteristics describe not only supposed "potential terrorists" but also lots of other people who will never attempt to commit an act of terrorism. Likewise, the report includes a table titled "Trajectories of Radicalization inside the United States," which lists characteristics typical of each stage of radicalization, based on actual people charged with committing or attempting to commit terrorist attacks. The descriptions and behaviors grouped in the "self-identification" stage, the second of four stages in the radicalization model, include things like "seeks more knowledge of Islam," "works at Islamic bookstore—Brooklyn," and "works as kitchen designer in Maryland" (54).

What the people described by the NYPD report do have in common, of course, is that they are Muslim or appear to be Muslim or Middle Eastern. As Leti Volpp has argued, "September 11 facilitated the consolidation of a new identity category that groups together persons who appear 'Middle Eastern, Arab, or Muslim.' This consolidation reflects a racialization wherein members of this group are identified as terrorists, and are disidentified as citizens."[25] In Volpp's formulation, the label "terrorist" becomes an implicitly racial category because it describes and corresponds directly to how "persons who appear 'Middle Eastern, Arab, or Muslim'" look. The NYPD model is designed to enable the disidentification of these people as citizens, a process accelerated by the fact that the people on which the model is based are accused terrorists. In other words, because the actual people described in the report are accused of committing or attempting to commit acts of terrorism, officers reading the report are encouraged to see descriptions like "seeks more knowledge of Islam" and "male Muslims" as fitting within a "trajectory of radicalization." This encouragement toward generalization detaches such descriptions from the specific people they describe, the actual people on which the NYPD model is based, and turns them into characteristics of terrorists in general. The radicalization model thereby allows racism to pass as reasoned judgment, assembling an inventory of characteristics of terrorists or "indicators" of terrorism that are derived from specific individuals and specific events but presented in a way that severs them from these origins.

This retrospective way of understanding a chain of events is the kind of thinking encouraged by the logic of plot. The NYPD radicalization model encourages law enforcement officials, in other words, to look for the plot in a Brooksian sense—to retroactively make causal connections between a string of seemingly disconnected actions and events. Again, for Brooks, the "anticipation of retrospection" is the "master trope" of the logic of plot.[26] The model encourages its audience to understand an individual's behavior as plotted or to see causal connections between his actions that link them together in a chain of events leading necessarily toward some simultaneously potential and already known event. Like characters in a novel, whose actions throughout the novel may suddenly become meaningful once the reader reaches the end, the actions and characteristics of the individuals described in the NYPD report only become legible as actions or characteristics of those who "are on the path of radicalization" retrospectively, once they have committed or tried to commit a terrorist act (9). Yet, in the moment when officers are detecting this supposed plot, any putative attack remains in the future; the model trains officers to anticipate that they may be able to look back on the things they detect as meaningful one day, without waiting for that day to arrive.[27]

The fact that the NYPD report is meant to be used as a model of potential behavior or as "a tool for predictability" only further exacerbates the obvious moral, ethical, and legal problems with this way of understanding terrorism (7). The report is meant to identify individuals who, according to the model, are more likely to attempt acts of terrorism before they attempt such acts. As Charles E. Allen, former chief intelligence officer for DHS, put it, such a tool provides law enforcement and governmental officials with the "capability to track emerging radicalization trends before they manifest into violence," data that can then be used "to identify those populations and locales where radicalization is occurring, as well as its scope."[28] By claiming to act as a predictive tool, the NYPD radicalization model provides law enforcement and governmental officials with justification for enlisting people in preordained terrorist plots—for emplotting them. It encourages the idea that anyone who fits the extremely loose criteria described by the model could potentially be involved in a terrorist plot. This provides officials with a way, as Frank Kermode puts it, to make meaning "in the middest": by providing a preordained end (a future terrorist attack), it gives them justification for reading the supposed end into the beginning, or into the middle, or into plotlessness.[29]

This is where my understanding of what it means to look for the plot differs from Brooks's influential formulation. Although I share Brooks's understanding of plot as "a structuring operation elicited in the reader," in the context of preparedness, I depart from his emphasis on readerly desire as the engine that drives plot.[30] Unlike the novels and short stories on which Brooks focuses to develop his concept of reading for the plot, the NYPD radicalization model doesn't tell a story, and so it doesn't, as Brooks puts it, rely on "the play of desire in time that makes us turn pages and strive toward narrative ends."[31] It isn't designed to make its audience wonder what will happen next. In fact, the idea that "the end" is already known, and that it is implied in every element of the unfolding plot the model supposedly makes visible, is an important aspect of the kind of thinking the NYPD report promotes. In other words, the radicalization model is designed to train its audience to detect the outlines of an already formed, already ongoing terrorist plot in the most innocuous of events and circumstances. Striving toward the end is not the engine that drives the movement of its plot—suspicion is.

Learning to See Something

If the NYPD radicalization model provides an example of how professional law enforcement officers learn to look for the plot, the DHS "If You See Something, Say Something" terrorism prevention campaign is an example of how the national security state imagines members of the public might learn to do so. The commonalities between these two examples of counterterrorism discourse reveal the extent to which this discourse—like, as we saw in chapter 3, preparedness discourse in general—deputizes citizens to behave as "professional" agents of the state. The materials associated with the "If You See Something, Say Something" campaign, DHS's most well-known publicity campaign, are centered on these responsibilities of the citizen-agent. The product of a New York City advertising firm, the slogan was originally created for and trademarked by the New York City Metropolitan Transportation Authority in 2003.[32] In 2010, DHS launched a nationwide campaign centered around the slogan, which, as of this writing, includes posters, web logos and banners, online videos, and television and radio public service announcements. The campaign posters are familiar to anyone who has been through an airport security checkpoint or who has ridden on a subway car or bus in almost any U.S. metropolitan area in the past decade. They feature the smiling, confident faces of citizens who remind us that "We all play a role in keeping our community safe" or that "Together, we can help keep our community safe" and to "Report suspicious activity to local authorities" (Figure 21).[33]

Figure 21. "If You See Something, Say Something" campaign poster examples.

Criticism of the "If You See Something, Say Something" campaign has been widespread. In 2004, for example, when the campaign was still associated with the New York City MTA, Latina media collective Fulana began a countercampaign called "If You Fear Something, You'll See Something." They displayed flyers, posters, stickers, and brochures with this slogan at MTA stations next to "If You See Something, Say Something" materials, reversing the causality of plotting implied by the campaign and exposing its reliance on suspicion.[34] The ACLU has also argued that the Suspicious Activity Reporting Initiative, an associated campaign from the Department of Justice, promotes racial, ethnic, and religious profiling.[35] And media studies scholar Deepa Kumar has argued that "If You See Something, Say Something" is an example of "banal nationalism" that serves to normalize militarism and offer some "atomized individuals"—Kumar emphasizes that the campaign's address is racialized—"a sense of belonging through the enactment of security rituals."[36]

Many other critics of the campaign have focused on the kinds of surveillance it encourages, critiquing it as an example of what security studies scholar Mark Andrejevic has termed *lateral surveillance* or "peer-to-peer monitoring, understood as the use of surveillance tools by individuals, rather than agents of institutions public or private, to keep track of one another."[37] "If You See Something, Say Something," these critics emphasize, asks people to surveil one another based on flimsy or nonexistent criteria, encouraging racial and religious profiling and normalizing militarism and surveillance as part of people's civic duty. The campaign also participates in what Rachel Hall has called the *aesthetics of transparency,* a rationality of governance that "understands security in terms of visibility."[38] The aesthetics of transparency not only seeks to make what is invisible or unseen visible; it also justifies the use of force and the stripping away of rights in pursuit of visibility. By enjoining people to keep an eye out for "suspicious activity," and through its association with airport security checkpoints, the campaign participates, as Lisa Parks has put it, in "a broader security regime in which looking authorizes touching and touching can become torture."[39]

I want to turn our attention from visual surveillance per se to the particular kind of seeing "If You See Something, Say Something" encourages. Like the radicalization model discussed in the previous section, the "If You See Something, Say Something" campaign relies on an understanding of terrorist attacks as plotted, as the end point of a sequence of events that gives shape and meaning to these events. The attacks against which the campaign urges people to remain vigilant are always both potential and already known. However, while the NYPD radicalization model encourages law enforcement officials to make sense of multiple facts, events, and behaviors by placing them in a linear sequence leading toward an implied end, "If You See Something, Say Something" invests its energy in training its audience to "recognize" the signs of a potential terrorist plot in everyday objects and activities that do not exist in a sequence. Instead of identifying a chain of interconnected events leading toward the end point of a terrorist attack, it attempts to focus people's attention on individual actions and objects, actions and objects it wants them to see as weighted with significance. In this way, "If You See Something, Say Something," as its title suggests, takes the disassociation of people from their own descriptions performed by the NYPD report one step further by encouraging people to keep an eye out not for specific kinds of people—for example, those "under the age of 35" or "male Muslims"—but rather for specific actions and objects. In this way, the campaign's materials sever the objects of terrorism from the figure of the terrorist while still relying on the viewer's (implicit, intuitive) association of the two.

We can get a sense of how this works by examining a series of online videos associated with the "If You See Something, Say Something" campaign. These videos, collectively titled *Take the Challenge*, focus on honing viewers' observational capacities. The series consists of three one-minute videos—"Bikes," "Toss," and "Hallway"—which all begin by "challenging" the viewer with an assignment. For example, the "Bikes" video, which depicts people on bikes riding around an obstacle course and jumping off ramps, asks the viewer to watch "how many riders in green jump the ramps."[40] The viewer is then supposed to count the number of bike riders wearing green t-shirts who he sees jump the ramps, and after about twenty-five seconds, the video's host reveals that the answer to the ostensible challenge is five riders. However, the video then "rewinds" and replays the footage the viewer just watched, visually highlighting other aspects of the scene with bright green arrows while the host asks the viewer if he noticed seemingly unrelated things like "the unicyclist" riding through the course, the "hidden message" of "BE ALERT" printed on two cyclists' shirts, or "the man dropping the suspicious backpack" (Figure 22). The other two videos in the series, "Toss" and "Hallway," are structured in the same way. They each ask the viewer to count something innocuous while something more significant, such as someone leaving a "suspicious" bag or package in the background of the scene, happens. All of the videos end with the campaign slogan by challenging the viewer to "be aware of your surroundings" and to "say something to local authorities . . . if you see something suspicious."

The real challenge of the *Take the Challenge* videos is therefore noticing what the video doesn't explicitly ask you to notice. The viewer may only understand that the suspicious backpack left by a trash can in the background of the video is meaningful once he reaches the end of the "Bikes" video, which appears first on the website. But if the viewer continues watching the other videos in the series, he should notice the general pattern. By the time the viewer gets to the third video, the idea is that he will know how to watch it and what to look for. It's important that there are three videos in the series, in other words, because watching each video means practicing how to pay attention. The videos thus train their viewers to look between the lines, to observe what happens around them and "correctly" in-

Figure 22. Still shot from the "Bike" *Take the Challenge* video.

terpret these happenings by identifying "suspicious" things. They train their viewers, in other words, in a visual hermeneutics of suspicion.[41] This way of seeing is one in which decontextualized, nonspecific actions and objects are seemingly made visible for "what they are": signs of a terrorist plot in progress. Even the *Take the Challenge* video titles themselves—"Bikes," "Toss," and "Hallway"—signal this investment in the potential significance of mundane objects and activities. As a style of what Eve Kosofsky Sedgwick termed *paranoid reading,* this observational practice demands the viewer place these actions and objects into a plot that explains them.[42] The *Take the Challenge* videos teach people that if they see a backpack abandoned by a trash can, there could be a reason for that; they encourage viewers to transform seemingly mundane actions and objects into symbols weighted with significance and intention. Importantly, this transformation occurs within the viewer. Learning to look for the plot doesn't change anything about the backpack itself. It changes how the viewer interprets, and thereby attempts to control his own reactions to, the backpack.

Similarly, a public awareness video that was featured on the campaign's website until 2019 dramatizes a number of what we might call "If You See Something, Say Something" scenarios.[43] These dramatizations depict unknown people in hoodies, whose faces viewers only indirectly glimpse, doing suspicious things like leaving backpacks in public places, breaking into storage units at night, taking pictures of train platforms and writing down the schedules of the security guards patrolling the platforms, and sneakily entering secure areas without authorization. Each dramatization then shows the people who observe these suspicious actions—the video calls them "people like you"—reporting what they have seen to the local authorities. The future attack suggested by the hooded people's suspicious behavior, and the reason why the observers contact local authorities in the first place, therefore, remains outside the dramatization's narrative, implied in a vague way but never depicted or specified. Like other materials associated with the campaign, the public awareness video never depicts a terrorist attack. Instead, it gestures toward various actions and objects associated with the contours of a generic terrorist plot in which the terrorists gather materials and information and leave things in public places. The effect is to teach viewers how to regard certain actions and objects with suspicion regardless of whether they are a signs of a future terrorist attack. Viewers should learn to notice things and then to report them immediately, without waiting to find out if they will lead to an attack or not.

The goal of both the public awareness video and the *Take the Challenge* videos is to train viewers to anticipate the end before it happens, a hallmark, as Sedgwick observes, of practices of paranoid reading.[44] Such practices rely on imprecision: the campaign trains people to see signs of impending terrorism in "something"— which is to say, in almost anything—and the (presumed) event of a terrorist attack isn't actually required to sanction the validity of the campaign's paranoid reading. The general ethos of the campaign is that it doesn't actually matter if the something viewers report turns out to be meaningful. Instead, the videos teach viewers how to provide random, decontextualized objects—"something"—with a narrative context. The videos teach people how to imaginatively control these objects by placing them within the structure of an ongoing terrorist plot, that is, a plot with a known ending. This context provides an overall frame, but it remains usefully vague.

This imprecision also allows the campaign to disavow the racial logic that drives preparedness. In encouraging viewers to report "something" before "something" bad happens, the campaign disconnects the objects and behaviors being observed from the people handling or performing them. Reading for the plot, the campaign insists, is just about learning to properly identify, interpret, and control objects, not people. And by teaching people to notice innocuous things and actions—backpacks, packages, using restricted stairwells, scribbling things in notebooks at train stations—the campaign relies on "evidence" of terrorism that is seemingly unrelated to race. What, after all, does an abandoned backpack have to do with race? This emphasis on the literal objects of (presumed) terrorism rather than on people is complemented by the campaign's corresponding focus on the subjects of national security—the smiling, confident people who observe and report the objects of terrorism. When campaign materials do depict people, they emphasize the people doing the observing rather than the people being observed (because, again, the campaign is supposedly about observing not people but rather "somethings"). For example, the campaign posters depict male and female "everyday" people of various races, ethnicities, and ages confidently looking back at the viewer or calling the authorities (Figure 21). They depict the campaign's audience, in other words—those who should, if they see something, say something—not the supposed signs of an impending terrorist plot.

This depiction of the campaign's putative audience is an example of what Sara Ahmed has called "diversity as public relations."[45] As we saw with the Active Shooter exercise materials discussed in chapter 3, the depictions of "diverse" people in the campaign materials seek to project an ethos of diversity and inclusion that, as Kumar has put it, "presents security nationalism in self-consciously politically correct terms."[46] The campaign's public awareness video makes this ethos explicit when it states, "Reported suspicious activity should not be based on a person's race, religion, or gender, but rather on behaviors that seem suspicious or out of the ordinary," a mantra that repeats across almost every iteration of the campaign and its materials on any platform.[47] And in a seemingly intentional reversal of the racial profiling the ACLU has argued the campaign encourages, almost all of this video's dramatizations feature a person of color observing and then reporting a white person doing something suspicious (Figure 23).[48] By depicting people of color as good citizens of the homeland, the campaign uses diversity, following Ahmed, as *a method of protecting whiteness*" by deflecting attention away from it.[49]

However, the public awareness video's depiction of people of color observing white people with suspicion also draws our attention to the racial dynamic of "If You See Something, Say Something" explicitly (only it's reversed). Unlike other preparedness materials I have discussed in this book, whiteness is not both universal and particular in this video—it is specifically embodied. Yet this embodiment still seeks to protect the whiteness at the center of the national security state. The public awareness video condenses this protection into the object of the hoodie, a garment worn exclusively by white men in the video. The hoodie, Mimi Thi Nguyen argues, is a visual sign "*fully schematized by racism*": it is "the excess assigned to [the Black] body" that both signals a threat and makes that body visible to state-sanctioned violence.[50] The white men in hoodies in this video are cloaked in this sign of what Treva B. Lindsey calls "Black

violability" to shield the state from charges of perpetuating this violence.[51] This strategy is designed to uphold whiteness as the center
of preparedness not only by deflecting attention away from it as a
racial category but also by literally shielding it from view. White
people in this video often have obscured faces, lurk in the shadows
or in dark corners, and are shot from a distance, from behind, or
from the side. Whiteness is not just protected from sight: it is that
which seeks to disappear from sight, to be unseen. This willful
(color) blindness also protects whiteness by refusing to acknowledge the relationship of the hoodie to Black bodies specifically. The
fungibility of bodies in the world of the video—a white man wearing
a hoodie is just the same as a Black man wearing a hoodie, a person
of color seeing and saying is just the same as a white person seeing and saying—presumes the hoodie can be detached from Black
bodies while still retaining its association with criminality, just as
it presumes a person of color can occupy the subject position of the
citizen of the homeland who sees and says with the same implicit
authority a white person can. Even though the video ostensibly reverses the racial dynamic implied by the campaign as a whole, it also
disavows this dynamic by metonymically displacing danger onto an
inanimate object—the hoodie—while simultaneously refusing to
see that object as always already overdetermined by the dynamic
the video attempts to reverse.

Studies have repeatedly shown that the "suspicious activities"
routinely reported to DHS disproportionately identify and call out
people of color; as Kumar puts it, the campaign "operates within
an ideological climate in which decades of association of black and
brown people with crime, drugs, and terrorism . . . create conscious,
but more often unconscious, responses that lead ordinary people,
as well as security personnel, to consistently identify [Black and
brown people] as suspicious."[52] However, the campaign's materials
attempt to reassure viewers that what they are performing is not, in
fact, an example of what Simone Browne has referred to as "racializing surveillance," or practices of surveillance that "reify boundaries,
borders, and bodies along racial lines."[53] There is, again, no direct
evidence of such racializing surveillance in the campaign materials
themselves, and the only specific direction viewers are given about
what they are supposed to notice is that they are *not* supposed to

Figure 23. Still shot of someone seeing something suspicious from the "If You See Something, Say Something" public awareness video.

notice "a person's race, religion, or gender." Racism is therefore everywhere absent from the campaign materials; it, along with gender- and religion-based discrimination, are literally the only "somethings" people are not supposed to notice in looking for the plot. Yet the visual aesthetics of the campaign, combined with how it encourages people to interpret specific objects and actions, reinforces the audience's associations, conscious or not, of suspicious behavior with people of color, especially, through the depiction of people wearing hoodies, with Black people. Precisely because these "somethings" remain so usefully vague, the campaign leaves it up to the viewer to decide what the real objects of seeing and saying are.

"Your Every Day"

The reluctance on the part of the "If You See Something, Say Something" campaign to depict or dramatize the terrorist attacks that are potentially anywhere and everywhere tells us a lot about how the national security state imagines everyday life in the homeland, its field of operations. As we have seen throughout this book, insisting that preparedness training is just a part of everyday life is a strategy many preparedness materials use to normalize disaster. The "If You

See Something, Say Something" campaign also presents an image of everyday life in the homeland to provide people with a reason for counterterrorism preparedness training in the first place. By depicting scenes of seemingly calm everyday life in which something happens, and then by training people to notice and interpret that something as suspicious regardless of whether it "actually" is, the campaign depicts the world of the viewer as one where terrorist violence, while only ever implied or suspected, is potentially everywhere. The everyday, normal world of the homeland is a world in which people must continually try to control and configure events, objects, and behaviors into plot points. Comparing this world to the world assumed by the State Department's failed "Think Again Turn Away" counterterrorism campaign, which was addressed to people considering joining Islamic terrorist groups, or to people outside the homeland, makes clear the ideological importance of the concept of "everyday life" for the national security state. While the everyday world of the homeland is seemingly calm, the world outside the homeland is violent and terrible, but obviously so. It requires no decoding, because, these materials suggest, you don't need the skills of a paranoid reader to understand it. It is uncomplicated in its brutality. Everyday life in the homeland is therefore both that which must be protected through counterterrorism efforts so that it does not become like everyday life outside the homeland, and that which, because it is already rife with suspicious objects, events, and behaviors that need decoding, is fundamentally unprotectable.

We catch a glimpse of DHS's imagination of the everyday world of the homeland and the people who live there through the *Protect Your Every Day* public service announcements (PSAs) associated with the "If You See Something, Say Something" campaign. There are several different Spanish- and English-language versions of these announcements, each of a different length, but all of them are based on the same concept. I focus on the ninety-second version in what follows. This ad, first released in 2015, features a variety of characters with different jobs—a firefighter, a teacher, a farmer, a manager, a barber, a waitress, a student, a mom—who speak directly to the camera and in voice-overs against footage of each of them going about their "every day" (these same characters are also depicted on "If You See Something, Say Something" posters [Figure 21]). The everyday people of the video tell us that they "are all part of your community" and emphasize that "every day we move in and out of each other's busy lives."[54] They tell us that the "every day" is full of "little details" like "the morning walk," "the bus stop friends," and "a hot cup of coffee," as well as "surprises" like "a flat tire" and "mid-day traffic." "There's always something unexpected," they state. Such everyday details and surprises, they assure us, are "fine." What isn't fine, however, is "when you experience a moment of uncertainty. Something you know shouldn't be there. Someone's behavior that doesn't seem quite right." Such moments, the every-day people of the PSA tell us, "are the moments to take a pause," be-cause "if something doesn't feel right, it's probably not." The video urges its viewers to pay attention to these moments when "some-thing doesn't feel right," because "a lot of little details can become a pattern." Viewers should pay attention to "one detail at a time" and "trust our instincts," "because," the people on the video assure us, "only you know what's not supposed to be in your every day." The PSA ends with the standard injunction of the campaign as a whole: the firefighter tells us, "If you see something suspicious, say some-thing to local authorities."

The *Protect Your Every Day* PSA reveals the extent to which the "If You See Something, Say Something" campaign imagines what these videos call the "every day" as in need of deciphering. The unex-pected "little details" of everyday life like traffic jams and bus delays are not opposed to the "moments of uncertainty" when something "doesn't seem quite right"—after all, the little details are also unex-pected, and both are normal aspects of everyday life. Rather, what differentiates these things from indicators of potential terrorist attacks is that indicators of potential terrorist attacks don't "feel right." They give the people of the homeland pause. Again, what makes something a "something" citizens of the homeland should pay attention to is not any quality of the "something" itself; it is how that "something" makes the observer feel. These little details *could* "become a pattern," but they may not. However, this doesn't matter; what matters is that viewers "trust our instincts" and try to "protect your every day."

The message of the *Protect Your Every Day* PSA is simply that: feel confident that the feelings of suspicion you may have about some objects are, if not factually correct, at least morally correct. Having these feelings "is not about paranoia, or being afraid," the video announces. Rather, it is "about standing up, and protecting our communities." The video matches its tone to this assertion. The lighting is bright and crisp, the sound track peaceful yet chipper, and the overall feel recalls a pharmaceutical company ad. The idea is not to scare viewers into complying but rather to assure them that their compliance means "standing up" against the terrorists. However, while the overall affective response the video wants to encourage is not paranoia, the structure of the campaign itself is unavoidably paranoid. This is not, again, because it encourages fear but rather because, as Sedgwick emphasizes, paranoia itself involves defensive projection of one's anxieties and desires onto specific objects.[55] The paranoid position is one from which objects, not the self, are carriers of bad affects. The purpose of the *Protect Your Every Day* PSA, then, is to defend this structure.

"Think Again Turn Away" assumes a different audience—and, as a result, adopts a completely different tone—than the *Protect Your Every Day* PSA. Launched by the U.S. Department of State in Arabic and Urdu in 2011, and in English in 2013, "Think Again Turn Away" was a social media campaign with accounts on Twitter, YouTube, Tumblr, Facebook, and Ask.fm. These accounts interacted with prominent Islamic extremist accounts and posted counter-messaging material, such as news articles and political cartoons critical of ISIS and firsthand accounts from former members of ISIS about its horrors.[56] According to an article about the campaign published on *Time* magazine's website, the Twitter account often tried to communicate with pro–Islamic State accounts, tweeting at them directly and taunting them with messages like "a picture of children standing around a crucified soldier in the street of an unidentified city" with the caption, "This is what children see under ISIS rule, this brand of honor and respect."[57] Another article, published on *Gizmodo*, explains how the Ask.fm account often "got real surly, real quick" when responding to pro-ISIS trolls, mocking their "English-language skills," calling ISIS "a disgrace . . . to humanity at large," and telling them they "clearly lack a soul, heart, morality, and an ounce of humanity."[58] The campaign garnered widespread criticism from the U.S. media for a lack of clear direction from the

Obama administration and for its revolving door of staffers, and it was eventually shuttered in 2016 after a negative report by a panel of social media and marketing experts.[59] As of this writing, the campaign's social media accounts have been deleted.[60]

If the "If You See Something, Say Something" campaign involves training people of the homeland to look for the plot even when nothing happens—to see plots without events—the "Think Again Turn Away" campaign involves something like the opposite. It involves confronting people outside the homeland with event after event, without the requirement of plotting. One of the more infamous videos created by the campaign, *Welcome to the Islamic State Land*, demonstrates what this looks like.[61] The video, which was viewed more than 844,000 times on YouTube before it was taken down, is a parodic recruiting ad for the Islamic State.[62] It begins with the line "Run, Do not walk to ISIS Land," and the English subtitles read that new recruits "can learn useful new skills" there, such as "blowing up mosques," "crucifying and executing Muslims," "plundering public resources," and "suicide bombings inside mosques!" These messages are interlaced with grainy images and footage of acts of violence: mutilated corpses on crosses in public squares, severed heads, CCTV footage of a bomb going off in a public place, people shot point-blank. The aesthetic is intentionally retro. The producers used a vintage filter so that the images and footage appear scratched and slightly sepia toned, as if they were shot on Super 8mm film instead of cell phones. The video closes with the line "Travel is inexpensive because you won't need a return ticket," which is juxtaposed with images of bloodied corpses and blurry footage of a person being thrown off a cliff.

Like all of the materials discussed in this chapter, *Welcome to the Islamic State Land* does not tell a story or have a plot. But unlike the "If You See Something, Say Something" campaign videos, *Welcome to the Islamic State Land* isn't invested in implying that there *is* a plot, in training its viewers how to look for the plot in everyday situations. The campaign addresses itself to anyone who could potentially be an ISIS recruit, and according to the criteria set out by radicalization models like the 2007 NYPD model discussed earlier in this chapter, this could be anyone who "appear[s] 'Middle Eastern, Arab, or Muslim'" living in the United States or United Kingdom or anyone who lives in a country in the Middle East.[63] This audience, the campaign implies, doesn't need to be taught how to look for the plot; the assumption is that, if they haven't planned a terrorist plot, they already know about such plots anyway. For this audience, the State Department's video simply depicts event after event (or the aftermath of event after event), without the need to imply that these events are all causally connected or that they could have been prevented if people had only recognized the warning signs. There is no need to inculcate a hermeneutics of suspicion in this audience, in other words. The campaign presumes that they don't need to *suspect* because they already *know*.

This is why *Welcome to the Islamic State Land* is so invested in showing viewers actual images and footage of violent atrocities. Unlike the vagaries of "If You See Something, Say Something," which enjoins viewers to always keep an eye out for "something," "Think Again Turn Away" presents a string of specific violent events to the viewer. These events are not re-created or acted, like the *Protect Your Every Day* PSAs or the "If You See Something, Say Something" public awareness videos. Instead, "Think Again Turn Away" was created by editing together footage posted online by extremist accounts. In turning this footage into a faux recruitment video, the producers of *Welcome to the Islamic State Land* highlight its status as found footage, as an archive of atrocities committed by ISIS. That is, the video's rhetorical positioning as a fake advertisement establishes a relationship between the video and its viewers in which the viewers are meant to balk at the violence the video depicts but not question its veracity. This framing sets up a relationship between the viewer and the video that Jaimie Baron refers to as the *archive effect*, which results from "an experience of reception" in which the viewer experiences footage "as coming from another time or from another context of use or intended use."[64] The video's repackaging of footage originally posted by extremist groups into a (fake) advertisement, then, reinforces for the viewer that this footage is the "real deal," an accurate record of history and of what really happened, precisely because it has been repackaged. Moreover, while the overall point of the video is to dissuade people from joining terrorist groups by exposing them to horror after horror, the archive effect ensures the video is not necessarily frightening. Its sarcastic reframing as a fake recruiting video means that viewers are meant to see the events depicted in the video at a remove, as being from another time and place. Viewers may be morally and ethically horrified, but the immediacy of fear is not the primary intended effect.

If the world of the homeland is a world of nebulous potential events that need to be decoded, of hazy plots that require people skilled in paranoid reading to detect, the world outside the homeland is a world of beheadings, shootings, and bombings. It is a world of specific events disconnected from plots or plotting because they are disconnected from interpretation. If you are a member of the video's target audience, the video suggests, you don't need to be taught to decipher the signs of potential violence because violence already surrounds you. "Think Again Turn Away" is evidence that the opposite of the everyday world imagined by the "If You See Something, Say Something" campaign is not, as Joseph Masco writes, "a *world without events*," one in which "accidents, malfunctions, acts of terror" have all been eliminated.[65] Rather, it is a world in which obviously bad events happen all the time and so do not need to be interpreted. It is a self-evidently terrible world.

The contrasting tones and styles of the *Protect Your Every Day* and *Welcome to the Islamic State Land* videos betray a mutual dependence suggested by the syntactic parallelism of the campaigns' titles ("If You See Something, Say Something" and "Think Again Turn Away"). For example, while *Protect Your Every Day*, as part of the "If You See Something, Say Something" campaign, invests its energies in earnestly training its audience how to see something in nothing, *Welcome to the Islamic State Land* hits its audience over the head with the specificity of violent event after violent event. *Protect Your Every Day* reassures and placates; *Welcome to the Islamic State Land* mocks and berates. *Protect Your Every Day* is slick and corporate, with a high production value; *Welcome to the Islamic State Land*, on the other hand, remixes content posted by extremist groups so that it looks "old" and less technologically advanced. The reassuring and placating tone of *Protect Your Every Day* presumes an audience that is susceptible to gentle persuasion and reassurance; the cynical criticism offered by "Think Again Turn Away," however, infantilizes its target audience, presuming they should be made to face the facts and to feel ashamed. Even the titles of these videos indicate each campaign's beliefs about its audience. While the people of the homeland already inhabit an everyday world that is theirs—*Protect Your Every Day*—the people addressed by *Welcome to the Islamic State Land* need to be welcomed to a "land" defined only by its relationship to a terrorist organization, an entire world of violence. These inversions make it clear that the grainy, dark world of *Welcome to the Islamic State Land* is necessary to sustain the crisp, sanitized world of *Protect Your Every Day*. These two videos are effectively two sides of the same counterterrorism coin; each one requires the other for its force and meaning.

The mutual dependence of "If You See Something, Say Something" and "Think Again Turn Away" also reminds us who is supposed to detect, disrupt, and thwart plots and who can't, won't, or doesn't need to do those things. The *Protect Your Every Day* video and the *Take the Challenge* videos train subjects to learn to see and understand objects in specific ways and, in so doing, to create plots that make sense of these objects. *Welcome to the Islamic State Land*, on the other hand, focuses on the objects that make up these plots and the effects of plotting, such as dead bodies, weapons, and explosives. It focuses on what has already been done rather than on who must learn to do something. This lends an air of the inevitable to *Welcome to the Islamic State Land* that the *Protect Your Every Day* video strives to avoid. The world outside the homeland, we are meant to believe, is one in which everything has already happened, while, in the world of the homeland, something is always about to happen. This vision of the homeland as always potentially dangerous is the assumption at the root of counterterrorism discourse, and it is what sustains the fundamental divisions this discourse proposes between "us" and "them." While the people of the homeland should be paranoid, this discourse seems to say, at least there is something "we" can do. "They" are already lost.

Coda: Say Something

This chapter has drawn out the formal logic of plot embedded in counterterrorism preparedness materials, a logic that encourages suspicion and paranoia, though not necessarily fear, in its target audience while also complimenting them for their acumen and correct feelings. This logic depends on an understanding of the everyday world of the homeland as a place of hidden, potential violence that only looks good in comparison to places outside the homeland where violence is supposedly ubiquitous. This logic of plot sustains what bell hooks has identified as a "fantasy of whiteness": the idea "that the threatening Other is always a terrorist." As hooks contends, this fantasy "enables many white people to imagine there is no representation of whiteness as terror, as terrorizing."[66]

Jordan Peele's 2017 film *Get Out*, however, provides one such representation. The plot of *Get Out* centers on the struggle to detect and survive the machinations of plotters—in this case, wealthy white people. Chris (Daniel Kaluuya), the Black protagonist, becomes ensnared in a plot devised by the Armitages, a family of white suburbanites who want to kidnap him, using their daughter Rose (Allison Williams) as bait, and remove most of his brain so that his body can become a "host" to the brain of the highest white bidder. Chris doesn't discover the full shape of the plot against him until it's almost too late, but he is able, just barely, to escape the Armitages' clutches, killing them all and burning their house down in the film's bloody final act. Drawing on the classic visual vocabulary of suspense, Peele embeds within the first two-thirds of the film a series of indicators—mostly unremarkable—that something is off in the home and world of the Armitages. Like the "If You See Something, Say Something" campaign, *Get Out* encourages its viewers, through Chris, to learn to look for the plot before it's too late. In addition to cannily employing the conventions of horror and suspense, Peele's portrait of plotting reverts the structure of suspicion implied by the documents and campaigns I have discussed in this chapter. In this film—one preview for which featured the tag line "Say Something"—the white characters, the presumed citizens of the homeland, are the plotters, and the Black characters must learn how to see and say. This reversal critiques the counterterrorism campaign's implicit argument that terrorism is not endemic to the United States, that it always arrives from elsewhere and is enacted by "other" people. As Kevin Lawrence Henry Jr. puts it in his review of the film, "*Get Out* makes clear that the real terrorism that threatens most US citizens is homegrown, normalized, and enlivened by white dominance and supremacy."[67]

Much of the film's training in looking for the plot, as in the "If You See Something, Say Something" campaign, revolves around learning to correctly interpret visual signs and cues. As critics have noted, *Get Out* is all about seeing, and seeing correctly (or incorrectly).[68] Chris is an up-and-coming photographer, and his camera provides some of the best evidence that something is seriously awry at the Armitages'. When he snaps a photo of the only other Black person at the Armitages' garden party, the oddly dressed Logan (Lakeith Stanfield), later revealed to be an acquaintance of Chris's named Andre, the flash causes a strange reaction: Andre suddenly snaps to awareness, his nose starts to bleed, and he screams at Chris to "get out!" while pushing him away. Photography in general also helps Chris finally to realize he's in danger. His discovery toward the end of the film of a pile of Polaroid snapshots of Rose and the other Black people she has lured into her family's trap is what finally convinces him he should try to leave the house. Seeing, with all its multiple valences—observing, revealing, knowing—is at the very crux of the film.

Chris's subject position as a Black man makes the film's emphasis on seeing and looking all the more significant. The film is centered on what, echoing hooks, we might call the "recognition of [the] agency [of] black spectators." For hooks, because "the politics of slavery, of racialized power relations, were such that the slaves were denied their right to gaze," the act of looking while Black, or of "manipulat[ing] one's gaze in the face of structures of domination that would contain it, opens up the possibility of agency."[69] Chris, who by the standards of the "If You See Something, Say Something" campaign is an out-of-place "something" in the Armitages' white suburban world, becomes in this film the agent of seeing and saying.[70] Moreover, because Chris is a photographer, he spends much of the film looking through his camera, and because Chris is the film's protagonist, audience members spend much of the film seeing the world from his perspective, or looking through his eyes. Indeed, Peele has indicated that while the film is "made . . . for Black audiences," one of his intentions in the film was also to "ask a white person to see the world through the eyes of a Black person for an hour and a half."[71] Not only is Chris afforded agency through his gaze; the film invites white spectators to inhabit this gaze as well.

As many commentators have noted, one of Peele's innovations is to utilize the generic conventions of horror to reveal to white viewers the everyday horror of racism in the United States and the violence against Black people it sanctions. In other words, Peele insists that white viewers identify with the subject position of Black people under white supremacy. And unlike the counterterrorism materials discussed in this chapter, viewers of *Get Out* are supposed to feel afraid. Peele uses this structure of identification to force white people to see something they might otherwise never see—the fact that white supremacy *is* horror—and, in the conventional response to horror movies, to then say something like "Don't go in there!" or "Get out!"

We might be tempted to argue that this persistent emphasis on the power of seeing indicates, as one critic put it, that "cameras [and vision more generally] . . . have the power to reveal" in this movie or to read Chris's talent for photography as a practice of counterveillance akin to Browne's "dark sousveillance."[72] However, Chris's gift for sight is precisely what makes him an attractive candidate for the Armitages' "procedure" in the first place. Jim Hudson (Stephen Root), the blind art dealer who purchases Chris at the Armitages' silent auction, wants to occupy his body because he wants Chris's "eye," "those things you see through," as he puts it. Although the film invites white viewers, as Peele puts it, "to see the world through the eyes of a Black person for an hour and a half," this invitation means that white audience members also metaphorically occupy Hudson's desired position throughout the film. In this reading, the invitation to see the world differently constitutes an attempted takeover of the Black gaze, an act of dispossession that tries to evacuate Black subjectivity. For white viewers, seeing the world through Chris's eyes isn't necessarily revelatory. It can be yet another way to refuse to see the operations of white supremacy.

Chris's "eye" also doesn't exactly help him in the face of the Armitages' plotting. In one scene, for example, Chris is taking some photographs in the backyard, and he uses his camera's zoom lens to look into a window where Georgina (Betty Gabriel), the Armitage family's supposed housekeeper, is fixing her hair. Chris suspects something is off with Georgina, but when he tries to look more closely at her using his camera, she turns her head to look at him in the backyard, and he quickly turns his lens away. By the time he looks back, Georgina is gone. Of course, by the end of the film, Chris knows that Georgina was acting strangely because she is a victim of the Armitages' procedure; Rose's grandmother's brain was implanted in her body. But at this point in the film, this scene of looking and being looked at doesn't provide Chris with any new information or knowledge. Although he has his suspicions, he doesn't see beyond appearances or understand anything more clearly. What's more, from Chris's perspective, the odd behaviors and actions of the Armitages and their friends—the "somethings" he notices—are not actually that unusual; they are common, everyday microaggressions and experiences of racism in the United States. As the actor who plays Chris, Daniel Kaluuya, puts it, "this film is how racism feels. You get paranoid and you can't talk about it. You can't voice it. No one around you gets it, so you can't speak about it."[73] Chris knows something is off at the Armitages', but he can't quite figure out what, and he so tries to convince himself, as he has in the past, that the everyday racism he encounters there is survivable.

Of course, Chris is right to be paranoid, and the audience knows this. The audience, for example, is meant to understand the scene with Georgina in the backyard for what it is: a portent of doom. Although the audience also doesn't know about Georgina at this point in the film, the suddenness of her turn toward Chris combined, at that exact moment, with a sudden orchestral blast on the film's sound track signals that there is more going on in this scene than meets the eye. There are many such signs throughout the film, including Chris's discomfort with the fact that Rose tells him she hasn't told her parents he is Black; the encounter with the cop who asks for Chris's ID on the drive upstate; Rose's father, Dean's (Bradley Whitford), persistent use of words and phrases like "my man" and "thang" around Chris; Chris's unplugged cell phone; Rose's mother, Missy's (Catherine Keener), teacup—the list goes on and on. All of these signs are imbued with dread because the audience knows they are watching a horror film. Reading the film's interest in sight as indicative of its belief in the power of seeing to reveal the truth forgets, in other words, that *Get Out* is a horror movie. And like many horror films, it emphasizes again and again what Richard Brody, in his review of the film, refers to as "the totemic and symbolic power of objects."[74] Things are often more than they seem in horror movies: a teacup is not just a vessel for tea, just as a man shouting at you to "get out" is not just having a seizure. This is why, although seeing may be at the crux of the film, a sharp eye and technologies that reproduce or enhance vision, like cameras, continually fail in this movie to help Chris fully understand what's going on. Understanding what's really going on involves more than "revealing the truth" of things by observing how they look. It means correctly interpreting these things as horrific, reading into these seemingly innocuous or strange objects, gestures, and behaviors the necessarily violent end all viewers of horror movies know must come. It means, in other words, acting according to one's training in the visual hermeneutics of suspicion and becoming a paranoid reader, someone who knows how to look for the plot.

Reading *Get Out* in relation to the "If You See Something, Say Something" materials, then, allows us to see how the campaign has borrowed from the visual hermeneutics of suspicion common in horror movies to attempt to train people in counterterrorism. "The totemic and symbolic power of objects," and the concomitant ability to "correctly" observe and interpret this power, is integral to both the campaign and the horror genre. Yet, however much "If You See Something, Say Something" borrows from horror, the affect "If You See Something, Say Something" is designed to produce is not horror but rather calm, cool resolve. To accomplish this, the campaign seeks to protect citizens of the homeland from the supposed terror they are being trained to detect by offering up the imagined relief of action: when people see something, they can say something about it to the authorities. The campaign allows people to simultaneously occupy the position of a viewer of a horror film—someone who can see something—and of a character in a horror film: someone who is in a position to say something about what he sees. It constitutes a fantasy not necessarily of total knowledge—of being able to predict what will happen—but rather of total control, one that relies on the visual hermeneutics of suspicion common in the horror genre for its epistemological weight and authority but that, unlike horror movies, is meant to nullify terror. Instead of screaming impotently at a figure on a screen, a citizen of the homeland can simply call her local authorities.

Peele's film is skeptical of this fantasy of control. Like any horror film, *Get Out* revels in the inability of the audience to control the events of the plot and prevent the bad end they know is coming. Indeed, the inability to control the bad events one knows are coming is a good encapsulation of the experience of horror in general. Horror films often produce suspense by relying on the contrast between what the audience knows—its ability to correctly interpret seemingly innocuous things as dreadful—and what the characters in the movie know: their inability to correctly interpret these things. When viewers watch a horror movie, they, as members of the audience, usually know they are watching a horror movie. And, assuming they are generally familiar with the overall structure of the genre, they know something is coming, even if they don't know exactly what. They can therefore use this knowledge to hypothesize the significance of odd objects, behaviors, and moments in the plot. But the characters in a horror movie don't usually know they are in a horror movie, and they often tell themselves not to "read too much into" anything. A teacup, they may convince themselves, is simply a teacup.[75] Of course, they are usually wrong, but you, as a viewer, can't do anything about it. This is what turns your suspense into dread; one of the sources of terror in horror films is that, as a viewer, you can interpret signs of impending doom for what they are, but you can't communicate this to the characters who don't yet realize the genre into which they have been emplotted. No matter how much you, like Andre, scream at Chris to "get out," he won't listen. You can see something, but you can't say anything.[76]

While *Get Out* implies that the fantasies of control offered by the national security state are futile at best, it also offers its viewers a complementary fantasy. This fantasy emphasizes the power of the hermeneutics of suspicion to detect terror, but it is ultimately not in keeping with the film's genre. The fantastical elements of the film are most clear in connection to the character of Rod (Lil Rel Howery). Rod is suspicious of the Armitages from the start, and when Chris tells Rod that Missy has hypnotized him without his permission, Rod suggests—more or less accurately, it turns out—that it could be because "white people love making people sex slaves and shit." Later, when Chris goes missing and Rod talks to Rose on the phone, he senses she is lying to him about Chris's whereabouts because, as he articulates it, "that TSA shit tingles." And it's Rod who swoops in at the end of the film in a borrowed airport security car to save Chris after he has finally escaped the clutches of the Armitages. *Get Out* therefore presents us with a hero who works for the TSA, one who, unlike Chris, is right about the Armitages and their intentions all along. He sees something, and he repeatedly says something about it, even though no one listens to him. He acts like a good citizen of the homeland and a dutiful agent of the state.

But no matter how much Rod acts like the ideal citizen-agent of the homeland, it is also true that he never acts in an official capacity. For one, we never see Rod actually working for TSA. While we know that Rod takes his professional responsibilities seriously because he tells Chris that he got "in trouble for patting down an old lady" even though "it's standard procedure," whenever we see him at work, he is always on break. He applies his "TSA shit" throughout the film to figure out what has happened to Chris, and he succeeds in correctly deducing what the Armitages are up to, but again, he does this during his time off the clock. And when he does try to file an official report and alert law enforcement to the fact that the Armitages, as he says, have "been abducting Black people, brainwashing them, and making them work for them as sex slaves and shit," he is laughed out of the building. Taking matters into his own hands, he uses an airport security car to find his friend, co-opting the resources of the national security state and law enforcement for his own purposes and succeeding. It is only when Rod works outside the confines of his job, in other words—when he applies what he knows in a different domain than airport security, and when he decides to stop following directions—that he is able to help Chris.[77]

Of course, to return to the beginning of the chapter, if we define a plot as a sequence of events linked together through probable cause and effect, none of what happens in this ending of the film— Chris managing to make it out of the Armitages' house alive and Rod rescuing him—makes for an especially consistent plot. The film's happy ending doesn't seem to make sense, given its genre, as horror films don't usually end well for their protagonists. The film's original ending, which Peele and the production team only decided to change at the last minute after test audiences reacted negatively to it, is more in keeping with the rest of the film and with its genre overall. In this ending, Chris is confronted after killing Rose with the flashing lights not of Rod's airport security vehicle but rather of the police. The police arrest him for murder, and the film ends with Rod visiting Chris in prison, where he learns that Chris can't remember enough about what happened to prove he was acting in self-defense when he killed the Armitages. Although Kaluuya claimed that this ending "resonated" with him "because it showed me how unfair the system is," when test audiences saw the film, it "punched everybody in the gut," as producer Sean McKittrick said. Marcus Henderson, who plays Walter, emphasized that audiences wanted Chris to "catch a break" from "reality."[78] In deciding to change the ending, in other words, Peele and the production team explicitly opted for wish fulfillment instead of realism or even the fulfillment of generic expectation. As Lil Rel Howery puts it, the film's original ending is "just too real."[79]

When comparing Get Out's two endings, we might therefore be tempted to argue that the theatrical release's plot breaks down or isn't as good. However, the very implausibility of this ending—that which might make viewers exclaim "get out!" in disbelief—points us toward the importance of Rod's role in the film. He is an agent of fantasy, although not the fantasy of whiteness, to borrow hooks's language, that "If You See Something, Say Something" enacts. While the horror at the root of the film is all too realistic, Rod's deux ex machina ending is explicitly fantastical. It constitutes a wish for an alternate universe in which Chris's escape *is* possible, a world in which he can survive. In this way, Get Out, through Rod, provides a vision of what it might look like if the TSA were to work to detect and stop the terrorism endemic to the United States, the terrorism bred and perpetuated by white supremacy, instead of terrorism imagined as coming from elsewhere. It provides a fantasy of the national security state turned against itself.[80] In providing this fantasy, Peele opts not to negate the national security state but rather to borrow its proliferative fiction-making capacity. He recognizes the power of making up stories about security, especially for those people constantly told that the somethings they see are nothings, that they are reading too much into things, that they should be less paranoid. To see the significance of one's suspicions realized in a well-plotted conspiracy—this is one of the satisfactions promised (to some people) by the national security state. Peele's film lays bare the assumptions embedded in this promise about who deserves or should receive such gratification.

Epilogue

The Uses of Fiction

This book has focused on the use of fiction and fictionality by the post-9/11 U.S. national security state. In recent years, literature scholars have become interested in questions about the uses of literature or fiction more generally. They have argued, for example, for the value of fiction in creating engaged citizens and strong democracies; they have turned to cognitive science and neuroscience to explain how fiction makes people more perceptive and helps them understand complex social relationships; and they have aimed to delineate the reasons why people read fiction and find it valuable.[1] It is no surprise that scholars seem to be making such arguments about fiction with increasing frequency today. As Thomas Koenigs has emphasized, the pedagogical value of fiction for K–12 as well as postsecondary education is currently being challenged in the United States to a greater degree than it has for more than a century.[2] It has perhaps therefore felt all the more urgent for scholars to insist on the value and purpose of fiction, on what it does in the world and why it matters.

Because of the effects of this current attitude toward fiction—including frequent disdain on the part of educational policy makers toward those who teach fiction and the concomitant shifting of resources away from the teaching of and scholarship about fiction in many educational contexts—I have been continually surprised while working on *Training for Catastrophe* about how seriously U.S. national security agencies and officials take fiction. From one perspective, as I state in the book's introduction, the post-9/11 U.S. national security state is one of the largest federal funders of fiction in the United States today. Many of the materials national security officials and agencies create for training people in disaster preparedness are fictions or explicitly fictional, even though they are not always narrative. And as their use in training exercises, games, and public awareness campaigns attests, these materials also communicate certain ideas about how people value fiction today and what purposes they think it serves. Namely, they show that fiction can be used to learn about disasters and to train people to expect some disasters as part of normal, everyday life—and to ignore or deny other disasters that are already part of normal, everyday life for millions of people.

While I have not sought in this book to delineate one single or unifying method through which this training happens, I have emphasized throughout how state agencies and officials create fictions of their own and borrow concepts from fiction more generally to do their political work. They treat fiction as simultaneously imaginary and real, eliciting people's consent to training scenarios and exercises that are both endowed with the authority of realism and relieved from the pressure of plausibility. They design these materials to encourage people to think about disasters in generic ways, as "professionals," training them in generic conventions that make some events legible as disasters and leave others invisible. They extol resilience, individualizing the burden of disaster response and characterizing members of their audience as "heroes" while displaying repugnance and disgust toward those who are most resilient. And they teach people to imagine terrorist attacks as plotted narratives with already known endings and, accordingly, to look for signs of impending doom in everyday objects and behaviors while ignoring the terrors of white supremacy enacted by the security state itself. Fiction is valuable for preparedness because it teaches people to think otherwise, to imagine what hasn't happened, to consider new possibilities and ways of being. Many literary critics have also made this argument about the value of fiction more generally. I hope *Training for Catastrophe* puts to rest the idea that such a use of fiction is necessarily progressive, radical, or critical. Imagining new possibilities can be used to constrain political action just as easily as it can be used to encourage it.

I want to end, nevertheless, with an example of encouragement, one that both embodies some of the main problems with preparedness as it is currently practiced and provides a model for confronting these problems. Stop Urban Shield is a coalition of community and social justice organizations in California's Bay Area that has worked since 2013 to stop Urban Shield, a SWAT team training and weapons expo. Urban Shield was created in 2007 by the Alameda County Sheriff's Office and was held every year from 2007 to 2018 in Alameda County around September 11. The expo, the largest of its kind in the world, was funded primarily by the Department of Homeland Security (DHS). It brought together local law enforcement officers and emergency responders from across the United States to train in emergency response and disaster preparedness and to make contact with weapons manufacturers and learn about their products. The centerpiece of the Urban Shield expo was the SWAT team competition, which was designed to train law enforcement officials and first responders in how to react to terrorist attacks and other violent situations.

Stop Urban Shield argued that although such activities were "billed as an emergency preparedness activity," these "war games perpetuate racist and xenophobic stereotypes, increase the use of militarized weaponry and tactics in everyday law enforcement, and cost taxpayers millions of dollars."[3] For example, Stop Urban Shield has reported that although the Urban Shield SWAT team training competition was focused on training teams to respond to terrorist threats, the majority of SWAT deployments by agencies who participated in Urban Shield SWAT training in 2014 and 2015 were to serve warrants, not to respond to terrorist attacks or other "critical incidents." Data collected by the ACLU show that SWAT team actions have disproportionate effects on people of color in the United States; from 2011 to 2012, 50 percent of people affected by SWAT team actions were Black or Latino, while only 20 percent were white.[4] Furthermore, the number of people killed by police every year in the United States far outweighs the number of those killed in terrorist events.[5] Nevertheless, Stop Urban Shield reported that in 2015, the

Alameda County Sheriff's Office spent $4.8 million on "Enhanced Homeland Security Exercise, Evaluation, and Training," the bulk of which paid for Urban Shield, and $0 on "Medical and Public Health," "Emergency Planning and Community Preparedness," or "Recovery."[6]

To address these problems, and to direct public funds away from the militarization of police and toward community preparedness and welfare efforts, Stop Urban Shield organized a series of protests and community actions in Oakland, California, the site of Urban Shield 2014. They were successful that year in stopping Urban Shield from being held in Oakland again. The Alameda County Sheriff's Office then moved the expo outside of Oakland to the Pleasanton Fairgrounds. Over the course of the next year, the Stop Urban Shield coalition grew to include more than two dozen endorsing organizations from across the Bay Area. The coalition held actions to disrupt Urban Shield 2015 and 2016, launched publicity campaigns educating people about the expo, and held their own community emergency preparedness workshops and events. In response to these actions, the Alameda County Board of Supervisors initiated a County Task Force on Urban Shield to evaluate its effectiveness and impact on the community, and on March 27, 2018, the Alameda County Board of Supervisors voted 5–1 to end Urban Shield.[7] After this vote, the Alameda County Sheriff's Office organized to reinstate Urban Shield in the name of holding on to more than $5 million in federal grant money from DHS. But in late February 2019, the County Board of Supervisors, following recommendations from an ad hoc committee, voted to overhaul the expo and center it on natural disaster preparedness and response instead of police training.[8] As a result, the Sheriff's Office lost federal grant funding for the initiative, effectively putting an end to efforts to resurrect Urban Shield. The Bay Area Urban Security Initiative, which distributed the grant funding that supported Urban Shield, was expected to issue a request for proposals to hold Urban Shield elsewhere in the Bay Area, but as of this writing, a new location for the expo has not been established.[9]

Stop Urban Shield also advocated for a vision of preparedness that centered on community building. As part of its efforts to end the expo, Stop Urban Shield organized a letter-writing campaign in

2016 involving community organizations in Alameda County. These organizations—which included a diverse array of groups, such as the California Nurses Association, the Interfaith Committee 4 Black Lives, the San Francisco Board of Supervisors, and UAW 2865, the union of University of California teaching assistants and other student workers—wrote to the Alameda County Board of Supervisors to express their concerns with Urban Shield and to argue for ending the expo.[10] These letters call for an end to the "militarized policing" and "war games" the Urban Shield SWAT training expo featured, and therefore for an end to Urban Shield altogether, but they don't call for an end to preparedness activities per se. Instead, they emphasize the need "for emergency response resources that prioritize health and well-being" and for "public investment in our communities, including basic social resources such as education." As these letters put it, "shifting disaster preparedness priorities toward community strength and resilience, and away from war games and militarization, is an important way to demonstrate a commitment to shoring up preparedness without making the county's communities vulnerable."[11] The letters of support, in other words, emphasize the need for preparedness programs that support health and well-being over militarization, social services over policing.

Of the community-oriented emergency preparedness resources mentioned in these letters that are still available (many of the organizations that created these resources have now folded, providing an object lesson in the difficulty of sustaining community-run preparedness efforts without consistent funding), most are not so different from the preparedness materials discussed throughout this book. They include tools like workshops about how to make an emergency preparedness kit, tip sheets about how to respond to wildfires or pandemics, and videos showing how to prepare for and respond to an earthquake if you are disabled.[12] The main distinction between these preparedness materials and those produced by agencies like DHS or the Federal Emergency Management Agency is simply that they are not, by and large, produced by the state. Instead, they are produced by nonprofit entities and local organizations (although sometimes using federal grant funds).[13]

However, the fact that these materials are produced by local organizations does not necessarily make them examples of a "good" kind of preparedness, as opposed to the "bad" kind of preparedness practiced by the federal government—a "good" use of fiction versus a "bad" use of fiction. Indeed, these materials share many of the same ideological commitments as preparedness materials produced by the state. For example, *Prepare to Prosper* is a video produced in association with the now-defunct Bay Area organization CARD, or Collaborating Agencies Responding to Disasters.[14] CARD was an organization dedicated to helping community groups provide resources for people with disabilities, and it promoted a "fear-free" philosophy of preparedness that emphasized "end[ing] the use of fear and threat of disasters as the 'motivation' for emergency preparedness."[15] CARD critiqued the philosophy of preparedness pursued by the U.S. federal government as trying to scare people into preparing for disasters by enjoining them to imagine the worst. CARD's materials, by contrast, emphasize the actions individuals can take to prepare for disasters when they stop reacting out of fear. In the *Prepare to Prosper* video, the host describes a harrowing experience he had during an earthquake when he couldn't evacuate a building because he uses a wheelchair and cannot take the stairs. The video demonstrates CARD's fear-free philosophy through its ironic "dramatic reenactments" of the earthquake. In enacting what happened on the day of the earthquake, the host shows the difficulties he faced in trying to leave the building. Such reenactments are common in workplace disaster-training videos. However, the host also pauses during the reenactment to wryly assure viewers not to worry, because "this is just a dramatic re-creation." The video then goes on to emphasize that, instead of preparing for the worst they can imagine, people should instead "prepare to prosper" or "to be the best you can be, in whatever circumstance." It also provides tips for disabled people and caretakers about becoming more prepared for earthquakes, such as making sure that floor space is clear so people in wheelchairs can navigate freely and quickly, that they store bottled water and preserved food in easily accessible places in their homes, and that they enter "the right frame of mind for a challenging situation."

The video's focus on people with disabilities, who are often excluded implicitly or explicitly from many preparedness materials, does fill a gap in state-sponsored preparedness discourse. Likewise, its specific recommendations for how to prepare for an earthquake are practical. However, the video's emphasis on what individuals should do to respond to disasters aligns it with many preparedness materials produced by the state. Its insistence, like the Active Shooter training exercise discussed in chapter 3, that the best way to prepare for disasters is to put yourself in the right frame of mind—and not, for instance, to advocate for compliance with the laws established by the Americans with Disabilities Act so that if an earthquake happens, people with disabilities will be able to evacuate—is in keeping with the philosophy of preparedness as it is practiced by the federal government, regardless of whether that philosophy is "fear-free." Again, there is nothing bad about tip sheets focused on how to make an emergency preparedness kit or about a video on what to do in the case of an earthquake if you are disabled, whether the federal government or local agencies and organizations produce such materials. However, when individual preparedness is positioned as the only viable response to disaster and to the need to plan for disasters, to the exclusion of the systemic social and political changes needed to address the causes and consequences of these disasters, then we are dealing with a deeply broken ideology of preparedness. The discussion of preparedness I have pursued in this book takes this depoliticization of disaster as its central target.

The purpose of this book has not been to critique preparedness in order to advocate for "better" preparedness materials, whatever that may mean. We don't necessarily need better materials focused on how individuals can prepare themselves for disaster, as comforting as the idea of these materials may be. We need collective action against the current practices of the U.S. national security state. I bring up the *Prepare to Prosper* video as an example only to demonstrate the pervasiveness of the idea that individual disaster preparedness is the best way to prepare for disasters. This belief contributes to the argument that preparedness can never fail to prepare people we saw in operation in chapter 1, to the creation of the kinds of implausible (at best) training scenarios discussed in chapter 2, to the popularity of workplace training scenarios like the Active Shooter exercise featured in chapter 3, to the ubiquity within preparedness discourse of the character of the hero discussed in chapter 4, and to the paranoia of the counterterrorism materials explored in chapter 5. These are all, of course, examples of preparedness materials produced by federal organizations and agencies. Likewise, the belief in individual responsibility contributes to preparedness materials produced by local organizations with an explicit social justice orientation, such as the *Prepare to Prosper* video.

However, the success of the Stop Urban Shield coalition itself proves the inadequacy of this approach as the *only* approach to preparedness. Stop Urban Shield did not succeed in shutting down the Urban Shield expo in Alameda County because it partnered with local organizations to produce better preparedness materials; it succeeded because it insisted on preparedness as a political issue and took political action against some of its current practices. Such political action necessarily involved critiquing Urban Shield, but it didn't end there. This book has shown how preparedness seeks to incorporate any criticism as part of the process of preparedness training itself. When preparedness discourse emphasizes criticizing preparedness training as one of the most important aspects of that same training, we need to seriously consider to what use critique can be put. Stop Urban Shield demonstrates that critique, while as necessary as ever, is not enough. Critique can help us understand how preparedness works and its history, expose its contradictions and failures, and connect it to other, overlapping systems of oppression and inequality, but this is not sufficient for confronting the scale of problems associated with preparedness in the United States today.[16]

Yet where critique ends, something else can begin. Walidah Imarisha has argued that "all organizing is science fiction. Organizers and activists dedicate their lives to creating and envisioning another world, or many other worlds."[17] In this statement, Imarisha is not arguing for a particular use of fiction, or even for the value of fiction more generally, so much as she is aligning collective action with the creation of fiction itself. Scholarship on the use or value of fiction today, as the examples cited at the beginning of this epilogue make clear, tends to emphasize the positive effects of reading fiction on the individual. Reading fiction, these arguments claim, makes people more engaged citizens, more empathetic or sympathetic people, and better at critical and creative thinking. Imarisha's statement, on the other hand, emphasizes an expansive, resolutely social definition of fiction, one that accommodates an understanding of its collective benefits. If I am advocating any uses of fiction in this book, I am advocating those that bring about the kind of collective action necessary to confront the U.S. national security state. Or, to put it more strongly, I am advocating for the use of fiction *that is* such collective action. This is one way of understanding what Stop Urban Shield accomplished. It envisioned and laid the foundation for a different world, one without Urban Shield, one that was only ever fictional—until it wasn't.

Acknowledgments

I am grateful to the many who have left their mark on this book. The University of California, Santa Barbara's vibrant intellectual life shaped me and this project in too many ways to track. I am thankful for Rita Raley, whose generosity, commitment, and laser insight has taught me so much; Bishnu Ghosh, who has shown me time and time again the power of beauty, community, and collaboration; and Alan Liu, whose kindness and rigor continue to inspire me every day. They believed in this project before I did, and their encouragement to be undisciplined has sustained me and my work throughout much of the past decade. Colin Milburn, Felice Blake, Aranye Fradenburg, and Candace Waid generously discussed my research and provided guidance at crucial moments. My involvement in the Risk Society Series and the Speculative Futures Research Group at UCSB informed this project's earliest stages, and I am grateful for the faculty and graduate students who organized and participated in those initiatives. For collegiality, camaraderie, and community, I thank Rahul Mukherjee, Alison Reed, Anne Cong-Huyen, Amanda Phillips, Steve Pokornowski, Marcel Brousseau, and Kate Kelp-Stebbins. I am beholden to Charlotte Becker and Megan Fernandes most of all for their enduring friendship. You continue to make me feel at home, wherever we are.

This project began to take on new life during my time at Clemson University, and I benefited enormously from conversations with friends and colleagues there, including Erin Goss, Jonathan Beecher Field, Susanna Ashton, Gabriel Hankins, Chenjerai Kumanyika, Cameron Bushnell, Elizabeth Rivlin, Brian McGrath, Kimberly Manganelli, Sarah Juliet Lauro, Rhondda Thomas, Walt Hunter, and Lindsay Turner. Angela Naimou, Michael LeMahieu, and Michele

Speitz all read parts of what would become this book and provided vital feedback and encouragement. The collegiality and generosity of many at the University of Miami make it an exceptional place to live and work. I owe special thanks to department chairs Pam Hammons and Tim Watson, who have offered extensive personal and institutional support. I am grateful to the numerous friends and colleagues at UM who read or listened to portions of this book, including Brenna Munro, Juan Chattah, Tracy Divine-Guzman, Simon Evnine, Catherine Judd, Anne Schmalstig, Dominique Reill, Frank Palmeri, Donette Francis, Sarah Cash, Hadassah St. Hubert, and Nathan Timpano. I have depended many times on the labor and knowledge of staff across the university. Special thanks go to Melissa Reittie, Lydia Starling, Kim Mehrtens, and Angie Callesis in the English department; Monica Metcalf in the Dean's Office; and Ony Dunnam de Gonzalez in the Center for Humanities. I thank Mihoko Suzuki, Hugh Thomas, and Meg Homer in the Center for Humanities for their tireless promotion of the humanities on campus and for their support of my research. John Funchion, Thomas Goodman, Tassie Gwilliam, and Frank Stringfellow daily offer indispensable advice, mentorship, and camaraderie. The dedication and savvy of Allison Schifani, Susanna Allés Torrent, and Lillian Manzor make working in the digital humanities at UM energizing, and I feel lucky to hatch schemes with them. Countless friends have made Miami home; I am especially grateful for Allison, Brenna, Nikki Naser, Pam, Gema Pérez-Sánchez, Krista Goff, Marina Magloire, Cae Joseph-Massena, and Mike Touchton. Friends farther afield provided crucial insights, much-needed advice, and words of encouragement; I am especially thankful for conversations with Shannon Brennan, Laurie Shannon, and Jan Radway and to Yumi Lee and Golnar Nikpour for the best group text chain in the world.

I was beyond fortunate to participate during summer 2016 in the First Book Institute at Penn State's Center for American Literary Studies. Sean Goudie and Priscilla Wald have been incredible interlocutors; this book would have been impossible without them. For helping me discover the book I wanted to write all along, I thank them, Tina Chen, and the other 2016 participants: Kelly Bezio, Brianna Burke, Danielle Christmas, Joseph Darda, Gordon Fraser, Kya Mangrum, and Matthew Schilleman. The University of Miami also provided support for the writing of this book, including a Center for the Humanities Faculty Fellowship, a Provost's Research Award in the Humanities, and a junior faculty research leave. I am grateful for invitations to present parts of this book from Katherine Buse, Ranjodh Singh Dhaliwal, Joshua Neves, Martin French, and Preston Stone and to audiences at the University of California, Davis, at Concordia University, and in the Critical Cultural Studies graduate collective at the University of Miami for listening. Bishnu, Bhaskar Sarkar, and anonymous readers at *Surveillance and Society, American Literature,* and *American Quarterly* all improved portions of what became this project or related pieces with their feedback.

This book has grown in parallel to my work with the WhatEvery1 Says project, which has been a fixture in my life for almost as long. The collaborative work of that project has often provided a much-needed respite from the solitary labor of writing. For their guidance, conviviality, and incredible perseverance, I thank my fellow PIs Alan, Scott Kleinman, and Jeremy Douglass. I owe special thanks as well to Abigail Droge, Dan Baciu, Giorgina Paiella, Tarika Sankar, Rebecca Baker, and Ashley Hemm for their leadership, scholarly and technical contributions to innumerable aspects of the project, and assistance with the many daily tasks of co-running a multi-institutional grant. I thank the research assistants who have contributed to the project over many years for showing us we could do so much more than we thought. I hope they recognize the traces of our time together in this book.

I am indebted to Danielle Kasprzak, Jason Weidemann, and Leah Pennywark at the University of Minnesota Press for their unflagging belief in and support of this project even at the earliest stages of its development. Gerry Canavan and an anonymous reader of the manuscript helped me to articulate what I cared most about in the book, shaping its form, sharpening its arguments, and greatly improving it. I also thank Anne Carter and Ana Bichanich for editorial and production assistance, Holly Monteith for her generous and sharp copyediting, and Celia Braves for her expertise in crafting the index.

Many have shared their love during the years of writing this book. My parents, Carol Williamson and Mel Thomas, have been steadfast in their support; my brother Evan Thomas, his partner

Keith Bynum, and Belle have provided much joy and laughter. The boisterous energy and encouragement of my large extended family have always been nourishing. Kristin Brubaker's cheer and care have buoyed my spirits for more than a decade. Kat Devlin, Shannon, Eleanor, and Henrietta will always be family. Muffet knows when I need a cat curled up next to me or a head bonk of encouragement. And to Jessica Rosenberg—my first, last, and best reader, my heart—I owe the greatest debt of gratitude of all. Your generosity, neon brilliance, and love make this book and so much more possible. You continue to light the way for me every day.

Notes

Preface

1. WHO, "Archived: WHO Timeline—COVID-19."
2. Bergen, "Americans Are Going to Demand to Know"; Dickinson, "Rolling Stone Timeline"; Frieden et al., "We Ran the CDC"; Hudspeth, "Coronavirus Response"; Karlawish, "A Pandemic Plan"; Lopez, "Trump Administration's Botched Coronavirus Response"; Maxmen and Tollefson, "Two Decades of Pandemic War Games."
3. Ibrahim, "Did Betsy DeVos Say Schools Can't Plan for a COVID-19 Outbreak?"
4. Benjamin, "Work of Art," 41.

Introduction

1. SIGMA Forum, "What Is SIGMA?" Information published or presented online changes all the time. This is especially true of government websites and online resources; many of the government sources I cite in this book have changed many times, often silently and without a change in web address, throughout the process of writing. To attempt to make the archive I gather and discuss available to others in some form, I have, whenever possible, archived websites and online resources I use as primary sources, as they appeared in late 2019 and early 2020, using the WayBack Machine. If sources had been archived recently and the archived version matched the live version, I used the existing archived link. The archived address for each source appears in the book's bibliography. In cases when it was not possible to archive a source, I include its live web address as it appeared in late 2019 or early 2020.
2. SIGMA Forum, "SIGMA Members."
3. Lang, "Sci-Fi Writers Take US Security Back to the Future"; Hall, "Sci-Fi Writers Join War on Terror"; Montgomery, "Sci-Fi Writers Dream Up Gadgets."
4. National Commission on Terrorist Attacks upon the United States, *9/11 Commission Report,* 336.
5. Quoted in Andrews, "Science Fiction in the National Interest."
6. Rumsfeld, "Defense.Gov Transcript."

7. Morris, *Unknown Known*.

8. George W. Bush first outlined this doctrine in a 2002 commencement address at West Point. See Bush, "Commencement Address."

9. Brian Massumi's work on preemption has been widely influential. See Massumi, *Ontopower*, esp. chapter 1, "The Primacy of Preemption: The Operative Logic of Threat," and chapter 6, "Fear (The Spectrum Said)." While a full accounting of Massumi's influence exceeds the work of this introduction, for notable work in literary and cultural studies that builds on and challenges his ideas about preemption, see Palumbo-Liu, "Preemption, Perpetual War"; Puar, *Terrorist Assemblages*; Grusin, *Premediation*; uncertain commons, *Speculate This!*; Masco, *Theater of Operations*, esp. "Introduction: The 'New' Normal."

10. Although I focus in this book on the fictional properties of preparedness material, I discuss the medial properties of preparedness documents as digital objects—focusing on what it means to update a document and on what it means to document events that haven't happened in the first place—in Thomas, "Preparedness Documents after the Fact."

11. See, e.g., Collier and Lakoff, "Vital Systems Security"; Walker and Cooper, "Geneaologies of Resilience"; Lakoff, "Preparing for the Next Emergency"; de Goede and Randalls, "Precaution, Preemption."

12. Lakoff, "Preparing for the Next Emergency," 253.

13. See Anderson, "Preemption, Precaution, Preparedness." The precautionary principle is an environmental doctrine that argues that regulatory action should be taken even if scientific evidence regarding the precise nature of environmental threats is disputed. For more on the precautionary principle, see Ewald, "Return of Descartes's Malicious Demon"; and de Goede and Randalls, "Precaution, Preemption."

14. Amoore, *Politics of Possibility*, 5. Aimee Bahng calls preparedness a "speculative science" that "work[s] to colonize the future," drawing our attention to the practices of speculation that link national security and finance and that have long underwritten the American project of (military, financial) empire. See Bahng, *Migrant Futures*, 169.

15. Jasbir K. Puar writes of September 11, 2001, "as an event in the Deleuzian sense, privileging lines of flight, an assemblage of spatial and temporal intensities." She argues that "the event-ness of September 11 refuses the binary of watershed moment and turning point of radical change, versus intensification of more of the same." See Puar, *Terrorist Assemblages*, xxvi.

16. Other countries have also developed their own preparedness programs and policies. For example, see Anderson and Adey, "Affect and Security," on preparedness in the United Kingdom.

17. As Andrew Lakoff and Stephen J. Collier have described, "civil defense and emergency management shared a similar field of intervention—potential future catastrophes—which made their techniques transferable." See Lakoff and Collier, "Infrastructure and Event," 257. Collier and Lakoff have also documented how the nuclear preparedness agencies established

during the Cold War—including the Federal Civil Defense Administration and the Office of Defense Mobilization—focused on what they call "vital systems security," or ensuring the continued functioning of important infrastructure in the event of an attack. This emphasis on nonmilitary defense laid the groundwork for the eventual integration of military and natural disaster preparedness techniques and activities. See Collier and Lakoff, "Vital Systems Security."

18. Civil Defense Preparedness Agency, "Civil Preparedness," 1.

19. For more information on these institutional reorganizations, see Homeland Security National Preparedness Task Force, "Civil Defense and Homeland Security"; Lakoff and Collier, "Vulnerability of Vital Systems."

20. Lee Clarke describes all-hazards planning like this: "The claim is that planning is generically similar across hazards so that to plan for the one is to plan for the many. Specifically, all hazards planning says that natural calamities are the same as technological, and especially nuclear, calamities." See Clarke, *Mission Improbable*, 74.

21. White House, "National Security Strategy of the United States," v.

22. Stephen Collier and Andrew Lakoff highlight another important element of the rise of preparedness as a central paradigm of U.S. national security: the development of what they call the "administrative tools for governing emergency." They document how the executive branch's emergency powers began to expand in the 1930s as a response to the Great Depression and how these new expanded powers were institutionalized in the 1940s with the creation of the Office of Emergency Management and in the 1950s with the creation of the Office of Defense Mobilization. These offices were created to allow the president to exercise immediate control and supervision over emergencies, which at the time mainly meant wartime emergencies. As the successors to these offices expanded their purviews to include the management of *any* emergency, the power of the executive branch to govern emergencies in general expanded as well. See Collier and Lakoff, "Vital Systems Security."

23. Robert P. Marzec refers to the securitization of natural disasters as "environmentality," "a militarized mentality" about the ecosystem that understands the "governance" of the environment as "a central military concern." It is, as Marzec puts it, "environmentalism turned into a policing action." See Marzec, *Militarizing the Environment*, 4.

24. See Amoore, *Politics of Possibility*, esp. chapter 1, "On Authority: Probabilities for a World of Possibility," and chapter 2, "On Risk: Securing Uncertain Futures," for more on the history of preparedness and related modes of anticipatory action and governance, specifically their relation to statistical calculation and probabilistic reasoning.

25. See, e.g., Grausam, *On Endings*; Belletto, *No Accident, Comrade*; Melley, *Covert Sphere*; Voelz, *Poetics of Insecurity*; Bahng, *Migrant Futures*, chapter 2, "Homeland Futurity: Speculations at the Border." Bahng's chapter opens with a discussion of the national security state's investment in fiction, or, as she puts it, "a fairly pervasive merger between science fiction

and the logics of preemption" (53). Amoore includes a chapter on literature and the importance of imagination for contemporary national security regimes like preparedness in *Politics of Possibility.*

26. Anderson, "Security and the Future." *Speculate This!,* by uncertain commons, defines the more general processes of speculation on which preparedness depends as "a modern apparatus for erasing the future by realizing it as eternal present" (chapter 1, "Prospects").

27. Johannes Voelz has made a similar connection between national security and fiction in the modern age. As he puts it, "modern literature is thus a cultural practice that is related to security in that both rely on fictionality." See Voelz, *Poetics of Insecurity,* 27.

28. DHS is not the only national security institution or agency that practices preparedness. Likewise, preparedness is not the only paradigm of national security under which we could classify the activities of DHS. Preparedness is less an institutionally specific set of protocols or policies than it is a philosophy of or approach to national security. Indeed, many within the broader national security community understand preparedness as a "culture." And like any culture, its practices are unevenly distributed and often modified in surprising and unexpected ways.

29. All of these numbers, however, pale in comparison to the 2017 enacted budget for the Department of Defense, which was more than $580 billion. See U.S. Department of Homeland Security, "FY 2019 Budget-in-Brief"; National Endowment for the Arts, *National Endowment for the Arts 2017 Annual Report*; National Endowment for the Humanities, "NEH Chairman William D. Adams's Statement on NEH FY17 Budget."

30. Pease, *New American Exceptionalism,* 4. Also see Rose, *States of Fantasy.* American studies scholarship on the nineteenth century, fiction, and national fantasy is also of a piece with this work on the twentieth century; see esp. Berlant, *Anatomy of National Fantasy*; Kaplan, *Anarchy of Empire in the Making of US Culture.*

31. Pease, *New American Exceptionalism,* 4.

32. Melley, *Covert Sphere,* "Preface."

33. Melley, *Covert Sphere,* "Introduction: The Postmodern Public Sphere."

34. Melley, "Zero Dark Democracy," 17, 36. See Jameson, *Political Unconscious.* In this view, literary texts are symbolic solutions to social and political problems that can only be felt unconsciously.

35. Melley, "Zero Dark Democracy," 17, 36.

36. This book joins the recent resurgence of interest in fictionality, or the concept of fiction, in literary studies. Much of this scholarship can be separated into two camps. The first emphasizes the development of the concept of literary fictionality by focusing on the rise of the European and American novel in the eighteenth century. See, e.g., Gallagher, "Rise of Fictionality"; Paige, *Before Fiction*; Koenigs, "Fictionality Risen." The second emphasizes a rhetorical approach to fictionality that seeks to separate out genres of fiction (the novel, short story, graphic novel, fictional film,

etc.) from fictionality as a discursive mode. See, e.g., Walsh, *Rhetoric of Fictionality*; Nielsen, Phelan, and Walsh, "Ten Theses about Fictionality."

I make two interventions into these discussions. First, while the majority of the work on fictionality in literary studies is focused on the history of the novel or on novelistic realism more broadly, I argue in chapter 2 that, to understand how the national security state values fiction, we need to move away from a conception of fictionality rooted primarily in the novel or in novelistic realism. Second, by analyzing how fictionality functions in contemporary U.S. culture outside of those contexts occupied by literature, film, and other entertainment media, I am also interested in how fictive discourse operates in ostensibly "nonfictional" contexts. However, my approach to fictive discourse is informed by literary criticism and cultural studies. Instead of separating kinds of fiction from the quality of fictionality more broadly, I examine the fictions preparedness materials produce.

37. Agamben, *State of Exception*, 22.

38. As Marzec has argued, during the Cold War, "'war' as the primary motivator for military activity [was] replaced by something more insidious and ubiquitous: 'security.'" See Marzec, *Militarizing the Environment*, 227. Donald Pease also dates the emergence of the U.S. state of exception to the early Cold War, emphasizing that it is characterized "by absolute independence from any juridical control and any reference to the normal political order." See Pease, *New American Exceptionalism*, 24.

39. See Collier and Lakoff, "Vital Systems Security," for a critique of arguments that align Agamben's concept of the state of exception too closely with U.S. national security during and after the Cold War. Collier and Lakoff argue that because "the organization for emergency management inherited from the Cold War is often rather under-equipped" and because "the more recent expansion of the purview of emergency management . . . has not involved grants of exceptional powers to the executive branch," "discussions of the 'state of exception' . . . do not fully capture the historical development or contemporary reality of emergency government in the US" (46, 45).

40. I take up a discussion of biopolitics and necropolitics in more detail in chapter 4. In the first volume of *The History of Sexuality*, Foucault famously describes biopower as "the power to 'make' live and 'let' die." See Foucault, *Will to Knowledge*, 138. Later, in his lectures that comprise *"Society Must Be Defended,"* Foucault reformulates and extends this description to "the more you kill" or "let . . . die will allow you to live more" (255).

41. As Mbembe asks, "is the notion of biopower sufficient to account for the contemporary ways in which the political, under the guise of war, of resistance, or of the fight against terror, makes the murder of the enemy its primary and absolute objective?" See Mbembe, "Necropolitics," 12.

42. Foucault's and Mbembe's concepts have been enormously influential in the study of U.S. national security. For important interventions, see Puar, *Terrorist Assemblages*; Nguyen, *Gift of Freedom*; Weheliye, *Habeas*

Viscus; Marzec, *Militarizing the Environment*; Grewal, *Saving the Security State*.

43. For a discussion of what "catastrophe" means from a security studies perspective, and what it means to engage in a politics of catastrophe, see Aradau and van Munster, *Politics of Catastrophe*. For an argument for using the term *emergency* instead of *catastrophe*, see Adey, Anderson, and Graham, "Governing Emergencies."

44. Massumi, *Ontopower*, 180, 200.

45. Massumi, 180.

46. Grusin, *Premediation*, 4, 2.

47. Grusin, 47. Joseph Masco also identifies fear or terror as the foundation of U.S. counterterrorism efforts since 1945, and he describes his book *Theater of Operations* as an exploration of "the conditions of possibility for the most powerful military state in human history to declare war on an emotion." Like Massumi and Grusin, Masco argues that the national security state "affectively channel[s]" fear and terror to control the populace: the state uses the vulnerability it creates to demand ever-greater investments in security. See Masco, *Theater of Operations*, 2.

48. Berlant, *Cruel Optimism*, 10. Speaking specifically of a post-9/11 U.S. national security context, Joseph Masco has referred to this as "a project of normalization through militarization." While Masco also focuses on the normalization of future threat, he emphasizes how the national security state seeks to train people to respond unthinkingly to potential disaster. "The goal of a national security system," Masco writes, "is to produce a citizen-subject who responds to officially designated signs of danger automatically, instinctively activating logics and actions learned over time through drills and media indoctrination." See Masco, *Theater of Operations*, 19, 18. As we will see in chapter 1, I argue that preparedness training is less about teaching people to respond automatically than it is about persuading people to take certain ways of thinking and feeling for granted.

49. Berlant, "Thinking about Feeling Historical," 5, 6.

50. See U.S. Department of Homeland Security, "Resilience."

51. Kumar, "See Something, Say Something," 153.

52. Masco, *Theater of Operations*, 28.

53. Kumar argues that "the 'homeland' . . . tends to be white, even if it is not explicitly articulated as such." Kumar, "See Something, Say Something," 162.

54. As Roderick A. Ferguson puts it, whiteness works in many institutional contexts today "not primarily through the denigration of minority difference but through its hegemonic affirmation—that is, through an appreciation of diversity *and through the avowal rather than the disavowal of whiteness*." See Ferguson, "Distributions of Whiteness," 1101.

55. Chow, *Protestant Ethnic*, 15. Mimi Thi Nguyen refers to this as "transnational multiculturalism," a term that focuses our attention on the imperial projects that U.S. liberal philosophies of multicultural tolerance undergird. See Nguyen, *Gift of Freedom*, chapter 3, "Race Wars, Patriot Acts."

56. See Kumar, *Islamophobia and the Politics of Empire*.

57. Puar, *Terrorist Assemblages*, xxxii.

58. Grewal, *Saving the Security State*, 16–17.

59. Browne, *Dark Matters*, 9, 8–9.

60. As Robyn Wiegman has argued, "far from operating as the opposite or resistant counter to the universal . . . the particular is the necessary contradiction that affords white power its historical and political elasticity." See Wiegman, "Whiteness Studies and the Paradox of Particularity," 149–50.

61. Ahmed, *What's the Use?*, 3.

62. See, e.g., Nussbaum, *Cultivating Humanity*; Zunshine, *Why We Read Fiction*; Felski, *Uses of Literature*; Nussbaum, *Not for Profit*. For a review of work in neuroscience on the benefits of reading fiction, see Paul, "Neuroscience of Your Brain on Fiction."

63. Landy, *How to Do Things with Fictions*, 10.

64. Marzec, *Militarizing the Environment*, 196.

65. Jameson, *Archaeologies of the Future*, 232.

66. Palumbo-Liu, "Preemption, Perpetual War," 154. Palumbo-Liu uses a capital *I* in "Imagination" because he is referring specifically to Kant's notion of the aesthetic Imagination.

67. Lorde, "A Litany for Survival."

1. Training in an Empiricist Epistemology of Fiction

1. Rumsfeld, "Defense.Gov Transcript."

2. Massumi, *Ontopower*, 9–10.

3. Anderson, "Security and the Future," 227.

4. Rumsfeld, "Transforming the Military."

5. As Johannes Voelz argues, security is fictional because "it is a practice that creates an arrangement with uncertainty." See Voelz, *Poetics of Insecurity*, 23.

6. Shapin and Schaffer, *Leviathan and the Air-Pump*, 36.

7. Daston and Galison, *Objectivity*, 262.

8. Box, "Robustness in the Strategy of Scientific Model Building," 201.

9. Box. Also cited in So, "All Models Are Wrong," 669. Louise Amoore and Rita Raley have emphasized the central role of computing and computational modes of thought to security more generally. As they put it, "the practice of security has historically embraced a computational capacity to act decisively and procedurally in the face of radical uncertainty." See Amoore and Raley, "Securing within Algorithms," 4.

10. Frigg, "Models and Fiction," 252, 255, 260. Frigg also provides a discussion of related literature in the philosophy of science that precedes his claim; see pages 255–56. For a related argument in the philosophy of science, see Toon, *Models as Make-Believe*. For a counterargument, see Magnani, "Scientific Models Are Not Fictions." Arguably, the long-standing concerns in science fiction studies with simulation and reality also mark

the relationship between models and fiction as a foundational issue in that field. I discuss how scholars in science fiction studies have thought about realism and reality in more detail in chapter 2.

11. Taylor, "Novel as Climate Model," 2.

12. Taylor, 3.

13. Franzen, "What If We Stopped Pretending the Climate Apocalypse Can Be Stopped?"

14. As I will discuss in more detail in chapter 2, this way of understanding the relationship between fiction and reality reverses Jean Baudrillard's perhaps more familiar claim that in the era of the hyperreal, models substitute for reality. See Baudrillard, *Simulacra and Simulation*, "Simulacra and Science Fiction."

15. Committee on Homeland Security and Governmental Affairs, "Preparing for a Catastrophe," 63. Future references to this document are cited parenthetically in the text.

16. Alexander, *Principles of Emergency Planning and Management*, 299.

17. Haddow, Bullock, and Coppola, *Introduction to Emergency Management*, 111–12.

18. Haddow, Bullock, and Coppola, 111–12. The use of the phrase "battlefield experience" in quotes in the original text explicitly connects preparedness training to military training. For more on the relationship between (computer) simulations and military training, see Crogan, *Gameplay Mode*.

19. Alexander, *Principles of Emergency Planning and Management*, 292. Alexander sounds very similar here to critics who describe the value of speculative and science fiction in terms of the genre's ability to, in Darko Suvin's famous formulation, achieve "cognitive estrangement" by employing "an imaginative framework alternative to the author's empirical environment." See Suvin, *Metamorphoses of Science Fiction*, 8.

20. Lakoff, "Preparing for the Next Emergency," 247.

21. Emergency Management Institute, "Emergency Management."

22. Kaplan and Ragle, *A River in Egypt*. The L.A. Earthquake Sourcebook contains an eclectic mix of personal essays on natural disaster preparedness, interviews with emergency planners and preparedness professionals, short academic pieces on everything from the geology of earthquakes to urban planning for natural disasters, and images of visual art and design pieces by Art Center College students. For more on the preparedness campaign itself, see Designmatters, "Los Angeles Earthquake."

23. Although this isn't entirely clear in the narrative, Marty's friend seems to represent the "devil's advocate" or cynical side of his personality. Marty and his friend look very similar to one another, only the friend is unshaven and wearing a red sweatshirt.

24. Kaplan and Ragle, *A River in Egypt*, 295, 298. Future references to this work are cited parenthetically in the text.

25. Dare to Prepare, "The 7 Steps to Earthquake Safety." For more on

the Earthquake Country Alliance, see Earthquake Country Alliance, "Welcome to Earthquake Country." Future references to this document are cited parenthetically in the text.

26. As Art Spiegelman emphasizes, graphic narratives "choreograph and shape time" through the interaction of image and text on the page. Quoted in Chute, "Comics as Literature?," 454.

27. Chute, 455; Darda, "Graphic Ethics," 34.

28. Camus, *Myth of Sisyphus*, 123.

29. Federal Emergency Management Agency, "IS-139 Exercise Design," 8.24.

30. Foucault, *Discipline and Punish*, 170, 131.

31. Foucault, 135.

32. Foucault, 138, 137, 164.

33. Foucault, 166.

34. Association of State and Territorial Health Officials, "Guide to Preparedness Evaluation," 10; Federal Emergency Management Agency, "IS-139 Exercise Design," 5.7; Association of State and Territorial Health Officials, "Guide to Preparedness Evaluation," 7.

35. Federal Emergency Management Agency, "Using Tabletop Exercises and Drills," 6; Association of State and Territorial Health Officials, "Guide to Preparedness Evaluation," 7.

36. Federal Emergency Management Agency, "Using Tabletop Exercises and Drills," 12; Federal Emergency Management Agency, "IS-139 Exercise Design," 8.3.

37. Ahmed, *Willful Subjects*, 57.

38. Bourdieu, *Logic of Practice*, 56. For Bourdieu, *habitus* refers to "acquired . . . permanent dispositions" that are "opposed as much to the mechanical necessity of things without history in mechanistic theories as [they are] to the reflexive freedom of subjects 'without inertia' in rationalist theories." See Bourdieu, *Sociology in Question*, 86, and Bourdieu, *Logic of Practice*, 56.

39. Ahmed, *Willful Subjects*, 57.

40. Ahmed, 73.

41. As Ahmed puts it, "we could think of will as a pressing device: bodies are pressed this way or that by the force of a momentum. The will in having direction becomes directive." See Ahmed, 57.

42. As many have argued, preparedness is one symptom of the neoliberalism of the national security state. In its fetishization of individual responsibility and flexibility in the face of disaster, preparedness both appeals to the individual's sense of purpose and autonomy and emphasizes that it is the individual's responsibility to prepare herself to withstand coming disaster. For more on preparedness and neoliberalism, see Walker and Cooper, "Geneaologies of Resilience."

43. Ahmed, *Willful Subjects*, 75.

44. Crogan, *Gameplay Mode*, 78.

45. U.S. Department of Homeland Security, "Homeland Security Exercise and Evaluation Program," 2-3.

46. U.S. Department of Homeland Security, 6-3.

47. Cazdyn, *Already Dead*, 7–8.

48. Cazdyn, 5. Lauren Berlant has called this the "stretched-out present"; see Berlant, *Cruel Optimism*, 5.

49. This understanding of training is closer to how Foucault discusses the concept in the second volume of *History of Sexuality*. Foucault emphasizes there that classical Greek thought conceived of *epimeleia heautou*, or care of the self, as a training regimen. It was considered to be a kind of "*askēsis* . . . a practical training that was indispensable in order for an individual to form himself as a moral subject" or to develop a productive relationship to the force of his own desires and pleasures so that they did not "turn seditious or rebellious." The care of the self as Foucault conceives it involved mastering a set of techniques—it was something that needed to be taught using tools like "[athletic] training, meditation, tests of thinking, examination of conscience, control of representations" and that needed to be continually practiced. However, unlike the kind of training Foucault discusses in *Discipline and Punish*, such practice was indistinguishable from the practice of living one's life. As Foucault puts it, "exercise was regarded as the actual practice of what one needed to train for; it was not something distinct from the goal to be reached." "Life as a whole," he writes, was understood through this framing "as a sort of continuous exercise." See Foucault, *Use of Pleasure*, 77, 72, 73, 74, 73.

50. U.S. Department of Homeland Security, "Homeland Security Exercise and Evaluation Program," Intro-1.

51. U.S. Department of Homeland Security.

52. Federal Emergency Management Agency, "IS-130.A"; the quote is from "Lesson 1 Exercise Evaluation Overview."

53. Federal Emergency Management Agency.

54. U.S. Department of Homeland Security, "Homeland Security Exercise and Evaluation Program," 1-2.

55. Kermode, *Sense of an Ending*, 101. Leif Sorensen describes the difference between apocalyptic and postapocalyptic narratives in similar terms: "post-apocalyptic narratives sidestep a full engagement with the finality of the apocalyptic and rewrite apocalyptic time as the occasion for the production of new stories." See Sorensen, "Against the Post-apocalyptic," 562.

56. Bahng, *Migrant Futures*, 53.

57. Researchers have done the most work on the effectiveness of preparedness training in the context of disaster preparedness for health care workers. In general, this research is inconclusive about the effectiveness of preparedness training. For systematic reviews of this literature, see Williams, Nocera, and Casteel, "Effectiveness of Disaster Training for Health Care Workers," and Potter et al., "Evidence Base for Effectiveness of Preparedness Training."

2. Realism

1. U.S. Department of Defense, "CONPLAN 8888 Counter-Zombie Dominance." Future references to this document are cited parenthetically in the text.

2. Federal Emergency Management Agency, "IS-139 Exercise Design"; Committee on Homeland Security and Governmental Affairs, "Preparing for a Catastrophe," 13.

3. Aristotle, *Poetics*, 50, 28.

4. For foundational work on the history of probability, see Foucault, *Order of Things*, esp. part III, "Representing," and Hacking, *Emergence of Probability*. For more on the relationship between Foucault's and Hacking's studies and literary form, see Patey, *Probability and Literary Form*, esp. Appendix A. For more on the link between probability, the novel, and realism, see Newsom, *A Likely Story*; Kavanagh, *Enlightenment and the Shadows of Chance*; Gallagher, "Rise of Fictionality"; Molesworth, *Chance and the Eighteenth-Century Novel*; Paige, *Before Fiction*. Finally, see Newsom, *A Likely Story*, and Paige, *Before Fiction*, for differing accounts of the historicity of the term *probability*.

5. See Kavanagh, *Enlightenment and the Shadows of Chance*, esp. chapter III, "*Vraisemblance*, Probability, and Opinion," and Alliston, "Female Quixotism and the Novel."

6. Gallagher, "Rise of Fictionality," 346. For more on this understanding of the relationship between plausibility and the suspension of disbelief, see Molesworth, *Chance and the Eighteenth-Century Novel*, and Paige, *Before Fiction*.

7. Gallagher details how eighteenth-century British novels separated themselves from fantastical or incredible narratives and became a genre in their own right only when they became plausible or "believable." As Gallagher claims, "fictionality only became visible when it became credible, because it only needed conceptualizing as the difference between fictions and lies became less obvious." See Gallagher, "Rise of Fictionality," 340.

8. Gallagher, *Nobody's Story*, xvi–xvii.

9. Another important figure from the Cold War era was Ramsay Potts, an air bomber in World War II who went on to become a prominent nuclear preparedness planner during the early Cold War. Potts focused much of his planning work on how to reduce the susceptibility of vital infrastructure like the electrical grid to attack and on how to increase its ability to recover from an attack. For more on Potts, see Collier and Lakoff, "Vital Systems Security," 30. We might also include Val Peterson, director of the Federal Civil Defense Administration from 1953 to 1957 and architect of the infamous Operation Alert national civil defense preparedness exercises that ran from 1954 to 1961, as an important figure. For more on Peterson and Operation Alert, see Orr, *Panic Diaries*, esp. chapter 3, "'Keep Calm!' for the Cold War: Diary of a Mental Patient," and Masco, *Theater of Operations*, esp.

chapter 1, "'Survival Is Your Business': Engineering Ruins and Affect in Nuclear America." Finally, we could include John Macy, who was appointed the first director of FEMA in 1979 and who developed the concept of all-hazards planning, which I discuss in the introduction. For more on Macy, see Haddow, Bullock, and Coppola, *Introduction to Emergency Management*, esp. chapter 1, "The Historical Context of Emergency Management."

10. In using the term *possibilistic*, I am following Louise Amoore, who argues that the "mode of risk" that informs both economics and security today follows "a possibilistic logic." This logic "does not deploy statistical probabilistic calculation in order to avert future risks but rather flourishes in conditions of declared constant emergency because decisions are taken on the basis of future possibilities, however improbable or unlikely." See Amoore, *Politics of Possibility*, 12. On the term *possibilistic*, see also Galperin, *Historical Austen*.

11. Davis uses this term to describe how Cold War civil defense preparedness exercises manufactured a sense of realism. These exercises, she notes, reveal "how realism results from calculated decisions." Davis understands what she calls the "'consensual reality'" of these exercises "not so much [as] an aesthetic—all or nothing—but [as] a technique capable of selective deployment" and that "could be stepped up incrementally." Importantly, she emphasizes, the consensual reality of these exercises was "not just at the discretion of planners but its deployment [was] also at the discretion of players who [could] selectively invoke it." See Davis, *Stages of Emergency*, chapter 2, "Rehearsals for Nuclear War," "Realism."

12. Baudrillard, *Simulacra and Simulation*, 123, 124.

13. As Guy Oakes writes, "the Cold War conception of nuclear reality represented an attempt to think about the unthinkable, to conceptualize an unintelligible event and rationalize a world that seemed to be irrational, by reducing the apparently unimaginable experience of nuclear war to a set of routines." See Oakes, *Imaginary War*, 79. Joseph Masco traces not only these routines but also the larger "affective culture" of post-9/11 U.S. national security to "generations of nuclear crises." Contemporary counterterrorism, he argues, has "amplif[ied] . . . a specific formulation, a concern with the atomic bomb, to one that views technology itself as a source of fear (including weapons, planes, computers, viruses, and box cutters). This formulation creates a terroristic menace of nearly infinite scope and capabilities, enabling a counterterrorism that seeks to be equally total." See Masco, *Theater of Operations*, 27.

14. For more on the relationship of preparedness to the Cold War, and on the role of training exercises in particular in this history, see Lakoff, "Preparing for the Next Emergency"; Lakoff and Collier, "Distributed Preparedness"; and Collier and Lakoff, "Vital Systems Security."

15. See McClanahan, "Future's Shock," for more on Kahn's influence beyond national security. McClanahan also emphasizes that Kahn borrowed the term *scenario*, which by the 1960s was an outdated term for a screenplay, from film production.

16. Lakoff, "Preparing for the Next Emergency," 260.

17. Kahn and Wiener, *Year 2000*, 4. Not surprisingly, Kahn was an avid science fiction fan.

18. See, e.g., McClanahan, "Future's Shock"; Grausam, *On Endings*; Belletto, *No Accident, Comrade*.

19. McClanahan, "Future's Shock," 44, and Belletto, *No Accident, Comrade*, 112.

20. Ghamari-Tabrizi, *Worlds of Herman Kahn*, 135. Kahn's work on this subject is voluminous; see esp. Kahn, "Modification of the Monte Carlo Method," and Kahn, "Applications of Monte Carlo."

21. Kahn, "Stochastic (Monte Carlo) Attenuation Analysis," 7.

22. Kahn, "Applications of Monte Carlo," 124.

23. Kahn and Mann, "Techniques of Systems Analysis," 127.

24. Albert Latter, quoted in Ghamari-Tabrizi, *Worlds of Herman Kahn*, 135. For more on systems analysis at RAND during this period, see Edwards, *Closed World*, esp. 113–45.

25. Kahn and Mann, "Techniques of Systems Analysis," 128.

26. Kahn and Mann, 36.

27. Kahn, "On Alternative World Futures," 55.

28. Christopher Newfield calls this prestige "numerical culture," which he "reductively" defines as the belief that numbers "enjoy epistemic superiority to narrative" because numbers lead to quantifiable results and products. See Newfield, "Trouble with Numerical Culture."

29. Kahn, "On Alternative World Futures," 25.

30. Kahn, *Thinking about the Unthinkable*, 145, 175.

31. See Amoore, *Politics of Possibility*, for a history of how, as she puts it, "low probability, high consequence events are made amenable to governing by risk" (56). While Amoore focuses on rationalities of risk management and calculation rather than aesthetics, she emphasizes throughout that regimes of security, such as preparedness, depend on the "imagination of possibilities" to a greater degree than on probability (24).

32. Kahn's understanding of the relationship between disaster scenarios and reality therefore diverges from how Richard Grusin has explained this relationship in his book *Premediation*. Grusin associates scenarios with prediction; he writes that scenarios "imagin[e] the real as something like a predetermined or preexisting state that can be predicted or forecast or planned." As a result, he argues that scenario creation "ultimately involves the creation or determination of distinctions between false or illusory possibilities on the one hand and the real or the actual on the other—only those possible scenarios that come true are real, while the others are proved false or illusory or wrong." For Kahn—and for preparedness materials more generally—there is no necessary relation between scenarios and what will actually happen. As this section argues, Kahn in fact worked to undo such an association between prediction and scenario building, arguing instead that possibility, not probability, is the only meaningful rubric for judging a scenario's usefulness. See Grusin, *Premediation*, 59, 61.

33. Kahn, "On Alternative World Futures," 25.
34. Kahn, *Thinking about the Unthinkable*, 145.
35. Kahn and Wiener, *Year 2000*, 17, 37.
36. Kahn and Wiener, 4.
37. Kahn, *On Thermonuclear War*, 253.
38. Kahn, "On Alternative World Futures," 25.
39. Kahn, 29.
40. As we will see in chapter 3, Kahn's dream of such a systematic "program" or "blueprint" for scenario building was not fully realized until the creation of the Homeland Security Exercise and Evaluation Program after 9/11. This agency produces standardized scenarios for use by both government agencies and the public in workplaces, schools, and community organizations.
41. U.S. Department of Homeland Security, "Homeland Security Exercise and Evaluation Program (HSEEP), Vol II," 13.
42. U.S. Department of Homeland Security, 13.
43. U.S. Department of Homeland Security, 14.
44. Federal Emergency Management Agency, "Risk Assessment," 3-1.
45. Federal Emergency Management Agency, Appendix A, A-1–A-47.
46. Federal Emergency Management Agency, 3-15, 3-16.
47. U.S. Department of Homeland Security, "Homeland Security Exercise and Evaluation Program (HSEEP), Vol II," 13.
48. Federal Emergency Management Agency, "Maximum of Maximums Table Top Exercise (TTX) Script." FEMA identifies seven different exercise types: four kinds of discussion-based exercises in which participants talk their way through exercises—seminars, workshops, tabletop exercises, and games—and three kinds of operations-based exercises in which participants enact the exercise—drills, functional exercises, and full-scale exercises. See U.S. Department of Homeland Security, "Homeland Security Exercise and Evaluation Program (HSEEP), Vol II," 2–5.
49. For more on this scenario and other "maximum of maximum" scenarios, see Graham, "Mothers of All Disasters."
50. U.S. Department of Homeland Security, "Homeland Security Exercise and Evaluation Program (HSEEP), Vol II," 2–5.
51. Federal Emergency Management Agency, "Maximum of Maximums Table Top Exercise (TTX) Script," 12, 2, 4, 9.
52. Federal Emergency Management Agency, "Metascenario Table Top Exercise Facilitator Notes," 4, 9, 7, 5.
53. Federal Emergency Management Agency, "Maximum of Maximums Table Top Exercise (TTX) Script," 4, 9.
54. Federal Emergency Management Agency, 1.
55. Barthes, "Reality Effect," 16.
56. Barthes.
57. For an elaboration of this point, see Paige, *Before Fiction*, 14–16. Similarly, as Jesse Molesworth has discussed, psychological studies of "prospect theory" demonstrate what he terms "a certain narrative bias" toward the

vividness of literary plots. "What prospect theory reveals over and over again," he writes, "is a certain narrative bias—a belief that narratives possess a vividness that makes them more likely to occur than non-narratives and that ordinary life may be best understood through the language of a literary plot. . . . When asked to make a logical judgment of probability, in other words, the test subjects instead made a literary judgment." The vividness of emplotment, in other words, makes narratives seem likely. I discuss emplotment in more detail in the fifth chapter. See Molesworth, *Chance and the Eighteenth-Century Novel*, 8.

58. As Jesse Molesworth puts it, a rhetorical understanding of realism understands realism as "a textual interface seeking to diminish, or even liquidate, the boundary between audience and text." See Molesworth, *Chance and the Eighteenth-Century Novel*, 14. Catherine Gallagher's *Nobody's Story* and "Rise of Fictionality" are perhaps the most influential examples of non-sci-fi literary criticism that develop a rhetorical understanding of realism. Yet, as I will discuss later in this chapter, for Gallagher, this understanding of realism is still tied to a specific notion of plausibility rooted in the genre of realist fiction. Molesworth's *Chance and the Eighteenth-Century Novel* and Paige's *Before Fiction* are two examples of more recent criticism that take a rhetorical understanding of realism for granted and develop it further.

59. Tomberg, "On the 'Double Vision' of Realism," 277. Tomberg traces the impulse to see reality as peculiarly science fictional back to J. G. Ballard's well-known remark that "we have annexed the future into our own present, as merely one of the manifold alternatives open to us." Ballard's remark also calls to mind Kim Stanley Robinson's observation that "we are all now living in a science fiction novel that we are all writing together." See Ballard, "Introduction to the French Edition of *Crash*," 8, and Canavan and Robinson, "Still, I'm Reluctant to Call This Pessimism," 255.

60. Tomberg, "On the 'Double Vision' of Realism," 263. David M. Higgins makes a similar point in "American Science Fiction after 9/11."

61. Chu, *Do Metaphors Dream of Literal Sleep?*, 1, 2.

62. Chu, 7.

63. Chu.

64. Chu uses the term *mimesis* throughout her book, but she approaches this term "not from the familiar context of its long and contentious past but from a context more alien and futuristic: science fiction." As a result, her book reconfigures the conception of reality that lies behind mimesis: "The objects of science-fictional representation, while impossible to represent in a straightforward manner, are absolutely real. . . . Instead of conceptualizing science fiction as a nonmimetic discourse that achieves the effect of cognitive estrangement through 'an imaginative framework,' I conceptualize science fiction as a mimetic discourse whose objects of representation are nonimaginary yet cognitively estranging." See Chu, 2, 3.

65. Miéville, "Cognition as Ideology," 238. Additional references to this text are cited parenthetically. Miéville traces the "charismatic authority of

the text" back as far as H. G. Wells's defense of invented science: "Wells, in his rather scandalous defence of invented science, has it that the writer 'must trick [the reader] into an unwary concession . . . and get on with his story while the illusion holds'" (238).

66. This understanding of the role the authority of the text plays in whether readers consider a text to be realistic also recalls J. R. R. Tolkien's discussion of this phenomenon in "On Fairy-Stories." In this essay, Tolkien argues that readers understand a world to be "real" if the "story-maker proves a successful 'subcreator' [Tolkien's word for someone who engages in world-building]." If the author does well, "he makes a Secondary World which your mind can enter. Inside it, what he relates is 'true': it accords with the laws of that world. You therefore believe it while you are, as it were, inside. The moment disbelief arises, the spell is broken; the magic, or rather art, has failed." See Tolkien, "On Fairy-Stories," 52.

67. Gallagher, "Rise of Fictionality," 340, 339.

68. Federal Emergency Management Agency, "Maximum of Maximums Table Top Exercise (TTX) Script," 1.

69. Federal Emergency Management Agency.

70. Warner, "The Mass Public and the Mass Subject," 257. This applies especially to coverage of disasters: as Warner writes, "disaster is popular because it is a way of making mass subjectivity available" (256).

71. Warner, *Publics and Counterpublics*, 72.

72. Warner, 73.

73. Warner, 114.

74. Warner, 114. This conception of world building differs from the arguably more common understanding of world building as dependent on the reality effect. As Mark J. P. Wolf notes, narratives that spend time building worlds concern themselves with "a wealth of details and events . . . which do not advance the story but which provide background richness and verisimilitude to the imaginary world," while narratives that do not concern themselves as much with world building give the story itself primary importance. See Wolf, *Building Imaginary Worlds*, 2.

75. Gallagher, "Rise of Fictionality," 346.

76. Gallagher, 349.

3. Thinking Generically

1. Emergency Management Institute, "Emergency Management"; Committee on Homeland Security and Governmental Affairs, "Preparing for a Catastrophe," 9.

2. Emergency Management Institute, "Emergency Management"; Federal Emergency Management Agency, "Principles of Emergency Management Supplement," 9. This understanding of professionalism is adapted from public administration scholar Dwight Waldo's oft-cited work on professionalism in public administration. See Waldo, "Scope of the Theory of Public Administration."

3. Waugh and Sadiq, "Professional Education for Emergency Managers"; Clement, "Essentials of Emergency Management and Homeland Security Graduate Education Programs." See also Plant, Arminio, and Thompson, "A Matrix Approach to Homeland Security Professional Education," and the foundational work on professionalism in emergency management, Drabek, *Professional Emergency Manager*.

4. Bledstein, *Culture of Professionalism*, 89, 105.

5. Freidson, *Professionalism*, 95.

6. See Berlant, *Female Complaint*, 3–4.

7. While the word *genre* comes to English most recently from the French and the word *generic* more directly from Latin, both *genre* and *generic* descend from the Latin *genus*, meaning "type" or "kind." Indeed, "kind; sort; style" is the first definition given of *genre* in the *Oxford English Dictionary*.

8. This understanding of genre is indebted to recent conversations about the inextricably formal and social qualities of genre as a concept. While debates about genre in literary studies are as old as the discipline itself, many critics have observed that something like a consensus in genre theory has emerged in recent years. Older debates about whether a genre is fundamentally a formal, social, or discursive phenomenon have largely fallen by the wayside as critics have attempted to grapple with genres as historically contingent and messily social discursive practices that are nonetheless organized around recognizable formal conventions. As Jeremy Rosen puts it, "literary genres, in this view, are not static categories or corpuses, established groups of texts that abide by fixed sets of rules, though they are nonetheless made up of typified, codifiable practices that constitute norms." See Rosen, *Minor Characters Have Their Day*, 11. Ted Underwood comes to a similar conclusion when he writes, "In short, it increasingly seems that a genre is not a single object we can observe and describe. It may instead be a mutable set of relations between works that are linked in different ways, and resemble each other to different degrees." See Underwood, "Life Cycles of Genres." For more on this emerging consensus, see Cohen, "Introduction"; Pavel, "Literary Genres as Norms and Good Habits"; Rieder, "On Defining SF, or Not"; Frow, *Genre*; Martin, *Contemporary Drift*.

9. Berlant, *Female Complaint*, 4.

10. Jerng, *Racial Worldmaking*, "Genre-Race Configurations: A Methodological Approach."

11. Bonilla-Silva, *White Supremacy and Racism*, 138. See also Chow, *Protestant Ethnic*; Ahmed, *On Being Included*.

12. In this way, the preparedness materials I discuss in this chapter operate as a form of what Jerng has called "racial worldmaking," which he defines as "narrative and interpretive strategies that shape how readers notice race so as to build, anticipate, and organize the world." For Jerng, racial worldmaking happens in large part through genre, and for him, as for me, the concept of genre names a world-making capacity. Jerng emphasizes

that genre works to teach readers "when, where, and how race is something to notice" and that "race has an organizing and shaping force that is often associated with genre." See Jerng, *Racial Worldmaking*, "Introduction: Racial Worldmaking."

13. Pease, *New American Exceptionalism*, 169.

14. Pease.

15. As Pease emphasizes, this claim taps into the "Virgin Land" myth about the founding of the United States, or the myth that the United States was settled on empty, unoccupied land. This myth ignores the dispossession of Indigenous people that actually made the founding and expansion of the United States possible, and it presents the country as a formerly inviolate whole that has been wounded by the attacks of September 11. See Pease, chapter 5, "From Virgin Land to Ground Zero: Mythological Foundations of the Homeland Security State."

16. Pease, 169.

17. Kumar, "See Something, Say Something," 162.

18. Clarke's novels to date include *The Scorpion's Gate, Breakpoint, Sting of the Drone,* and *Pinnacle Event.* Clarke has described his work as "Tom Clancy–like." See Middle East Institute, "Sting of the Drone."

19. Clarke, *Sting of the Drone*, 199.

20. Clarke, *Pinnacle Event*, 29, 32, 33.

21. Hepburn, *Intrigue*, 29.

22. Terdoslavich, *Jack Ryan Agenda*, 15.

23. Clarke, *Breakpoint*, 1.

24. Clarke, *Sting of the Drone*, 195.

25. Keefe, "Insider"; Middle East Institute, "Sting of the Drone"; Clarke, "Richard Clarke Writes Mideast Thriller."

26. Hepburn, *Intrigue*, 24.

27. See Poot, "On Cliffhangers," 64. Poot defines the cliffhanger as "a place where the narrative discourse stops too soon" or as an "[act] of deliberate disruption . . . where the text breaks off, seemingly in the wrong place" (52). Poot's article is one of only a few discussions of the cliffhanger specifically in literary scholarship and/or narrative theory; see Poot's footnote 2 for a list of others.

28. Nussbaum, "Tune in Next Week." Also cited in Poot, "On Cliffhangers," 51.

29. Clarke, *Scorpion's Gate*, 4.

30. Clarke, 6.

31. Clarke, 10.

32. Clarke.

33. Poot, "On Cliffhangers," 60.

34. See Hepburn, *Intrigue*, chapter 2, "Thrills: Fear and Catharsis as Ideological Effects."

35. Berlant, *Female Complaint*, 4.

36. As Jeremy Rosen suggests, while critics often value literary works for their subversion or eschewal of genre conventions, it is precisely to

"the common features that constitute a genre's central conventions" that critics should turn if they want to understand how particular genres, and the individual texts of which they are constituted, "convey a shared social logic." See Rosen, *Minor Characters Have Their Day*, 7. Similarly, Jerng argues that the conventionality of genre, or "precisely . . . what critics most demean about genre fiction," is what accounts for "the complexity of its worldmaking practices." See Jerng, *Racial Worldmaking*, "Genre-Race Configurations: A Methodological Approach."

37. Keefe, "Insider."

38. Keefe.

39. National Commission on Terrorist Attacks upon the United States, *The 9/11 Commission Report*, xv.

40. National Commission on Terrorist Attacks upon the United States, 4.

41. National Commission on Terrorist Attacks upon the United States, 20.

42. National Commission on Terrorist Attacks upon the United States, 7.

43. Clarke, *Against All Enemies*, 3, 14.

44. Clarke, 1.

45. Clarke, 33.

46. "Instructive" is from *Politics and Prose*, "Richard A. Clarke 'Sting of the Drone'"; "prophetic" is from an editorial review of *Sting of the Drone* by Stephen Coonts quoted on the cover of the paperback edition; "insider's expertise" is from an editorial review of *Scorpion's Gate* quoted on the paperback cover; and the quote about *Against All Enemies* is from Clarke, "Clarke Urges 'Debate' on Terror Preparations," 4:30.

47. Keefe, "Insider."

48. Clarke, *Pinnacle Event*, 56.

49. Clarke, 56.

50. Clarke, 62.

51. Clarke, 64.

52. Clarke, 82.

53. Winant, *New Politics of Race*, 64, 65.

54. U.S. Department of Homeland Security, "Homeland Security Exercise and Evaluation Program," Intro-2.

55. U.S. Department of Homeland Security, 3-12. For more on the history of the scenario form in national security, see McClanahan, "Future's Shock," and Davis, *Stages of Emergency*.

56. U.S. Department of Homeland Security, "National Planning Scenarios," iii. Future references to this document are cited parenthetically. For a shortened, earlier draft of this document, see Homeland Security Council, "Planning Scenarios."

57. Alexander, *Principles of Emergency Planning and Management*, 299.

58. Taylor, *The Archive and the Repertoire*, 28. Taylor uses the term *scenario* more generally than I do to describe "a paradigmatic setup that relies

on supposedly live participants, structured around a schematic plot, with an intended (though adaptable) end" (13). She discusses the term in the context of first-contact narratives in Latin America and scenes of colonial encounter.

59. Taylor, 28, 32. Taylor describes the portability of the scenario in terms of a "hauntology" that works to reproduce hegemonic power structures and relations. "The scenario," she writes, "makes visible, yet again, what is already there: the ghosts, the images, the stereotypes." In this way, the scenario "promotes certain views while helping to disappear others" (28).

60. Federal Emergency Management Agency, "Emergency Management Institute Mission."

61. Federal Emergency Management Agency, "IS-907: Active Shooter: What You Can Do."

62. To download course materials, see Federal Emergency Management Agency. Figures 8–10 are taken from Federal Emergency Management Agency, "Active Shooter: What You Can Do, Course Downloads: Visuals," 28, 31, 36.

63. Berlant, "Thinking about Feeling Historical," 6, 5, 6.

64. The fact that active shooter drills are common not only in American workplaces but also, and perhaps even more so, in American schools is evidence of the extent to which "active shooter scenarios" are viewed as ordinary and unexceptional. The Education Department's National Center for Education Statistics estimates that 96 percent of American schools conducted lockdown drills in 2015 and 2016. See Williamson, "When Active-Shooter Drills Scare the Children They Hope to Protect."

65. Federal Emergency Management Agency, "IS-139 Exercise Design," 1.5.

66. Federal Emergency Management Agency, 1.

67. In her book *Stages of Emergency,* about Cold War civil defense, Tracy Davis focuses not on "practice" but rather on the closely related and more theater- and performance-studies-inflected term *rehearsal.* As I do in relation to preparedness training exercises, Davis argues that for the designers of civil defense exercises, rehearsal was understood as a form of persuasion: "The measurable, and reproducible, manifestation of persuasion is action: enacting a set of ideas through rehearsal imprinted behaviors upon the body, and in so doing created cognitive conditioning and a corporeal memory more likely to be reproduced in an emergency. Persuasion may have conditioned the public to believe, but rehearsal would enable the public to behave, not only in an orderly but in a constructively predictable manner." See Davis, *Stages of Emergency,* "The 'Deferred Event.'"

68. To view the pocket card, see Federal Emergency Management Agency, "Active Shooter: What You Can Do, Pocket Card."

69. Guillory, "Memo and Modernity," 111.

70. Blanchfield, "Market Can't Solve a Massacre."

71. Federal Emergency Management Agency, "Principles of Emergency Management Supplement," 9.

72. Seltzer, *Official World*, 16.

73. Federal Emergency Management Agency, "Principles of Emergency Management Supplement," 9.

74. U.S. Department of Homeland Security, "Homeland Security Exercise and Evaluation Program," 2-4.

75. Max Weber described this particular form of life more than a century ago as one in which "business with its continuous work has become a necessary part of [bourgeois professionals'] lives." For such a professional, the highest reward is "the irrational sense of having done [one's] job well." See Weber, *Protestant Ethic and the Spirit of Capitalism*, 32, 33.

76. Federal Emergency Management Agency, "IS-907: Active Shooter: What You Can Do, Instructor Guide," 13, 52.

77. Federal Emergency Management Agency, "IS-907: Active Shooter: How to Respond."

78. Federal Emergency Management Agency, 2.

79. Federal Emergency Management Agency, "IS-907: Active Shooter: What You Can Do, Instructor Guide" 36, 38.

80. Federal Emergency Management Agency, 20, 33.

81. Flatley, "Reading for Mood," 144.

82. Berlant, *Cruel Optimism*, 20.

83. Flatley, "Reading for Mood," 144.

84. Zhang, "Notes on Atmosphere," 122. A full discussion of the multiple verging and diverging meanings of related terms like *atmosphere, mood*, and *environment*, and the relationship of these terms to concepts like Raymond Williams's structure of feeling or Sianne Ngai's tone, is beyond the scope of this chapter. For considerations of these differences, see Flatley, "Reading for Mood," and Highmore, *Cultural Feelings*.

85. For this reason, Flatley, in "Reading for Mood," names a method of reading called "reading for mood" that involves "a speculative recreation of the understanding of the reader's mood embedded in a given textual practice, its theory-in-practice of the mood of its readers" (150). My reading of the Active Shooter exercise is one such example of reading for mood.

86. Federal Emergency Management Agency, "IS-139 Exercise Design," 4.25.

87. Federal Emergency Management Agency, 6.2.

88. Haddow, Bullock, and Coppola, *Introduction to Emergency Management*, 112.

89. Alexander, *Principles of Emergency Planning and Management*, 299, 297.

90. Mallard and Lakoff, "How Claims to Know the Future Are Used to Understand the Present," 370.

91. Federal Emergency Management Agency, "IS-139 Exercise Design," 5.7, 5.5.

92. Alexander, *Principles of Emergency Planning and Management*, 288.

93. Federal Emergency Management Agency, "IS-139 Exercise Design," 6.14.

94. In their interviews with preparedness exercise designers and participants, Peter Adey, Ben Anderson, and Stephen Graham also show how exercises are often designed to "punctuate" boredom with excitement. Exercise designers are often careful "to build news media [into the exercise] that feel realistic and are structured and articulated in such a way that they give the most optimum delivery and the most effective affect." See Adey, Anderson, and Graham, "Governing Emergencies," 111.

95. Quoted in Adey, Anderson, and Graham, 111.

96. Federal Emergency Management Agency, "Principles of Emergency Management Supplement"; Waugh and Sadiq, "Professional Education for Emergency Managers"; Oyola-Yemaiel and Wilson, "Three Essential Strategies," 82.

97. Liu, *Laws of Cool*, 76.

98. As I will discuss in more detail in chapter 5, this form of visual representation is, following from Sara Ahmed, "*a method of protecting whiteness.*" See Ahmed, *On Being Included*, 147.

99. Bonilla-Silva, *White Supremacy and Racism*, 138.

100. Grewal, *Saving the Security State*, 185, 190.

101. Grewal, 188.

102. Emergency Management Institute, "FY 2015 Annual Report," 4. For examples of scholarship about training participant self-assessment, see Rutty and Rutty, "Did the Participants of the Mass Fatality Exercise *Operation Torch* Learn Anything?," and Berlin and Carlström, "Three-Level Collaboration Exercise."

103. Rutty and Rutty, "Did the Participants of the Mass Fatality Exercise *Operation Torch* Learn Anything?," 220.

104. Select Bipartisan Committee to Investigate the Preparation for and Response to Hurricane Katrina, *A Failure of Initiative*, ix. Future references to this document are cited parenthetically in the text.

105. Committee on Homeland Security and Governmental Affairs, "Preparing for a Catastrophe," 2. Future references to this document are cited parenthetically in the text.

106. Lakoff, "Preparing for the Next Emergency," 270.

107. Lakoff, 248.

108. At the same time as it relies on images of Black suffering for rhetorical impact, the report also tries to deny the significance of the fact that Black people and poor people constituted most of the victims of the storm by claiming such a thing was to be expected. It mentions that "the dead in New Orleans were 62 percent black," for example, and claims this number was actually slightly better than expected, because "66 percent" of "the total parish population" at the time of the storm was Black. Likewise, the report mentions that "the analysis found that the percentage of dead bodies

found in poorer New Orleans and St. Bernard Parish neighborhoods—as measured by poverty rates and median household incomes—was roughly equivalent to their percentage in the overall population" (114, 115).

4. Character

1. Holling, "Resilience and Stability of Ecological Systems," 16.

2. In their comprehensive genealogy of the concept of resilience, Jeremy Walker and Melinda Cooper trace its first appearance in U.S. national security policy discourse to the aftermath of the oil crisis of the 1970s, in a proposal for a decentralized energy grid. They show how the concept began to cohere and become institutionalized in the 1990s through the development of critical infrastructure protection as a major area of concern for national security. After 9/11 and the creation of DHS, the concept of resilience became part of the conceptual foundation of preparedness, a development they map by comparing the 2002 *National Strategy for Homeland Security* to the 2007 *National Strategy for Homeland Security.* See Walker and Cooper, "Geneaologies of Resilience."

3. White House, "International Strategy for Cyberspace," 3; U.S. Department of Homeland Security, "NIPP 2013," 1.

4. U.S. Department of Homeland Security, "National Preparedness Goal," 1.

5. U.S. Department of Homeland Security, "Our Mission."

6. U.S. Department of Homeland Security, "Resilience."

7. As this book goes to press in early 2021, the page that originally included these quotes, which listed individual and community preparedness programs sponsored by DHS, is no longer accessible. See U.S. Department of Homeland Security, "Individual and Community Preparedness Awards," for a description of these awards.

8. E.g., "As we have seen in tragic incidents both at home and abroad, anyone can contribute to safeguarding the Nation from harm. Our national resilience can be improved, for example, by raising awareness of the techniques that can save lives through such basic actions as stopping life-threatening bleeding." U.S. Department of Homeland Security, "National Preparedness Goal," 2. Deepa Kumar describes the emphasis on resilience within national security contexts as a form of "emotion management" and emphasizes how the Obama administration focused on resilience as a way to signal a more liberal approach to the war on terror than the Bush administration. See Kumar, "See Something, Say Something," 153.

9. Joseph, "Resilience as Embedded Neoliberalism," 40.

10. Walker and Cooper, "Geneaologies of Resilience," 154.

11. O'Malley, "Resilient Subjects," 505; Grove, "On Resilience Politics," 6.

12. As Walker and Cooper put it, "resilience risks becoming the measure of one's fitness to survive in the turbulent order of things." See Walker and Cooper, "Genealogies of Resilience," 156.

13. For more on the resilient subject in security studies discourse, see Aranda et al., "Resilient Subject," and Evans and Reid, "Dangerously Exposed."

14. Glover, "Flesh Like One's Own," 255. Repugnance, or the act of recoiling from something in disgust, is an obsolete figurative meaning of *resilience*. See *Oxford English Dictionary Online (OED)*, s.v. "resilience."

15. Puar, *Terrorist Assemblages*, 35.

16. Foucault, *Will to Knowledge*, 137.

17. Mbebme, "Necropolitics," 27.

18. Mbebme, "Necropolitics," 40. As Glover puts it, "in the end, resilience can only mean a capacity for suffering combined with a refusal to lie down, to stay down, and to die." Glover, "Flesh Like One's Own," 255.

19. Glover, "Flesh Like One's Own," 237. Gerry Canavan and Jessica Hurley have also discussed these connections between the zombie, bio- and necropolitics, and Blackness. See Canavan, "We Are the Walking Dead," and Hurley, "History Is What Bites."

20. Many have argued the horizon of possibility for Black studies as a discipline and one of its greatest contributions has been its assumption of and insistence on the humanity of Black people despite a history and an everyday reality that positions Black people as objects. As a starting point, see Spillers, "Mama's Baby, Papa's Maybe," and Spillers, "Crisis of the Negro Intellectual"; Hartman, *Scenes of Subjection*, esp. her discussion of the humanity of the enslaved in the introduction; the genealogies Fred Moten traces in *In the Break*, 1n1; Denise Ferreira da Silva's discussion of violence and the excess of The Thing in "To Be Announced"; Weheliye, *Habeas Viscus*, esp. chapter 1, "Blackness: The Human"; Sharpe, "Black Studies."

21. Miller, *Ariadne's Thread*, 48.

22. In his extended close reading of the *OED* entry for "character," Miller emphasizes that the term refers to a written mark as well as to a person or person-like entity in a work of fiction. Focusing on the word's etymological connections to the Greek verb *charassein*, meaning "to make sharp" or "to engrave," and on its historical connections in English to writing, engraving, and symbology in general, Miller reminds us that to characterize means to make a mark and to make a representation of something else, two meanings that are overlapping, though not coterminous. All characters, fictional and symbological, are both specific and general. See Miller, *Ariadne's Thread*, 55–60. For more on the etymology of *character*, see Ahmed, "Willful Parts."

23. In this conception of character, I am following from Aaron Kunin's conception of character in his article "Characters Lounge." Kunin develops his approach to character transhistorically through readings of a wide range of materials, including Shakespeare, Dickens, and a contemporary comic book. He differentiates his formalist conception of character—he describes a character as "a formal device that collects every example of a kind of person" (291)—from Deidre Shauna Lynch's idea of the "economy" of

character and Alex Woloch's influential theory of "character-space." While other models of character generally encourage readers to see characters as individual people, Kunin's argument emphasizes that we can also understand character typologically. See also Lynch, *Economy of Character*, and Woloch, *The One vs. the Many*.

24. As Mbembe reminds us via Elias Canetti, "the survivor is the one who has taken on a whole pack of enemies and managed not only to escape alive, but to kill his or her attackers. This is why, to a large extent, the lowest form of survival is killing." See Mbembe, "Necropolitics," 36.

25. As I will discuss in the last section of this chapter, Lorde's poem performs what Christina Sharpe has called "wake work." See Sharpe, *In the Wake*.

26. Lorde, "A Litany for Survival."

27. American College of Emergency Physicians, "Disaster Hero"; U.S. Department of Homeland Security, "Disaster Master." The Ready.gov Be a Hero! campaign also included materials aimed at adults, such as the *Hero* ad, designed for airing on ESPN. See U.S. Department of Homeland Security, "Ready.Gov ESPN 'Hero.'"

28. Quotes are from the *Disaster Hero* home page; see American College of Emergency Physicians, "Disaster Hero."

29. U.S. Department of Homeland Security, "Be a Hero! Youth Emergency Preparedness, Grades 9–12," 2.

30. U.S. Department of Homeland Security. The full quote from the booklet reads as follows: "By the final lesson, students will become 'heroes' as they develop their own emergency preparedness campaign project."

31. U.S. Department of Homeland Security, "Disaster Master."

32. There are at least two ways of understanding the genre of these games from a games studies perspective. First, as examples of what Ian Bogost has called "persuasive games," *Disaster Hero* and *Disaster Master* are designed to "mount meaningful procedural rhetorics"—meaning they are designed to persuade their players of something (in this case, that preparedness is important and that the games can teach the player how to properly prepare for a disaster). See Bogost, *Persuasive Games*, 57. Bogost uses the term *persuasive games* to both expand on and depart from the earlier term *serious games*, which describes games designed for use in education, government, and industry. For more on serious games, see Abt, *Serious Games*, and Sawyer, "Serious Games." Second, we can also understand these games as offshoots of the lineage of war games, a genre that calls our attention to the long-running and mutually beneficial partnership between the gaming industry and the military. For more on this relationship, see Dyer-Witheford and de Peuter, *Games of Empire*, and Crogan, *Gameplay Mode*.

33. Frow, *Character and Person*, 13.

34. Douglass, "Enlightening Interactive Fiction," 135. For more on the "player character" in interactive fiction, which is similar to but not exactly identical with the "you" addressed in *Disaster Master*, see Montfort,

"Fretting the Player Character." Inversely, literary critics have long emphasized how apostrophe, in addressing an absent or voiceless entity, is a rhetorical trope that creates its own fictional addressee. As Barbara Johnson puts it, "apostrophe is thus both direct and indirect: based etymologically on the notion of turning aside, of digressing from straight speech, it manipulates the I/thou structure of direct address in an indirect, fictionalized way." See Johnson, "Apostrophe, Animation, and Abortion," 30. If we understand the mode of address *Disaster Master* employs as apostrophe—instead of viewing the player's "you" as a "character" in the game—we can see how the game doesn't so much draw the player into the fictional world of the text as it creates an ideal, fictionalized player for itself.

35. American College of Emergency Physicians, "Disaster Hero."

36. U.S. Department of Homeland Security, "Disaster Master."

37. Perlin, "Can There Be a Form between a Game and a Story?," 15; Ryan, "Will New Media Produce New Narratives?," 348.

38. John Frow has suggested that if something like "identification" with a character does happen in games, it happens not at the level of the characters' personalities but rather at the level of the "process of the game," a kind of "internalization of the logic of the program." This is an internalization that, he argues, the player can usually only achieve by controlling a character or avatar. See Frow, *Character and Person*, 48.

39. Juul, *Art of Failure*, 9.

40. Phillips names the complicated tension between death and pleasure in video games—or how games use player death to motivate players and to keep them interested and entertained—*mechropolitics*. As Phillips writes, "mechropolitics makes death fun, not merely as a visual spectacle but as a cooperative activity performed with a machine and encouraged by the mechanics of game and system design." Phillips, "Shooting to Kill," 4.

41. Berlant, *Cruel Optimism*, 97.

42. Office of the Press Secretary, "President Remembers 9/11 Heroes."

43. Office of the Press Secretary, "President's Remarks to the Nation."

44. For a full transcript of the speech, see Goodman, "Full Text September 11, 2011." For a video of the speech, see Curtis, "President Obama at Kennedy Center."

45. See Abramson, "Donald Trump Honors 9/11 Victims," for a full transcript of the speech.

46. Office of the Press Secretary, "President Remembers 9/11 Heroes."

47. Goodman, "Full Text September 11, 2011."

48. Abramson, "Donald Trump Honors 9/11 Victims."

49. Frow, *Character and Person*, 16.

50. Hunter, "Reading Character," 233. Quoted in Frow, *Character and Person*, 20.

51. See Forster, *Aspects of the Novel*. Many scholars have tied the development of "round" characters, and of a particular mode of characterization that privileges psychological depth and subjectivity, to the rise of the

realist novel in the eighteenth and nineteenth centuries. For examples of this work, see Lynch, *Economy of Character*; Miller, *Ariadne's Thread*, particularly chapter 2, "Character"; Vermeule, *Why Do We Care about Literary Characters?*

52. Goodman, "Full Text September 11, 2011."

53. Office of the Press Secretary, "President Remembers 9/11 Heroes;" Abramson, "Donald Trump Honors 9/11 Victims."

54. Kunin, "Characters Lounge," 291.

55. For a similar understanding of how character works in medieval and early modern fiction, see Elizabeth Fowler's *Literary Character*. Fowler develops the concept "social person" to describe characterization in this era: "social persons are models of the person, familiar concepts of social being that attain currency through common use" (2).

56. Kunin, "Characters Lounge," 291.

57. The "final girl" trope refers to a common convention of horror films in which one character, usually a girl, survives the slaughter and is left to tell the tale. Carol Clover coined the term in her book *Men, Women, and Chain Saws*.

58. Office of the Press Secretary, "President Remembers 9/11 Heroes."

59. Goodman, "Full Text September 11, 2011"; Abramson, "Donald Trump Honors 9/11 Victims."

60. Office of the Press Secretary, "President Remembers 9/11 Heroes"; Abramson, "Donald Trump Honors 9/11 Victims."

61. Goodman, "Full Text September 11, 2011."

62. McGurl, "Zombie Renaissance."

63. Glover, "Exploiting the Undead," 107, 108.

64. These figures come from Fraustino and Ma, "CDC's Use of Social Media and Humor." This campaign is not the only example of zombie-themed preparedness material. As discussed in chapter 2, the Joint and Combined Warfighting School created CONPLAN 8888, a "counter-zombie dominance" scenario, in 2009 to teach trainees how to create disaster training scenarios. See U.S. Department of Defense, "CONPLAN 8888 Counter-Zombie Dominance." The University of Florida also made headlines in 2009 when it posted "a plan to deal with a campus zombie attack" among other disaster preparedness plans on a university website. See Crabbe, "Thank Goodness!" These zombie-focused preparedness materials were published toward the end of what Sarah Juliet Lauro has called the "era of the millennial zombie," which roughly coincided with the first decade of the twenty-first century. Lauro notes that this decade, which witnessed a sharp rise in the popularity and ubiquity of the zombie, now seems to be over. See Lauro, *Transatlantic Zombie*.

65. Silver et al., *Preparedness 101*, 3. Future references to this work are given parenthetically in the text.

66. However, as Fraustino and Ma report, while the zombie campaign was effective in generating buzz about the CDC and preparedness, it was

much less effective at encouraging people to take action to prepare for anything. See Fraustino and Ma, "CDC's Use of Social Media and Humor," 235–36.

67. And zombies are also good allegorical figures. As McGurl emphasizes, zombies "make for good allegories, their very flatness propelling us into speculation about what they might mean 'on another level." See McGurl, "Zombie Renaissance."

68. Glover, "Flesh Like One's Own," 253.

69. Glover, 254.

70. Canavan, "We Are the Walking Dead," 433.

71. Glover, "Flesh Like One's Own," 254.

72. Glover, 450.

73. Glover, 255.

74. Bergson, *Laughter*, 31. As Lauren Berlant and Sianne Ngai have pointed out, Alenka Zupančič revises Bergson by pointing out "that the *question* of what's living, what's mechanical, and who needs to know is what really haunts the comedic and makes it an uncanny scene of aesthetic, moral, and political judgment." See Berlant and Ngai, "Comedy Has Issues," 234, and Zupančič, *Odd One In*, 113–20.

75. Zupančič, *Odd One In*, 27.

76. As Bergson observes, "every comic character is a *type*," and "it is comic to fall into a ready-made category" or "to crystallise into a stock character." See Bergson, *Laughter*, 101.

77. Zupančič, *Odd One In*, 29.

78. The rash of zombie horror comedy films from the first decade or so of the twenty-first century—including *Shaun of the Dead* (2004), *Zombieland* (2009), and *Warm Bodies* (2013)—makes the comical aspect of all zombies explicit. In addition to their delight in gore, these films also use the mechanical, shambling, dim-witted nature of zombies for comedic effect. Interestingly, they also tend to individualize zombies, either by turning them into something resembling a realist character by giving them interiority and motivation *(Warm Bodies)*, or by showing living people impersonate or imitate zombies for laughs (all three). This move illustrates Zupančič's assertion that "in comedy, the abstract and the concrete have switched places at the very outset." See Zupančič, *Odd One In*, 29. What is funny about making a zombie human or a human a zombie is that the zombie becomes an abstract device that allows us to see the fundamentally mechanical nature of life itself.

79. This scene's style is also campy, a mode related to but not coterminous with comedy. As Susan Sontag asserted, "camp is the glorification of 'character,'" where we understand "character" as "a state of continual incandescence—a person being one, very intense thing." Sontag, "Notes on 'Camp,'" 285, 286. As a zombie, Mrs. Clements is being very much—and only—"herself" here; as we would expect of a zombie, there is no depth to or development of her character.

80. Ngai, *Our Aesthetic Categories*, 7, 185.

81. Discussing the role of the zombie in Haitian literature, Glover writes, "While it is certainly true that the zombie refuses the notion of the ready-made hero as some sort of whole and transcendent figure destined to lead the masses to revolution, it must also be acknowledged that the hero always remains dormant in the zombie, hence the creature's inherent ambivalence and, ultimately, its usefulness to the Haitian novel." While Glover is using the term *hero* to mean the protagonist of a story or a folk hero, her argument emphasizes that the ambivalence of the zombie—its status as both living and dead—means the zombie is never only an object of exploitation and dehumanization. The chapter's last section returns to this idea in its interest in what survival means to those who, like the zombie, survive past all expectation. See Glover, "Exploiting the Undead," 106.

82. Office of Public Health Preparedness and Response, "Zombie Preparedness."

83. Glover, "Flesh Like One's Own," 255.

84. See *OED*, s.v. "repugnance."

85. In a discussion of the appearance of the zombie in twentieth- and twenty-first-century film, Jessica Hurley shows how the visual history of zombies in film is a history of how "whiteness comes to cover over blackness." Hurley argues that this "attempt to bury the past under a surface layer of whiteness, however, always fails" and that "even in its most white suburban forms the zombie is neither fully white nor fully black but composed of the tension between the two." See Hurley, "History Is What Bites," 318. Blackface, while visually the inverse of the whitewashing Hurley describes, is also a representation of the tension between Black and white skin.

86. Lott argues that minstrelsy was based on "a dialectic of romance and repulsion," especially in connection to the "imaginary" relationships the form encouraged between white and Black(-faced) men. Lott also emphasizes the minstrel show's reliance on juvenile humor to achieve repulsion, or how "the minstrel show's 'black' body offered a terrible return to the gorging and mucus-mongering of early life." See Lott, *Love and Theft*, 90, 153. While Lott draws attention to the potential of humor to form solidarities across class and racial lines, Saidiya Hartman argues that "on the minstrel stage, the comic inversions, bawdy humor, and lampooning of class hierarchies nonetheless operated within the confines of the tolerable, particularly since this transgression of order occurred by reproducing the abject status of blackness." See Hartman, *Scenes of Subjection*, 29.

87. Moten, *In the Break*, 1.

88. Hartman, *Scenes of Subjection*, 32.

89. The zany style of the comic also contributes to its distancing effect. Sianne Ngai argues that although "zaniness always seems to revolve around our experience of a zany character," the zany also "immediately activates the spectator's desire for distance. In fact, what is most striking about zaniness is how the image of dangerously strenuous activity it projects often seems designed to block sympathy or identification as a subjective response." See Ngai, *Our Aesthetic Categories*, 9, 8.

90. Lakoff, "Preparing for the Next Emergency," 271.
91. Lorde, "A Litany for Survival."
92. Gumbs, "Speculative Poetics," 133, 141.
93. Lothian, *Old Futures*, "Breeding (Afro)Futures."
94. Berlant, *Cruel Optimism*, 169.
95. Hartman, *Wayward Lives*, 227, 228.
96. Sharpe, *In the Wake*, 18.
97. As Gumbs emphasizes, the enduring popularity of "A Litany for Survival" "is so much of the way that Audre Lorde survives into the present." See Gumbs, "Speculative Poetics," 132. Gumbs's piece focuses mainly on Lorde's poem "Prologue," whose speaker she reads as another kind of undead figure: a vampire.

5. Looking for the Plot

1. Federal Emergency Management Agency, "Mission Areas."
2. Federal Emergency Management Agency.
3. Federal Emergency Management Agency.
4. House Committee on Homeland Security, "Terror Threat Snapshot (March 2017)"; House Committee on Homeland Security, "Working with Communities to Disrupt Terrorist Plots"; U.S. Department of Homeland Security, "Preventing Terrorism"; U.S. Department of Homeland Security, "Department of Homeland Security Strategy for Countering Violent Extremism," 1. For recent examples of rhetoric about "foiling terrorist plots" from the press, see Johnson, "Feds Unseal Charges in Foiled NYC Terror Plot"; Gajanan, "3 Men Charged in Foiled ISIS Terror Plot"; and Crimesider Staff, "New Details about Christmas Terror Plot."
5. Wendy Veronica Xin suggests that this overlap is part of the nature of a plot itself. As she writes, plot is "both the structure and the content of affective desires," both "a sequence of events" and "a series of intents"—both the structure of a narrative and the intent or design behind such a structure. See Xin, "Reading for the Plotter," 95, 97.
6. House Committee on Homeland Security, "Terror Gone Viral," 3.
7. This understanding of plot is often traced back to Aristotle. He argued that a well-formed plot, which he defined as the "story of action" (or, depending on the translation, the "structure of the incidents") in a tragedy, is one in which the incidents are linked through a "probable or necessary sequence." See Aristotle, *Poetics*, 23, 27. While it is beyond the scope of this chapter to rehash the influence of Aristotelian notions of plot on modern literary criticism, it's worth pointing out that this definition of plot is what unites both formalist or structuralist accounts of plot—Propp, Frye, Todorov, Barthes, Pavel—and accounts that emphasize plot as a dynamic experience that emerges in concert with the reader, such as in James, Forster, Lukács, Crane, Ricoeur, or Brooks. In other words, many of the different ways of understanding what a plot is that modern literary critics have developed rely on the basic idea that the events of a plot are connected to

one another via probable cause and effect. The importance of probability and causality to plot also continues to inform discussions of plot in literary criticism today. Yoon Sun Lee, for example, has emphasized that "plots ask and answer questions about causality as manifested in particular sequences." See Lee, "Bad Plots and Objectivity in Maria Edgeworth," 35.

8. Brooks, *Reading for the Plot*, 23. Brooks defines plot as "a structuring operation elicited by, and made necessary by, those meanings that develop through succession and time" (12). A plot is "the dynamic shaping force of the narrative discourse"—it is what both propels a reader forward through a narrative and allows the reader to make sense of what happens along the way (13). Seymour Chatman, writing in 1978, claimed that this tendency to read a plot into disconnected events was a function of literary reading itself. Even though "modern authors claim to reject or modify the notion of strict causality" in their plots, he argued, when reading these narratives, readers nevertheless possess a "powerful tendency to connect the most divergent events." See Chatman, *Story and Discourse*, 47. Robert L. Belknap makes a similar claim when he writes that "the integrity of the work [meaning the believability of a narrative's plot] comes in part from the fact that the causes the narrator cites make sense of some aspect of the reader's extra-literary experience." See Belknap, *Plots*, 23–24.

9. Brooks, *Reading for the Plot*, 13.

10. Puar writes, "Discourses of counterterrorism . . . illuminate the production of imbricated normative patriot and terrorist corporealities that cohere against and through each other." Because of this imbrication, "the terrorist and . . . the patriot . . . are not distant, oppositional entities, but 'close cousins.'" See Puar, *Terrorist Assemblages*, xxxii, 38.

11. This structure of disavowal is related to that of the fetish, particularly as it is discussed in the work of psychoanalytic film theorists Christian Metz and Laura Mulvey. Following from Freud, Metz writes that the structure of disavowal involved in the fetish "consists in making the seen retrospectively unseen by a disavowal of the perception, and in *stopping the look*, once and for all, on an object, the fetish." In this account, the fetish object substitutes for the seen that must be made retrospectively unseen (for Freud, this is the child's perception of the mother's lack of a penis), functioning, as Mulvey puts it, as "a red flag, symptomatically signaling a site of psychic pain." But, as Mulvey also emphasizes, the structure of disavowal at the root of the fetish depends on "the ability to disavow what is known and replace it with belief and the suspension of disbelief." As I have argued in this book, preparedness materials eschew belief and the suspension of disbelief in favor of generating consent and imparting correct feeling. As we will see in this chapter, counterterrorism preparedness materials not only focus on teaching people to see (and unsee) certain objects "correctly"; they also emphasize that people should feel good about these habits of perception. See Metz, "Photography and Fetish," 86, and Mulvey, "Some Thoughts on Theories of Fetishism," 6, 7.

12. As Mimi Thi Nguyen writes, the terrorist as she is imagined by the

U.S. security state "is the inhuman other produced by the basic division of the race that underlies the premise of total war. This figure is notably a foreign or alien body, rendered . . . as a viral contagion presumably programmed to destroy." See Nguyen, *Gift of Freedom*, 163. See Puar, *Terrorist Assemblages*, for a discussion of the "racialized queerness" of the terrorist, especially the introduction, "Homonationalism and Biopolitics," and chapter 1, "The Sexuality of Terrorism." See Kumar, *Islamophobia and the Politics of Empire*, for a history of the imbrication of Islamophobia and the twin projects of European and American empire and for discussions of legalized racism and hysteria about "homegrown terrorism." And as Arun Kundnani argues, "the war on terror . . . could not be sustained without the racialized dehumanization of its Muslim victims," which is "inseparable from the longer histories of racism in the US and the UK." See Kundnani, *Muslims Are Coming!*, 10, 11.

13. Weheliye, *Habeas Viscus*, 6.

14. In this way, the materials in this chapter contribute to a consideration of, as Toby Beauchamp puts it in his study of the surveillance practices of the national security state in relation to transgender politics, "how . . . visibility works as a part of biopower to produce the very category" of, in this case, the terrorist. See Beauchamp, *Going Stealth*, 20.

15. Peirce, *Philosophical Writings of Peirce*, 108. Peirce distinguishes between icons, indexes, and symbols. Icons resemble the thing they symbolize; indexes do not resemble the objects they stand in for but rather denote them through a material or "actual" connection; and symbols are connected to their objects via processes of interpretation, custom or habit, and law. Counterterrorism preparedness training therefore seeks to teach people to regard certain "suspicious" objects as indices of terrorism "by blind compulsion," as Peirce puts it (108). Perceiving a sign as an index automatically is one of the markers of indexicality for Peirce. For an excellent discussion of how these categories can overlap in the same object, see Nguyen, "Hoodie as Sign, Screen, Expectation, and Force." For an extended discussion of the history of Peirce's thought on the icon in particular, see Ghosh, *Global Icons*, 62–68.

16. Sharpe, *In the Wake*, 15.

17. Sharpe, "Black Studies," 66.

18. Silber and Bhatt, "Radicalization in the West," 5. Future references to this work are cited parenthetically in the text.

19. Fuchs, "New York City Settles Lawsuits."

20. Muslim American Civil Liberties Coalition for Truth and Justice, "NYPD Statement of Clarification."

21. See Bjelopera, "American Jihadist Terrorism," 1; Dyer et al., "Countering Violent Islamic Extremism," 3–11; Senate Committee on Homeland Security and Governmental Affairs, "Report on Violent Islamist Extremism," esp. 4. For evidence of the continuing influence of the model on federal agencies and organizations, see National Institute of Justice, "Radicalization and Violent Extremism," and Klausen, "A Behavioral Study of

the Radicalization Trajectories." For an excellent summary of the impact of the NYPD report and others like it at the federal level, see Patel, *Rethinking Radicalization*.

22. See American Civil Liberties Union, "Raza v. City of New York" and Raza v. City of New York. For more on the NYPD model's relationship to scholarship on radicalization, its influence beyond the NYPD, and a thorough critique of its assumptions, see Kundnani, *Muslims Are Coming!*, chapter 4, "The Myth of Radicalization."

23. As the ACLU has argued, the report's repeated emphasis on the idea that "potential terrorists" are "unremarkable" provides the foundation for unwarranted surveillance of Muslims living in the United States. If "anyone" (who looks or is Muslim or like he or she might be from the Middle East), even "unremarkable" people, can be a terrorist, and if we must, as the NYPD report claims, "identify the al-Qaeda inspired threat at the point where radicalization begins," then, the report implicitly claims, unwarranted surveillance of these groups of people is justified. See Silber and Bhatt, "Radicalization in the West," and Raza v. City of New York.

24. Chatman, *Story and Discourse*, 46.

25. Volpp, "Citizen and the Terrorist," 1576. Additionally, Jasbir Puar has argued that "this disidentification is a process of sexualization as well as of racialization of religion." "At this historical juncture," Puar argues, "the invocation of the terrorist as a queer, non-national, perversely racialized other has become part of the normative script of the US war on terror." See Puar, *Terrorist Assemblages*, 38, 37.

26. Brooks, *Reading for the Plot*, 23. This retrospective way of understanding plot is not to unique to Brooks. As Yoon Sun Lee has summarized, the general tendency in literary criticism about plot has been to "place more weight on the ending than on any other part of the story, since the ending is where poetic justice is supposedly executed." See Lee, "Bad Plots and Objectivity in Maria Edgeworth," 35. Here we might also think of classic works of narrative theory and literary criticism that emphasize the importance of the ending to storytelling in general, including Propp, *Morphology of the Folktale*; Benjamin, "Storyteller"; and Kermode, *Sense of an Ending*.

27. Michael Bernstein has criticized this anticipation of retrospection— this tendency to understand narratives, whether historical or fictional, only from the perspective of the end—as what he terms *backshadowing*. Backshadowing, Berstein writes, "is a kind of retroactive foreshadowing in which the shared knowledge of the outcome of a series of events by narrator and listener is used to judge the participants in those events *as though they too should have known what was to come*." See Bernstein, *Foregone Conclusions*, 16.

28. Allen, "Threat of Islamic Radicalization to the Homeland," 9.

29. Kermode writes, "Men in the middest make considerable imaginative investments in coherent patterns which, by the provision of an end, make possible a satisfying consonance with the origins and with the middle." See Kermode, *Sense of an Ending*, 17.

30. Brooks, *Reading for the Plot*, 37.

31. Brooks, xiii.

32. Allen Kay, chairman and chief executive of Korey Kay and Partners advertising agency, supposedly came up with the slogan on September 12, 2001. See Fernandez, "A Phrase for Safety after 9/11 Goes Global."

33. See U.S. Department of Homeland Security, "Campaign Materials." DHS launched the campaign in conjunction with the U.S. Department of Justice's Nationwide Suspicious Activity Reporting Initiative (NSI), which standardizes how reports about "behaviors and indicators of terrorism and terrorism-related crime" are documented, analyzed, and shared with federal agencies. The idea behind the shared launch, as DHS puts it, was to "[train] state and local law enforcement to recognize" and properly report such behaviors. See U.S. Department of Homeland Security, "About the Campaign." Figure 21 is taken from the "If You See Something, Say Something" campaign overview booklet. See U.S. Department of Homeland Security, "If You See Something, Say Something Campaign Overview."

34. Fulana, "If You Fear Something."

35. ACLU of Northern CA, "Gill v. DOJ (Challenge to Federal Suspicious Activity Reporting)."

36. Kumar, "See Something, Say Something," 155.

37. Andrejevic, "Work of Watching One Another," 488. For work specifically about "If You See Something, Say Something" that builds on Andrejevic's concept of lateral surveillance, see Hay, "Many Responsibilities of the New Citizen-Soldier"; Chan, "New Lateral Surveillance and a Culture of Suspicion"; Reeves, "If You See Something, Say Something."

38. Hall, "Of Ziploc Bags and Black Holes," 320. Hall uses examples from airport security to develop the concept of the aesthetics of transparency, including body scanners, security checkpoints, and the insistence on storing liquids in a transparent Ziploc bag.

39. Parks, "Points of Departure," 186. Also quoted in Browne, *Dark Matters*, 158. See Browne for more on the politics of visibility and vision at the airport. She argues that discrimination at the airport can be thought of as "'racial baggage,' where certain acts and certain looks at the airport weigh down some travelers, while others travel lightly" (132).

40. See U.S. Department of Homeland Security, "Take the Challenge."

41. The phrase "hermeneutics of suspicion" is Paul Ricoeur's, who used it to describe the critical attitudes and methods of Marx, Nietzsche, and Freud. See Ricoeur, *Freud and Philosophy*. For more on Ricoeur's hermeneutics of suspicion, see Sedgwick, "Paranoid Reading and Reparative Reading."

42. As Sedgwick writes, paranoid reading is "inescapably narrative"; it is a way of knowing that "acts as though its work would be accomplished if only it could finally, this time, somehow get its story truly known." See Sedgwick, "Paranoid Reading and Reparative Reading," 17.

43. As of this writing, this video is available for viewing on YouTube. See U.S. Department of Homeland Security, "'If You See Something, Say Something (TM)' Public Awareness Video."

44. Sedgwick writes, "Because there must be no bad surprises, and because to learn of the possibility of a bad surprise would itself constitute a bad surprise, paranoia requires that bad news be always already known." See Sedgwick, "Paranoid Reading and Reparative Reading," 10.

45. Ahmed, *On Being Included*, 143.

46. Kumar, "See Something, Say Something," 161.

47. U.S. Department of Homeland Security, "'If You See Something, Say Something (TM)' Public Awareness Video."

48. Kumar has also discussed the role of people of color in this video; see Kumar, "National Security Culture."

49. Ahmed, *On Being Included*, 147.

50. Nguyen, "Hoodie as Sign, Screen, Expectation, and Force," 799, 796.

51. Lindsey defines Black violability as "a construct that attempts to encapsulate both the lived and historical experiences of Black people with state-initiated and state-sanctioned violence." See Lindsey, "Let Me Blow Your Mind," 66, and Lindsey, "Post-Ferguson," 234.

52. Kumar, "See Something, Say Something," 161.

53. Browne, *Dark Matters*, 16.

54. To watch versions of the videos, see U.S. Department of Homeland Security, "Protect Your Every Day Public Service Announcement."

55. Sedgwick is building on Melanie Klein's ideas about the paranoid position, which Sedgwick describes as "a position of terrible alertness to the dangers posed by the hateful and envious part-objects that one defensively projects onto, carves out of, and ingests from the world around one." Sedgwick, "Paranoid Reading and Reparative Reading," 8.

56. For more about the campaign, see Rogers, "Think Again, Turn Away."

57. Katz, "Think Again Turn Away."

58. Knibbs, "State Department Tried to Fight ISIS."

59. Miller, "Panel Casts Doubt."

60. For a snapshot of the "Think Again Turn Away" Twitter account from October 9, 2014, see "Think AgainTurn Away (@ThinkAgain_DOS)."

61. The video is now archived at vlogger, *Welcome to the Islamic State Land*.

62. For more about the video, see Miller and Higham, "In a Propaganda War against ISIS."

63. Volpp, "Citizen and the Terrorist," 1576.

64. Baron, *Archive Effect*, 7, 9.

65. Masco, *Theater of Operations*, 31, 33.

66. hooks, "Representations of Whiteness in the Black Imagination," 44, 45.

67. Henry, "A Review of *Get Out*," 334. As many commentators on the film have noted, *Get Out* is a rare example of what Robin R. Means Coleman terms "Black horror," or films that "have an added narrative focus that calls attention to racial identity, in this case Blackness—Black culture, history, ideologies, experiences, politics, language, humor, aesthetics, style, music, and the like." See Coleman, *Horror Noire*, 7. For more on Black film

and Black horror, see Sobande, "Dissecting Depictions of Black Masculinity in *Get Out*," and Due, "*Get Out* and the Black Horror Aesthetic."

68. See, e.g., Cruz, "In *Get Out*, the Eyes Have It"; Brody, "*Get Out*"; Landsberg, "Horror Vérité."

69. hooks, "Oppositional Gaze," 116, 115. In this essay, hooks is responding to Manthia Diawara's influential formulation of Black spectatorship, which he calls a "resisting spectatorship." hooks's larger argument is that Diawara's formulation is implicitly male and that Black female spectatorship is different from Black male spectatorship. She argues that Black female spectatorship constitutes an "oppositional gaze." For more on Black spectatorship, see Diawara, "Black Spectatorship," and Diawara, "Black British Cinema."

70. I am grateful to an anonymous reviewer for this insight.

71. Quoted in Due, "*Get Out* and the Black Horror Aesthetic," 8; quoted in Zinoman, "Jordan Peele on a Truly Terrifying Monster."

72. Cruz, "In *Get Out*, the Eyes Have It." For Simone Browne, "dark sousveillance" refers not only to practices of "observing those in authority (the slave patroller or the plantation overseer, for instance) but also to the use of a keen and experiential insight of plantation surveillance in order to resist it." See Browne, *Dark Matters*, 22.

73. Yamato, "Jordan Peele on 'Get Out.'"

74. Brody, "*Get Out*."

75. Susan Smith terms this form of suspense, which is felt on behalf of a character, *vicarious suspense*. See Smith, *Hitchcock*, 18–20. In his book on the films of Alfred Hitchcock, Richard Allen emphasizes this form of suspense as something that both horror and thrillers have in common. In both genres, "the nature of the mysterious situation is one that does engender concern about the future on the part of the audience in the form of the anxious anticipation that characterizes suspense. . . . Characteristically, as in the horror film, the mystery is not merely something that we are curious to resolve, but it contains something threatening. We want to find out the source of the mystery, in order to confront our fears, but we also fear the outcome, and hence we may also wish not to have the secret revealed." See Allen, *Hitchcock's Romantic Irony*, 43. For other influential treatments of the role of suspense in film, see Carroll, "Toward a Theory of Film Suspense," and Carroll, "Paradox of Suspense."

76. Elizabeth A. Patton argues that this dread is symbolized in the film through the depiction of the sunken place, or the place Chris goes when Missy hypnotizes him. Patton writes that "the sunken place acts as a space of containment where Chris is forced to view his life through a screen." See Patton, "*Get Out* and the Legacy of Sundown Suburbs in Post-Racial America," 360. In this formulation, if Chris goes to the sunken place, he will become a spectator of his own life, able to see what's happening but unable to do anything. He will become like a viewer of horror movies.

77. Simone Browne has identified the Black female TSA worker, or the

"Black and sassy TSA agent," as "common archetype" in contemporary U.S. culture and cataloged her appearance in a wide variety of media from the past twenty years. Browne emphasizes that while this figure "may be a signifier of state power, that power is merely perceived," because Black women in general are "not able to access the very thing that [the Black female TSA agent] is tasked with protecting . . . 'freedom of movement.'" See Browne, *Dark Matters*, 147, 150, 151. Rod, as a Black male character, is a riff on this stereotype. While he is funny, and his warnings are perceived by others in the film as ridiculous, he is also the only person who correctly understands why the Armitages are dangerous. What's more, again, unlike the characters Browne discusses, we never see Rod at work in the film; the work he performs is for the benefit of his friend, not the national security state. As a man, Rod has enough freedom of movement to leave his job, steal a car from the airport, and rescue Chris.

78. Chitwood, "'Get Out' Filmmakers Explain Why They Changed the Ending."

79. Desta, "Jordan Peele's Get Out Almost Had an Impossibly Bleak Ending."

80. Producer Sean McKittrick's stated reasoning about why audiences disliked the original ending suggests another reading of the theatrical release's ending, however. For McKittrick, the original ending was troubling to audiences because "we weren't in the Obama era" anymore. After the 2016 presidential election, McKittrick explains, "we were in this new world where all the racism crept out from under the rocks again," and audiences didn't want to see that reflected onscreen. See Chitwood, "'Get Out' Filmmakers Explain Why They Changed the Ending." In this way, we can also read Rod's rescue of Chris as symptomatic of a longing for institutional authority and validity—for a return to a (mythic) time when TSA agents, and the national security state they represent, were the "good guys" acting in the country's best interests. I am grateful to Gerry Canavan for this insight.

Epilogue

1. On the relationship of fiction to citizenship, see, e.g., Nussbaum, *Cultivating Humanity*, and Nussbaum, *Not for Profit*. On cognitive and neuroscience and fiction, see Zunshine, *Why We Read Fiction*, and Paul, "Neuroscience of Your Brain on Fiction." On the value of reading fiction more generally, see Felski, *Uses of Literature*, and Landy, *How to Do Things with Fictions*.

2. Koenigs, "Fictionality Risen."

3. Stop Urban Shield Coalition, "Urban Shield," 2. For more on Stop Urban Shield, see Stop Urban Shield, "Stop Urban Shield"; Stop Urban Shield, "Our Fight"; and Solomon, "The Five-Year Fight to Shut Down 'War Games Training' in the Bay Area."

4. See Stop Urban Shield, "Stop Urban Shield PowerPoint," for more details about these statistics. For more information about the disproportionate effects of SWAT team actions on people of color in the Bay Area, see Critical Resistance for Stop Urban Shield Coalition, "People First!"

5. Khazan, "In One Year."

6. Stop Urban Shield, "Infographic."

7. Stop Urban Shield, "We Put an End to Urban Shield!" For more on these events, see Stop Urban Shield, "Timeline."

8. See Stop Urban Shield, "We Defended Our Victory Against Urban Shield!," and Hegarty, "Alameda County Leaders Support New Direction for Urban Shield."

9. See Hegarty, "Alameda County Loses Federal Money for Urban Shield." As of this writing, although the Urban Shield website exists, it is mainly a placeholder page. It contains no information about the expo, and the expo's social media accounts appear to be inactive. See Urban Shield, "Urban Shield."

10. See Stop Urban Shield, "Letters to the Alameda County Board of Supervisors."

11. These quotes are from the letter of support from UAW Local 2865, but all of the letters of support include some version of this language.

12. See City of Oakland, "Handling Emergencies," and City of Oakland, "Learn, Lead, Lift Train the Trainer Workshop."

13. *The L.A. Earthquake Sourcebook*, discussed in chapter 1, is an example of preparedness material produced by a nonprofit entity (the ArtCenter College of Design) with some funding from the federal government. Likewise, Oakland's Learn, Lead, Lift program, which has organized emergency kit–making workshops, is an example of a locally run organization that has been funded by federal grants. In 2014–15, for example, its activities were supported by the Urban Area Security Initiative (UASI) grant, funded by DHS. This is the same federal initiative that funded Urban Shield. For more information about Learn, Lead, Lift, see City of Oakland, "Welcome to Learn Lead Lift Project."

14. As of this writing, this video is available on YouTube. See SF DEM, "Prepare to Prosper (with Audio Description)."

15. Bernstein Crisis Management, "CARD."

16. I am referring not only to what I have spent the majority of this book doing but also, somewhat obliquely, to debates in literary studies over the past ten to fifteen years about the value and use of critique and to related debates about the "anti-hermeneutic turn" more broadly. On the limits of critique, see Latour, "Why Has Critique Run out of Steam?," and Felski, *The Limits of Critique*. The phrase "anti-hermeneutic turn" is Julie Orlemanski's; see Orlemanski, "Scales of Reading," for a comprehensive discussion of so-called post-critical approaches ranging from surface reading to the descriptive turn.

17. Imarisha, "Introduction," 3.

Bibliography

Abramson, Alana. "Donald Trump Honors 9/11 Victims for First Time as President." *Time*, September 2017. https://web.archive.org/web/20191231181545/https://time.com/4935852/president-trump-9-11-september-speech-transcript-memorial/.

Abt, Clark C. *Serious Games*. New York: Viking, 1970.

ACLU of Northern CA. "Gill v. DOJ (Challenge to Federal Suspicious Activity Reporting)." December 8, 2016. https://web.archive.org/web/20191231181906/https://www.aclunc.org/our-work/legal-docket/gill-v-doj-challenge-federal-suspicious-activity-reporting.

Adey, Peter, Ben Anderson, and Stephen Graham. "Governing Emergencies: Beyond Exceptionality." *Theory, Culture, and Society* 32, no. 3 (2015): 3–17. https://doi.org/10.1177/0263276414565719.

Agamben, Giorgio. *State of Exception*. Translated by Kevin Attell. Chicago: University of Chicago Press, 2005.

Ahmed, Sara. *On Being Included: Racism and Diversity in Institutional Life.* Durham, N.C.: Duke University Press, 2012.

Ahmed, Sara. *What's the Use? On the Uses of Use*. Durham, N.C.: Duke University Press, 2019.

Ahmed, Sara. "Willful Parts: Problem Characters or the Problem of Character." *New Literary History* 42, no. 2 (2011): 231–53. https://doi.org/10.1353/nlh.2011.0019.

Ahmed, Sara. *Willful Subjects*. Durham, N.C.: Duke University Press, 2014.

Alexander, David. *Principles of Emergency Planning and Management*. Edinburgh: Terra, 2002.

Allen, Charles E. "Threat of Islamic Radicalization to the Homeland." Senate Committee on Homeland Security and Governmental Affairs, March 2007.

Allen, Richard. *Hitchcock's Romantic Irony*. New York: Columbia University Press, 2007.

Alliston, April. "Female Quixotism and the Novel: Character and Plausibility, Honesty and Fidelity." *The Eighteenth Century* 52, no. 3 (2011): 249–69. https://doi.org/10.1353/ecy.2011.0021.

American Civil Liberties Union. "Raza v. City of New York—Legal Challenge to NYPD Muslim Surveillance Program." August 3, 2017. https://

web.archive.org/web/20191231190337/https://www.aclu.org/cases/
  raza-v-city-new-york-legal-challenge-nypd-muslim-surveillance
  -program.
American College of Emergency Physicians. "Disaster Hero." 2013. https://
  web.archive.org/web/20191231181428/http://www.disasterhero.com/.
Amoore, Louise. *The Politics of Possibility: Risk and Security beyond Proba-*
  bility. Durham, N.C.: Duke University Press, 2013.
Amoore, Louise, and Rita Raley. "Securing with Algorithms: Knowledge,
  Decision, Sovereignty." *Security Dialogue* 48, no. 1 (February 1, 2017):
  3–10. https://doi.org/10.1177/0967010616680753.
Anderson, Ben. "Preemption, Precaution, Preparedness: Anticipatory
  Action and Future Geographies." *Progress in Human Geography* 34, no. 6
  (2010): 777–98. https://doi.org/10.1177/0309132510362600.
Anderson, Ben. "Security and the Future: Anticipating the Event of Terror." *Geoforum* 41, no. 2 (2010): 227–35. https://doi.org/10.1016/j
  .geoforum.2009.11.002.
Anderson, Ben, and Peter Adey. "Affect and Security: Exercising Emergency in 'UK Civil Contingencies.'" *Environment and Planning D:*
  Society and Space 29, no. 6 (2011): 1092–1109. https://doi.org/10.1068/
  d14110.
Andrejevic, Mark. "The Work of Watching One Another: Lateral Surveillance, Risk, and Governance." *Surveillance and Society* 2, no. 4 (2004).
  https://doi.org/10.24908/ss.v2i4.3359.
Andrews, Arlan. "Science Fiction in the National Interest." Interview by
  Brooke Gladstone. *On the Media*, June 28, 2007. Podcast. https://www
  .wnyc.org/story/129496-science-fiction-in-the-national-interest/?tab
  =transcript.
Aradau, Claudia, and Rens van Munster. *Politics of Catastrophe: Geneaolo-*
  gies of the Unknown. London: Routledge, 2011.
Aranda, Kay, Laetitia Zeeman, Julie Scholes, and Arantxa Santa-María
  Morales. "The Resilient Subject: Exploring Subjectivity, Identity and
  the Body in Narratives of Resilience." *Health* 16, no. 5 (2012): 548–63.
  https://doi.org/10.1177/1363459312438564.
Aristotle. *Poetics.* Translated by Anthony Kenny. Oxford: Oxford University Press, 2013. Kindle.
Association of State and Territorial Health Officials. "Guide to Preparedness Evaluation Using Drills and Table Top Exercises." https://pdf4pro
  .com/view/guide-to-preparedness-evaluation-using-drills-and-2304cf
  .html.
Bahng, Aimee. *Migrant Futures: Decolonizing Speculation in Financial*
  Times. Durham, N.C.: Duke University Press, 2018.
Ballard, J. G. "Introduction to the French Edition of *Crash*." In *Crash*, 5–9.
  1974. Reprint, London: Triad/Panther, 1985.
Baron, Jaimie. *The Archive Effect: Found Footage and the Audiovisual Expe-*
  rience of History. New York: Routledge, 2013.
Barthes, Roland. "The Reality Effect." In *French Literary Theory Today: A*

Reader, edited by Tzvetan Todorov, translated by R. Carter, 11–17. Cambridge: Cambridge University Press, 1982.

Baudrillard, Jean. *Simulacra and Simulation*. Translated by Sheila Faria Glaser. Ann Arbor: University of Michigan Press, 1994.

Beauchamp, Toby. *Going Stealth: Transgender Politics and U.S. Surveillance Practices*. Durham, N.C.: Duke University Press, 2019.

Belknap, Robert L. *Plots*. New York: Columbia University Press, 2016.

Belletto, Steven. *No Accident, Comrade: Chance and Design in Cold War American Narratives*. Oxford: Oxford University Press, 2012.

Benjamin, Walter. "The Storyteller: Reflections on the Works of Nikolai Leskov." In *Illuminations*, edited by Hannah Arendt, translated by Harry Zohn, 83–109. 1936. Reprint, New York: Schocken Books, 1969.

Benjamin, Walter. "The Work of Art in the Age of Its Technological Reproducibility." In *"The Work of Art in the Age of Its Technological Reproducibility," and Other Writings on Media*, edited by Michael W. Jennings, Brigid Doherty, and Thomas Y. Levin, translated by Edmund Jephcott, Rodney Livingstone, Howard Eiland et al., 19–55. Cambridge, Mass.: Harvard University Press, 2008.

Bergen, Peter. "Americans Are Going to Demand to Know Why US Wasn't Prepared for This Pandemic." CNN, March 19, 2020. https://www.cnn.com/2020/03/19/opinions/coronavirus-commission-investigation-opinion-bergen/index.html.

Bergson, Henri. *Laughter: An Essay on the Meaning of the Comic*. Translated by Cloudesley Brereton and Fred Rothwell. 1911. Reprint, New York: Dover, 2005.

Berlant, Lauren. *The Anatomy of National Fantasy: Hawthorne, Utopia, and Everyday Life*. Chicago: University of Chicago Press, 1991.

Berlant, Lauren. *Cruel Optimism*. Durham, N.C.: Duke University Press, 2011.

Berlant, Lauren. *The Female Complaint: The Unfinished Business of Sentimentality in American Culture*. Durham, N.C.: Duke University Press, 2008.

Berlant, Lauren. "Thinking about Feeling Historical." *Emotion, Space, and Society* 1 (2008): 4–9.

Berlant, Lauren, and Sianne Ngai. "Comedy Has Issues." *Critical Inquiry* 43, no. 2 (2016): 233–49. https://doi.org/10.1086/689666.

Berlin, Johan M., and Eric D. Carlström. "The Three-Level Collaboration Exercise—Impact of Learning and Usefulness." *Journal of Contingencies and Crisis Management* 23, no. 4 (2015): 257–65. https://doi.org/10.1111/1468-5973.12070.

Bernstein, Michael André. *Foregone Conclusions: Against Apocalyptic History*. Berkeley: University of California Press, 1994.

Bernstein Crisis Management. "CARD—A New Angle on Disaster Preparedness." Bernstein Crisis Management, August 2, 2012. https://web.archive.org/web/20191231192554/https://www.bernsteincrisismanagement.com/card-a-new-angle-disaster-preparedness/.

Bjelopera, Jerome P. "American Jihadist Terrorism: Combating a Complex Threat." Congressional Research Service, January 2013. https://web.archive.org/web/20191231200605/https://fas.org/sgp/crs/terror/R41416.pdf.

Blanchfield, Patrick. "The Market Can't Solve a Massacre." *Splinter*, March 14, 2018. https://splinternews.com/the-market-cant-solve-a-massacre-1823745509.

Bledstein, Burton J. *The Culture of Professionalism: The Middle Class and the Development of Higher Education in America*. New York: W. W. Norton, 1978.

Bogost, Ian. *Persuasive Games: The Expressive Power of Videogames*. Cambridge, Mass.: MIT Press, 2007.

Bonilla-Silva, Eduardo. *White Supremacy and Racism in the Post–Civil Rights Era*. Boulder, Colo.: Lynne Rienner, 2001.

Bourdieu, Pierre. *The Logic of Practice*. Translated by Richard Nice. Stanford, Calif.: Stanford University Press, 1990.

Bourdieu, Pierre. *Sociology in Question*. Translated by Richard Nice. London: Sage, 1993.

Box, George E. P. "Robustness in the Strategy of Scientific Model Building." In *Robustness in Statistics*, edited by R. L. Launer and G. N. Wilkinson, 201–36. New York: Academic Press, 1976.

Brody, Richard. "'Get Out': Jordan Peele's Radical Cinematic Vision of the World through a Black Man's Eyes." *New Yorker*, March 2, 2017. https://www.newyorker.com/culture/richard-brody/get-out-jordan-peeles-radical-cinematic-vision-of-the-world-through-black-eyes.

Brooks, Peter. *Reading for the Plot: Design and Intention in Narrative*. Cambridge, Mass.: Harvard University Press, 1984.

Browne, Simone. *Dark Matters: On the Surveillance of Blackness*. Durham, N.C.: Duke University Press, 2015.

Bush, George. "Commencement Address at the United States Military Academy at West Point," June 2002. https://web.archive.org/web/20171205023711/http://www.presidentialrhetoric.com/speeches/06.01.02.html.

Camus, Albert. *The Myth of Sisyphus, and Other Essays*. Translated by Justin O'Brien. 1942. Reprint, New York: Vintage International, 1992.

Canavan, Gerry. "'We Are the Walking Dead': Race, Time, and Survival in Zombie Narrative." *Extrapolation* 51, no. 3 (2010): 431–53. https://doi.org/10.3828/extr.2010.51.3.7.

Canavan, Gerry, and Kim Stanley Robinson. "Still, I'm Reluctant to Call This Pessimism." In *Green Planets: Ecology and Science Fiction*, 243–60. Middletown, Conn.: Wesleyan University Press, 2014.

Carroll, Noël. "The Paradox of Suspense." In *Suspense: Conceptualizations, Theoretical Analyses, and Empirical Explorations*, edited by Peter Vorderer, Hans Jürgen Wulff, and Mike Friedrichsen, 1st ed., 71–92. New York: Routledge, 1996.

Carroll, Noël. "Toward a Theory of Film Suspense." In *Theorizing the Moving Image*, 94–117. Cambridge: Cambridge University Press, 1996.

Cazdyn, Eric. *The Already Dead: The New Time of Politics, Culture, and Illness.* Durham, N.C.: Duke University Press, 2012.

Chan, Janet. "The New Lateral Surveillance and a Culture of Suspicion." In *Surveillance and Governance: Crime Control and Beyond*, edited by Mathieu Deflem, 223–29. Bingley, U.K.: JAI Press, 2008.

Chatman, Seymour Benjamin. *Story and Discourse: Narrative Structure in Fiction and Film.* Ithaca, N.Y.: Cornell University Press, 1978.

Chitwood, Adam. "'Get Out' Filmmakers Explain Why They Changed the Ending." *Collider*, February 2018. https://collider.com/get-out -alternate-ending-explained/.

Chow, Rey. *The Protestant Ethnic and the Spirit of Capitalism.* New York: Columbia University Press, 2002.

Chu, Seo-Young. *Do Metaphors Dream of Literal Sleep? A Science-Fictional Theory of Representation.* Cambridge, Mass.: Harvard University Press, 2010.

Chute, Hillary. "Comics as Literature? Reading Graphic Narrative." *PMLA* 123, no. 2 (2008): 452–65. https://doi.org/10.1632/pmla.2008.123.2.452.

City of Oakland. "Handling Emergencies." https://web.archive.org/web/ 20191231182023/https://www.oaklandca.gov/resources/emergency -preparedness-handling-hazards-2.

City of Oakland. "Learn, Lead, Lift Train the Trainer Workshop." May 30, 2015. https://web.archive.org/web/20191231183918/https://solar .oaklandnet.com/core/Activity/Details/2686.

City of Oakland. "Welcome to Learn Lead Lift Project." http://www2 .oaklandnet.com/government/o/OFD/s/EmergencyPreparedness/ LearnLeadLift/index.htm.

Civil Defense Preparedness Agency. "Civil Preparedness—a New Dual Mission." 1972. https://web.archive.org/web/20191231193356/https:// www.hsdl.org/?view&did=34735.

Clarke, Lee. *Mission Improbable.* Chicago: University of Chicago Press, 1999.

Clarke, Richard. *Against All Enemies: Inside America's War on Terror.* New York: Free Press, 2004.

Clarke, Richard. *Breakpoint.* New York: G. P. Putnam's Sons, 2007.

Clarke, Richard. "Clarke Urges 'Debate' on Terror Preparations." Interview with Libby Lewis. *All Things Considered*, March 27, 2004. Radio broadcast. https://www.npr.org/templates/story/story.php?storyId =1794680.

Clarke, Richard. *Pinnacle Event.* New York: St. Martin's Press, 2015.

Clarke, Richard. "Richard Clarke Writes Mideast Thriller." Interview with Steve Inskeep. *Morning Edition*, October 25, 2005. Radio broadcast. http://www.npr.org/templates/story/story.php?storyId=4973276.

Clarke, Richard. *The Scorpion's Gate.* New York: G. P. Putnam's Sons, 2005.

Clarke, Richard. *Sting of the Drone*. New York: St. Martin's Press, 2014.

Clement, Keith E. "The Essentials of Emergency Management and Homeland Security Graduate Education Programs: Design, Development, and Future." *Journal of Homeland Security and Emergency Management* 8, no. 2 (2011). https://doi.org/10.2202/1547-7355.1902.

Clover, Carol. *Men, Women, and Chain Saws: Gender in the Modern Horror Film*. Princeton, N.J.: Princeton University Press, 1992.

Cohen, Ralph. "Introduction: Notes toward a Generic Reconstitution of Literary Study." *New Literary History* 34, no. 3 (2003): v–xvi. https://doi.org/10.1353/nlh.2003.0041.

Coleman, Robin R. Means. *Horror Noire*. New York: Routledge, 2011.

Collier, Stephen J., and Andrew Lakoff. "Vital Systems Security: Reflexive Biopolitics and the Government of Emergency." *Theory, Culture, and Society* 32, no. 2 (2015): 19–51. https://doi.org/10.1177/0263276413510050.

Committee on Homeland Security and Governmental Affairs. "Preparing for a Catastrophe: The Hurricane Pam Exercise." January 2006. https://web.archive.org/web/20170420132004/http://biotech.law.lsu.edu/blaw/FEMA/CHRG-109shrg26749.pdf.

Crabbe, Nathan. "Thank Goodness! UF Has a Plan for Zombie Invasions." *Gainesville Sun*, October 2, 2009. https://www.gainesville.com/news/20091002/thank-goodness-uf-has-a-plan-for-zombie-invasions.

Crimesider Staff. "New Details about Christmas Terror Plot in San Francisco Feds Say They Foiled." *CBS News*, January 5, 2018. https://www.cbsnews.com/news/new-details-about-christmas-terror-plot-in-san-francisco-feds-say-they-foiled/.

Critical Resistance for Stop Urban Shield Coalition. "People First! An Oakland Power Projects Report on Policing and Emergencies." 2018. https://web.archive.org/web/20191231195212/http://stopurbanshield.org/wp-content/uploads/2018/03/CR-SUS-DRAFT-v3.pdf.

Crogan, Patrick. *Gameplay Mode: War, Simulation, and Technoculture*. Minneapolis: University of Minnesota Press, 2011.

Cruz, Lenika. "In *Get Out*, the Eyes Have It." *The Atlantic*, March 3, 2017. https://www.theatlantic.com/entertainment/archive/2017/03/in-get-out-the-eyes-have-it/518370/.

Curtis, Colleen. "President Obama at Kennedy Center: America Does Not Give In to Fear." September 11, 2011. https://obamawhitehouse.archives.gov/blog/2011/09/11/president-obama-kennedy-center-america-does-not-give-fear.

Darda, Joseph. "Graphic Ethics: Theorizing the Face in Marjane Satrapi's *Persepolis*." *College Literature* 40, no. 2 (2013): 31–51. https://doi.org/10.1353/lit.2013.0022.

Dare to Prepare. "The 7 Steps to Earthquake Safety." In *The L.A. Earthquake Sourcebook*, edited by Judith Lewis and David Ulin, 290–314. Los Angeles, Calif.: Designmatters, 2008.

da Silva, Denise Ferreira. "To Be Announced: Radical Praxis or Knowing (at) the Limits of Justice." *Social Text* 114 31, no. 1 (2014): 43–62. https://doi.org/10.3138/9781442616455-032.

Daston, Lorraine, and Peter Galison. *Objectivity*. New York: Zone Books, 2007.

Davis, Tracy. *Stages of Emergency: Cold War Nuclear Civil Defense*. Durham, N.C.: Duke University Press, 2007. Kindle.

de Goede, Marieke, and Samuel Randalls. "Precaution, Preemption: Arts and Technologies of the Actionable Future." *Environment and Planning D: Society and Space* 27, no. 5 (2009): 859–78. https://doi.org/10.1068/d2608.

Designmatters. "The Los Angeles Earthquake: Get Ready." September 29, 2008. https://web.archive.org/web/20191231191054/https://designmattersatartcenter.org/proj/the-los-angeles-earthquake-get-ready/.

Desta, Yohana. "Jordan Peele's *Get Out* Almost Had an Impossibly Bleak Ending." *Vanity Fair*, March 3, 2017. https://www.vanityfair.com/hollywood/2017/03/jordan-peele-get-out-ending.

Diawara, Manthia. "Black British Cinema: Spectatorship and Identity Formation in Territories." *Public Culture* 3, no. 1 (1990): 33–48. https://doi.org/10.1215/08992363-3-1-33.

Diawara, Manthia. "Black Spectatorship: Problems of Identification and Resistance." *Screen* 29, no. 4 (1988): 66–79. https://doi.org/10.1093/screen/29.4.66.

Dickinson, Tim. "Rolling Stone Timeline: Coronavirus in America." *Rolling Stone*, May 8, 2020. https://www.rollingstone.com/politics/politics-news/rolling-stone-timeline-coronavirus-america-982944/.

Douglass, Jeremy. "Enlightening Interactive Fiction: Andrew Plotkin's *Shade*." In *Second Person: Role-Playing and Story in Games and Playable Media*, edited by Pat Harrigan and Noah Wardrip-Fruin, 129–36. Cambridge, Mass.: MIT Press, 2010.

Drabek, Thomas E. *The Professional Emergency Manager: Structures and Strategies for Success*. Boulder, Colo.: Institute of Behavioral Science, University of Colorado, 1987.

Due, Tananarive. "*Get Out* and the Black Horror Aesthetic." In *Get Out: The Complete Annotated Screenplay*, by Jordan Peele, 6–15. Los Angeles, Calif.: Inventory Press, 2019.

Dyer, Carol, Ryan E. McCoy, Joel Rodriguez, and Donald N. Van Duyn. "Countering Violent Islamic Extremism." *FBI Law Enforcement Bulletin* 76, no. 12 (2007).

Dyer-Witheford, Nick, and Greig de Peuter. *Games of Empire: Global Capitalism and Video Games*. Minneapolis: University of Minnesota Press, 2009.

Earthquake Country Alliance. "Welcome to Earthquake Country." 2020. https://www.earthquakecountry.org/.

Edwards, Paul N. *The Closed World: Computers and the Politics of Discourse in Cold War America*. Cambridge, Mass.: MIT Press, 1996.

Emergency Management Institute. "Emergency Management: Definition,

Vision, Mission, Principles." https://training.fema.gov/hiedu/docs/emprinciples/0907_176%20em%20principles12x18v2f%20johnson%20(w-0%20draft).pdf.

Emergency Management Institute. "FY 2015 Annual Report." 2015. https://web.archive.org/web/20191231193632/https://training.fema.gov/docs/emi_annual_report-fy2015.pdf.

Evans, Brad, and Julian Reid. "Dangerously Exposed: The Life and Death of the Resilient Subject." *Resilience* 1, no. 2 (2013): 83–98. https://doi.org/10.1080/21693293.2013.770703.

Ewald, François. "The Return of Decartes's Malicious Demon: An Outline of a Philosophy of Precaution." In *Embracing Risk: The Changing Culture of Insurance and Responsibility*, edited by Tom Baker and Jonathan Simon, 273–301. Chicago: University of Chicago Press, 2002.

Federal Emergency Management Agency. "Emergency Management Institute Mission." December 2014. https://web.archive.org/web/20191231181640/https://training.fema.gov/mission.aspx.

Federal Emergency Management Agency. "IS-130.A: How to Be an Exercise Evaluator." February 2018. https://web.archive.org/web/20191231183441/https://training.fema.gov/is/courseoverview.aspx?code=IS-130.a.

Federal Emergency Management Agency. "IS-139 Exercise Design." Exercise Management Institute, 2003. http://www.iaem.com/documents/Exercise%20Design-IS-139-002.pdf.

Federal Emergency Management Agency. "IS-907: Active Shooter: How to Respond." 2015. https://web.archive.org/web/20191231194642/https://www.dhs.gov/sites/default/files/publications/active-shooter-how-to-respond-2017-508.pdf.

Federal Emergency Management Agency. "IS-907: Active Shooter: What You Can Do." December 2015. https://training.fema.gov/is/courseoverview.aspx?code=IS-907.

Federal Emergency Management Agency. "IS-907: Active Shooter: What You Can Do, Course Downloads: Visuals." 2015. https://training.fema.gov/is/courseoverview.aspx?code=IS-907.

Federal Emergency Management Agency. "IS-907: Active Shooter: What You Can Do, Instructor Guide." 2015. https://training.fema.gov/is/courseoverview.aspx?code=IS-907.

Federal Emergency Management Agency. "IS-907: Active Shooter: What You Can Do, Pocket Card." 2015. https://www.dhs.gov/sites/default/files/publications/active-shooter-pocket-card-508.pdf.

Federal Emergency Management Agency. "Maximum of Maximums Table Top Exercise (TTX) Script." 2013. https://www.fema.gov/media-library-data/20130726-1833-25045-2267/mom_ttx_video_inject_scripts_final_508.pdf.

Federal Emergency Management Agency. "Metascenario Table Top Exercise Facilitator Notes." 2013. https://www.fema.gov/media-library

-data/20130726-1833-25045-3146/mom_ttx___facilitator_notes_final_
508.pdf.

Federal Emergency Management Agency. "Mission Areas." May 2, 2018.
https://www.fema.gov/mission-areas.

Federal Emergency Management Agency. "Principles of Emergency Management Supplement." September 2007. https://www.fema.gov/media
-library-data/20130726-1822-25045-7625/principles_of_emergency
_management.pdf.

Federal Emergency Management Agency. "Risk Assessment: A How-to
Guide to Mitigate Potential Terrorist Attacks against Buildings."
January 2005. https://www.fema.gov/media-library-data/20130726
-1524-20490-7395/fema452_01_05.pdf.

Federal Emergency Management Agency. "Using Tabletop Exercises and
Drills to Reveal Training Needs." https://www.hsdl.org/?view&did
=454079.

Felski, Rita. *The Limits of Critique*. Chicago: University of Chicago Press,
2015.

Felski, Rita. *Uses of Literature*. Malden, Mass.: Blackwell, 2008.

Ferguson, Roderick A. "The Distributions of Whiteness." *American Quarterly* 66, no. 4 (2014): 1101–6. https://doi.org/10.1353/aq.2014.0064.

Fernandez, Manny. "A Phrase for Safety after 9/11 Goes Global." *New York
Times*, May 5, 2010. https://www.nytimes.com/2010/05/11/nyregion/
11slogan.html.

Flatley, Jonathan. "Reading for Mood." *Representations* 140, no. 1 (2017):
137–58. https://doi.org/10.1525/rep.2017.140.1.137.

Forster, E. M. *Aspects of the Novel*. 1929. Reprint, New York: Penguin
Books, 1974.

Foucault, Michel. *Discipline and Punish: The Birth of the Prison*. Translated
by Alan Sheridan. New York: Vintage Books, 1995.

Foucault, Michel. *The Order of Things: An Archaeology of the Human Sciences*. 1966. Reprint, New York: Routledge, 2002.

Foucault, Michel. *"Society Must Be Defended": Lectures at the Collège de
France, 1975–76*. Edited by Mauro Bertani and Alessandro Fontana.
Translated by David Macey. 1997. Reprint, New York: Picador, 2003.

Foucault, Michel. *The Use of Pleasure*, vol. 2 of *The History of Sexuality*.
Translated by Robert Hurley. New York: Vintage Books, 1990.

Foucault, Michel. *The Will to Knowledge*, vol. 1 of *The History of Sexuality*.
Translated by Robert Hurley. 1976. Reprint, New York: Vintage Books,
1990.

Fowler, Elizabeth. *Literary Character: The Human Figure in Early English
Writing*. Ithaca, N.Y.: Cornell University Press, 2003.

Franzen, Jonathan. "What If We Stopped Pretending the Climate Apocalypse Can Be Stopped?" *New Yorker*, September 8, 2019. https://www
.newyorker.com/culture/cultural-comment/what-if-we-stopped
-pretending.

Fraustino, Julia Daisy, and Liang Ma. "CDC's Use of Social Media and Humor in a Risk Campaign 'Preparedness 101: Zombie Apocalypse.'" *Journal of Applied Communication Research* 43, no. 2 (2015): 222–41. https://doi.org/10.1080/00909882.2015.1019544.

Freidson, Eliot. *Professionalism: The Third Logic.* Chicago: University of Chicago Press, 2001.

Frieden, Tom, Jeffrey Koplan, David Satcher, and Richard Besser. "We Ran the CDC. No President Ever Politicized Its Science the Way Trump Has." *Washington Post,* July 14, 2020. https://www.washingtonpost.com/outlook/2020/07/14/cdc-directors-trump-politics/.

Frigg, Roman. "Models and Fiction." *Synthese* 172, no. 2 (2010): 251–68. https://doi.org/10.1007/s11229-009-9505-0.

Frow, John. *Character and Person.* New York: Oxford University Press, 2014.

Frow, John. *Genre.* New York: Routledge, 2015.

Fuchs, Chris. "New York City Settles Lawsuits Concerning Muslim Surveillance, Will Institute Reforms." *NBC News,* January 8, 2016. https://www.nbcnews.com/news/asian-america/new-york-city-settles-lawsuits-concerning-muslim-surveillance-will-institute-n492811.

Fulana. "If You Fear Something, You'll See Something (2004)." Hemispheric Institute Special Collections, 2004. https://hemisphericinstitute.org/en/hidvl-collections/item/1240-if-you-fear-something-youll-see-something.

Gajanan, Mahita. "3 Men Charged in Foiled ISIS Terror Plot on New York City." *Time,* October 6, 2017. http://time.com/4973294/terror-plot-new-york-city-isis/.

Gallagher, Catherine. *Nobody's Story: The Vanishing Acts of Women Writers in the Marketplace, 1670–1820.* Berkeley: University of California Press, 1994.

Gallagher, Catherine. "The Rise of Fictionality." In *The Novel: Vol. 1. History, Geography, Culture,* edited by Franco Moretti, 336–63. Princeton, NJ: Princeton University Press, 2006.

Galperin, William H. *The Historical Austen.* Philadelphia: University of Pennsylvania Press, 2003.

Ghamari-Tabrizi, Sharon. *The Worlds of Herman Kahn: The Intuitive Science of Thermonuclear War.* Cambridge, Mass.: Harvard University Press, 2005.

Ghosh, Bishnupriya. *Global Icons: Apertures to the Popular.* Durham, N.C.: Duke University Press, 2011.

Glover, Kaiama L. "Exploiting the Undead: The Usefulness of the Zombie in Haitian Literature." *Journal of Haitian Studies* 11, no. 2 (2005): 105–21.

Glover, Kaiama L. "'Flesh Like One's Own': Benign Denials of Legitimate Complaint." *Public Culture* 29, no. 2 (2017): 235–60. https://doi.org/10.1215/08992363-3749045.

Goodman, Bonnie K. "Full Text September 11, 2011: President Barack

Obama's Speech at the 9-11 'A Concert for Hope' in Washington, DC."
History Musings (blog), September 11, 2011. https://web.archive.org/
web/20191231181737/https://historymusings.wordpress.com/2011/
09/11/full-text-september-11-2011-president-barack-obama-speech
-9-11-a-concert-for-hope-kennedy-center-washington/.

Graham, David A. "The Mothers of All Disasters." *Atlantic*, September 2, 2015. https://www.theatlantic.com/national/archive/2015/09/
the-disaster-next-time/403063/.

Grausam, Daniel. *On Endings: American Postmodern Fiction and the Cold War*. Charlottesville: University of Virginia Press, 2011.

Grewal, Inderpal. *Saving the Security State: Exceptional Citizens in Twenty-First Century America*. Durham, N.C.: Duke University Press, 2017.

Grove, Kevin. "On Resilience Politics: From Transformation to Subversion." *Resilience* 1, no. 2 (2013): 146–53. https://doi.org/10.1080/216932
93.2013.804661.

Grusin, Richard. *Premediation: Affect and Mediality after 9/11*. New York: Palgrave Macmillan, 2010.

Guillory, John. "The Memo and Modernity." *Critical Inquiry* 31, no. 1 (2004): 108–32. https://doi.org/10.1086/427304.

Gumbs, Alexis Pauline. "Speculative Poetics: Audre Lorde as Prologue for Queer Black Futurism." In *The Black Imagination: Science Fiction, Futurism and the Speculative*, edited by Sandra Jackson and Julie E. Moody Freeman, 130–46. New York: Peter Lang, 2011.

Hacking, Ian. *The Emergence of Probability: A Philosophical Study of Early Ideas about Probability, Induction, and Statistical Inference*. 2nd ed. New York: Cambridge University Press, 2006.

Haddow, George D., Jane A. Bullock, and Damon P. Coppola. *Introduction to Emergency Management*. 4th ed. Amsterdam: Elsevier, 2011.

Hall, Mimi. "Sci-Fi Writers Join War on Terror." *USA Today*, May 31, 2007. https://usatoday30.usatoday.com/tech/science/2007-05-29-deviant
-thinkers-security_N.htm.

Hall, Rachel. "Of Ziploc Bags and Black Holes: The Aesthetics of Transparency in the War on Terror." *Communication Review* 10, no. 4 (2007): 319–46. https://doi.org/10.1080/10714420701715381.

Hartman, Saidiya. *Scenes of Subjection: Terror, Slavery, and Self-Making in Nineteenth-Century America*. 1st ed. New York: Oxford University Press, 1997.

Hartman, Saidiya. *Wayward Lives, Beautiful Experiments: Intimate Histories of Social Upheaval*. 1st ed. New York: W. W. Norton, 2019.

Hay, James. "The Many Responsibilities of the New Citizen-Soldier." *Communication and Critical/Cultural Studies* 4, no. 2 (2007): 216–20. https://
doi.org/10.1080/14791420701296604.

Hegarty, Peter. "Alameda County Leaders Support New Direction for Urban Shield." *East Bay Times*, February 26, 2019. https://www.eastbaytimes.
com/2019/02/26/alameda-county-leaders-support-new-direction-for
-urban-shield/.

Hegarty, Peter. "Alameda County Loses Federal Money for Urban Shield." *East Bay Times*, March 15, 2019. https://www.eastbaytimes.com/2019/03/15/alameda-county-loses-federal-money-for-urban-shield/.

Henry, Kevin Lawrence, Jr. "A Review of *Get Out*: On White Terror and the Black Body." *Equity and Excellence in Education* 50, no. 3 (2017): 333–35. https://doi.org/10.1080/10665684.2017.1336952.

Hepburn, Allan. *Intrigue: Espionage and Culture*. New Haven, Conn.: Yale University Press, 2005.

Higgins, David M. "American Science Fiction after 9/11." In *Cambridge Companion to American SF*, edited by Eric Carl Link and Gerry Canavan, 44–57. New York: Cambridge University Press, 2015.

Highmore, Ben. *Cultural Feelings: Mood, Mediation, and Cultural Politics*. New York: Routledge, 2017.

Holling, C. S. "Resilience and Stability of Ecological Systems." *Annual Review of Ecology and Systematics* 4, no. 1 (1973): 1–23. https://doi.org/10.1146/annurev.es.04.110173.000245.

Homeland Security Council. "Planning Scenarios: Executive Summaries." July 2004. https://web.archive.org/web/20191231195257/https://www.hsdl.org/?view&did=453531.

Homeland Security National Preparedness Task Force. "Civil Defense and Homeland Security: A Short History of National Preparedness Efforts." September 2006. https://training.fema.gov/hiedu/docs/dhs%20civil%20defense-hs%20-%20short%20history.pdf.

hooks, bell. "The Oppositional Gaze: Black Female Spectators." In *Black Looks: Race and Representation*, 1st ed., 115–31. Boston: South End Press, 1992.

hooks, bell. "Representations of Whiteness in the Black Imagination." In *Killing Rage*, Reprint ed., 31–50. New York: Holt Paperbacks, 1996.

House Committee on Homeland Security. "Terror Gone Viral: Overview of the 100+ ISIS-Linked Plots against the West, 2014–2016." Majority Staff Report. July 2016. https://www.hsdl.org/?view&did=794343.

House Committee on Homeland Security. "Terror Threat Snapshot (March 2017)." March 2017. https://web.archive.org/save/https://www.hsdl.org/?view&did=799368.

House Committee on Homeland Security. "Working with Communities to Disrupt Terrorist Plots." March 2010. https://web.archive.org/web/20191231200358/https://www.hsdl.org/?view&did=489182.

Hudspeth, Mark. "The Coronavirus Response: Why Wasn't America Ready?" *CBS News*, April 26, 2020. https://www.cbsnews.com/news/the-coronavirus-response-why-wasnt-america-ready/.

Hunter, Ian. "Reading Character." *Southern Review* 16, no. 2 (1983): 226–43.

Hurley, Jessica. "History Is What Bites." *Extrapolation* 56, no. 3 (2015): 311–33. https://doi.org/10.3828/extr.2015.17.

Ibrahim, Nur. "Did Betsy DeVos Say Schools Can't Plan for a COVID-19 Outbreak That 'Hasn't Happened Yet'?" *Snopes*, July 22, 2020. https://www.snopes.com/fact-check/devos-schools-covid-19/.

Imarisha, Walidah. Introduction to *Octavia's Brood: Science Fiction Stories from Social Justice Movements*, edited by Walidah Imarisha and adrienne maree brown. Oakland, Calif.: AK Press, 2015.

Jameson, Fredric. *Archaeologies of the Future: The Desire Called Utopia and Other Science Fictions*. New York: Verso, 2005.

Jameson, Fredric. *The Political Unconscious: Narrative as a Socially Symbolic Act*. Ithaca, N.Y.: Cornell University Press, 1982.

Jerng, Mark C. *Racial Worldmaking: The Power of Popular Fiction*. New York: Fordham University Press, 2017. Kindle.

Johnson, Barbara. "Apostrophe, Animation, and Abortion." *Diacritics* 16, no. 1 (1986): 29–47. https://doi.org/10.2307/464649.

Johnson, Kevin. "Feds Unseal Charges in Foiled NYC Terror Plot; Concerts, Subway Targeted." *USA Today*, October 6, 2017. https://www.usatoday.com/story/news/politics/2017/10/06/feds-unseal-charges-foiled-nyc-terror-plot-concerts-subway-targeted/741323001/.

Joseph, Jonathan. "Resilience as Embedded Neoliberalism: A Governmentality Approach." *Resilience: International Policies, Practices, and Discourses* 1, no. 1 (2013): 38–52. https://doi.org/10.1080/21693293.2013.765741.

Juul, Jesper. *The Art of Failure: An Essay on the Pain of Playing Video Games*. Cambridge, Mass.: MIT Press, 2013.

Kahn, Herman. "Applications of Monte Carlo." RAND Corporation, April 1956. https://web.archive.org/web/20200126190109/https://www.rand.org/pubs/research_memoranda/RM1237.html.

Kahn, Herman. "Modification of the Monte Carlo Method." RAND Corporation, November 1949.

Kahn, Herman. "On Alternative World Futures: Some Basic Techniques, Issues, and Themes." Hudson Institute, 1966.

Kahn, Herman. *On Thermonuclear War*. Princeton, N.J.: Princeton University Press, 1960.

Kahn, Herman. "Stochastic (Monte Carlo) Attenuation Analysis." RAND Corporation, July 1949. https://web.archive.org/web/20200126190323/https://www.rand.org/pubs/papers/P88.html.

Kahn, Herman. *Thinking about the Unthinkable*. New York: Horizon Press, 1962.

Kahn, Herman, and Irwin Mann. "Techniques of Systems Analysis." RAND Corporation, 1956. https://www.rand.org/pubs/research_memoranda/RM1829-1.html.

Kahn, Herman, and Anthony J. Wiener. *The Year 2000: A Framework for Speculation on the Next Thirty-Three Years*. London: Macmillan, 1967.

Kaplan, Amy. *The Anarchy of Empire in the Making of U.S. Culture*. Cambridge, Mass.: Harvard University Press, 2002.

Kaplan, Marty, and Darren Ragle. *A River in Egypt*. In *The L.A. Earthquake Sourcebook*, edited by Judith Lewis and David Ulin, 290–314. Los Angeles, Calif.: Designmatters, 2008.

Karlawish, Jason. "A Pandemic Plan Was in Place. Trump Abandoned It—and Science—in the Face of Covid-19." *Stat*, May 17, 2020. https://www

.statnews.com/2020/05/17/the-art-of-the-pandemic-how-donald
-trump-walked-the-u-s-into-the-covid-19-era/.

Katz, Rita. "Think Again Turn Away: The State Department Is Fumbling
Online." *Time*, September 2014. https://web.archive.org/web/
20191231191232/https://time.com/3387065/isis-twitter-war-state
-department/.

Kavanagh, Thomas M. *Enlightenment and the Shadows of Chance: The
Novel and the Culture of Gambling in Eighteenth-Century France.* Baltimore: Johns Hopkins University Press, 1993.

Keefe, Patrick Radden. "The Insider." *Boston Globe*, May 2005.

Kermode, Frank. *The Sense of an Ending.* 1967. Reprint, Oxford: Oxford
University Press, 2000.

Khazan, Olga. "In One Year, 57,375 Years of Life Were Lost to Police
Violence." *Atlantic*, May 8, 2018. https://www.theatlantic.com/health/
archive/2018/05/the-57375-years-of-life-lost-to-police-violence/
559835/

Klausen, Jytte. "A Behavioral Study of the Radicalization Trajectories of
American 'Homegrown' Al Qaeda–Inspired Terrorist Offenders." August 2016. https://web.archive.org/web/20191231200529/https://www
.ncjrs.gov/pdffiles1/nij/grants/250417.pdf.

Knibbs, Kate. "The State Department Tried to Fight ISIS on Ask.Fm, and It
Didn't Go Well." *Gizmodo*, December 2015. https://web.archive.org/
web/20191231191138/https://gizmodo.com/the-state-department
-tried-to-fight-isis-on-ask-fm-and-1746071495.

Koenigs, Thomas. "Fictionality Risen: Early America, the Common Core
Curriculum, and How We Argue about Fiction Today." *American Literature* 89, no. 2 (2017): 225–53. https://doi.org/10.1215/00029831-3861493.

Kumar, Deepa. *Islamophobia and the Politics of Empire.* Chicago: Hay-
market Books, 2012.

Kumar, Deepa. "National Security Culture: Gender, Race and Class in the
Production of Imperial Citizenship." *International Journal of Communication* 11 (May 12, 2017): 2154–77.

Kumar, Deepa. "See Something, Say Something: Security Rituals, Affect,
and US Nationalism from the Cold War to the War on Terror." *Public
Culture* 30, no. 1 (2018): 143–71. https://doi.org/10.1215/08992363
-4189203.

Kundnani, Arun. *The Muslims Are Coming! Islamophobia, Extremism, and
the Domestic War on Terror.* New York: Verso, 2014.

Kunin, Aaron. "Characters Lounge." *Modern Language Quarterly* 70, no. 3
(2009): 291–317. https://doi.org/10.1215/00267929-2009-001.

Lakoff, Andrew. "Preparing for the Next Emergency." *Public Culture* 19,
no. 2 (2007): 247–71. https://doi.org/10.1215/08992363-2006-035.

Lakoff, Andrew, and Stephen J. Collier. "Distributed Preparedness: The
Spatial Logic of Domestic Security in the United States." *Environment
and Planning D: Society and Space* 26 (2008): 7–28. https://doi
.org/10.1068/d446t.

Lakoff, Andrew, and Stephen J. Collier. "Infrastructure and Event: The Political Technology of Preparedness." In *Political Matter: Technoscience, Democracy, and Public Life*, edited by Bruce Braun and Sarah J. Whatmore, 243–66. Minneapolis: University of Minnesota Press, 2010.

Lakoff, Andrew, and Stephen J. Collier. "The Vulnerability of Vital Systems." In *Securing "the Homeland": Critical Infrastructure, Risk and (In)Security*, edited by Myriam Dunn Cavelty and Kristian Søby Kristensen, 17–39. New York: Routledge, 2008.

Landsberg, Alison. "Horror Vérité: Politics and History in Jordan Peele's *Get Out* (2017)." *Continuum* 32, no. 5 (2018): 629–42. https://doi.org/10.1080/10304312.2018.1500522.

Landy, Joshua. *How to Do Things with Fictions*. Oxford: Oxford University Press, 2012.

Lang, Jenna. "Sci-Fi Writers Take US Security Back to the Future." *Guardian*, June 5, 2009. https://www.theguardian.com/books/booksblog/2009/jun/05/sigma-science-fiction-us-security.

Latour, Bruno. "Why Has Critique Run Out of Steam? From Matters of Fact to Matters of Concern." *Critical Inquiry* 30, no. 2 (2004): 225–48. https://doi.org/10.1086/421123.

Lauro, Sarah. *The Transatlantic Zombie: Slavery, Rebellion, and Living Death*. New Brunswick, N.J.: Rutgers University Press, 2015.

Lee, Yoon Sun. "Bad Plots and Objectivity in Maria Edgeworth." *Representations* 139, no. 1 (2017): 34–59. https://doi.org/10.1525/rep.2017.139.1.34.

Lindsey, Treva B. "Let Me Blow Your Mind: Hip Hop Feminist Futures in Theory and Praxis." *Urban Education* 50, no. 1 (2015): 52–77. https://doi.org/10.1177/0042085914563184.

Lindsey, Treva B. "Post-Ferguson: A 'Herstorical' Approach to Black Violability." *Feminist Studies* 41, no. 1 (2015): 232–37. https://doi.org/10.15767/feministstudies.41.1.232.

Liu, Alan. *The Laws of Cool: Knowledge Work and the Culture of Information*. Chicago: University of Chicago Press, 2004.

Lopez, German. "The Trump Administration's Botched Coronavirus Response, Explained." *Vox*, April 2, 2020. https://www.vox.com/policy-and-politics/2020/3/14/21177509/coronavirus-trump-covid-19-pandemic-response.

Lorde, Audre. "A Litany for Survival." In *The Black Unicorn: Poems*, 31. New York: W. W. Norton, 1978.

Lothian, Alexis. *Old Futures: Speculative Fiction and Queer Possibility*. New York: New York University Press, 2018. Kindle.

Lott, Eric. *Love and Theft: Blackface Minstrelsy and the American Working Class*. New York: Oxford University Press, 2013.

Lynch, Deidre Shauna. *The Economy of Character: Novels, Market Culture, and the Business of Inner Meaning*. Chicago: University of Chicago Press, 1998.

Magnani, Lorenzo. "Scientific Models Are Not Fictions." In *Philosophy and Cognitive Science*, edited by Lorenzo Magnani and Ping Li, 1–38. Studies in Applied Philosophy, Epistemology, and Rational Ethics. Berlin: Springer, 2012.

Mallard, Grégoire, and Andrew Lakoff. "How Claims to Know the Future Are Used to Understand the Present: Techniques of Prospection in the Field of National Security." In *Social Knowledge in the Making*, edited by Charles Camic, Neil Gross, and Michèle Lamont, 339–77. Chicago: University of Chicago Press, 2010.

Martin, Theodore. *Contemporary Drift: Genre, Historicism, and the Problem of the Present*. New York: Columbia University Press, 2017.

Marzec, Robert P. *Militarizing the Environment: Climate Change and the Security State*. Minneapolis: University of Minnesota Press, 2015.

Masco, Joseph. *The Theater of Operations: National Security Affect from the Cold War to the War on Terror*. Durham, N.C.: Duke University Press, 2014.

Massumi, Brian. *Ontopower: War, Powers, and the State of Perception*. Durham, N.C.: Duke University Press, 2015.

Maxmen, Amy, and Jeff Tollefson. "Two Decades of Pandemic War Games Failed to Account for Donald Trump." *Nature*, August 4, 2020. https://www.nature.com/articles/d41586-020-02277-6.

Mbembe, Achille. "Necropolitics." Translated by Libby Meintjes. *Public Culture* 15, no. 1 (2003): 11–40. https://doi.org/10.1215/08992363-15-1-11.

McClanahan, Annie. "Future's Shock: Plausibility, Preemption, and the Fiction of 9/11." *Symploke* 17, nos. 1–2 (2009): 41–62. https://doi.org/10.1353/sym.2009.0011.

McGurl, Mark. "The Zombie Renaissance." *N+1*.

Melley, Timothy. *The Covert Sphere: Secrecy, Fiction, and the National Security State*. Ithaca, N.Y.: Cornell University Press, 2012. Kindle.

Melley, Timothy. "Zero Dark Democracy." In *Narrating 9/11: Fantasies of State, Security, and Terrorism*, 17–39. Baltimore: Johns Hopkins University Press, 2015.

Metz, Christian. "Photography and Fetish." *October* 34 (1985): 81–90. https://doi.org/10.2307/778490.

Middle East Institute. "Sting of the Drone: A Book Event Featuring Richard A. Clarke." May 29, 2014. https://web.archive.org/web/20191231190739/https://www.mei.edu/events/sting-drone-book-event-featuring-richard-clarke.

iéville, China. "Cognition as Ideology: A Dialectic of SF Theory." In *Red Planets: Marxism and Science Fiction*, edited by Mark Bould and China Miéville, 231–48. Middletown, Conn.: Wesleyen University Press, 2009.

Miller, Greg. "Panel Casts Doubt on U.S. Propaganda Efforts against ISIS." *Washington Post*, December 2, 2015. https://www.washingtonpost.com/world/national-security/panel-casts-doubt-on-us-propaganda-efforts-against-isis/2015/12/02/ab7f9a14-9851-11e5-94f0-9eeaff906ef3_story.html.

Miller, Greg, and Scott Higham. "In a Propaganda War Against ISIS, the

U.S. Tried to Play by the Enemy's Rules." *Washington Post*, May 8, 2015. https://www.washingtonpost.com/world/national-security/in-a -propaganda-war-us-tried-to-play-by-the-enemys-rules/2015/05/08/ 6eb6b732-e52f-11e4-81ea-0649268f729e_story.html.

Miller, J. Hillis. *Ariadne's Thread: Story Lines*. New Haven, Conn.: Yale University Press, 1992.

Molesworth, Jesse. *Chance and the Eighteenth-Century Novel: Realism, Probability, Magic*. Cambridge: Cambridge University Press, 2010.

Montfort, Nick. "Fretting the Player Character." In *Second Person: Role-Playing and Story in Games and Playable Media*, edited by Pat Harrigan and Noah Wardrip-Fruin, 139–46. Cambridge, Mass.: MIT Press, 2010.

Montgomery, David. "Sci-Fi Writers Dream Up Gadgets and Contingency Plans for Homeland Security." *Washington Post*, May 2009. https:// www.washingtonpost.com/wp-dyn/content/article/2009/05/21/ AR2009052104379.html.

Morris, Errol, dir. *The Unknown Known*. 2013. New York: Radius-TWC, 2014. Amazon Prime Video.

Moten, Fred. *In the Break: The Aesthetics of the Black Radical Tradition*. Minneapolis: University of Minnesota Press, 2003.

Mulvey, Laura. "Some Thoughts on Theories of Fetishism in the Context of Contemporary Culture." *October* 65 (1993): 3–20. https://doi.org/10 .2307/778760.

Muslim American Civil Liberties Coalition for Truth and Justice. "NYPD Statement of Clarification (Added, Summer 2009)." *MACLC's Weblog* (blog), September 5, 2009. https://web.archive.org/web/20191231184335/ https://maclc1.wordpress.com/2009/09/05/nypd-statement-of -clarification-added-summer-2009/.

National Commission on Terrorist Attacks upon the United States. *The 9/11 Commission Report*. Washington, D.C.: National Commission on Terrorist Attacks upon the United States, 2006. https://govinfo.library .unt.edu/911/report/911Report.pdf.

National Endowment for the Arts. *National Endowment for the Arts 2017 Annual Report*. Washington, D.C.: National Endowment for the Arts, April 2018. https://web.archive.org/web/20200126191247/https://www .arts.gov/sites/default/files/2017%20Annual%20Report.pdf.

National Endowment for the Humanities. "NEH Chairman William D. Adams's Statement on NEH Fy17 Budget." May 2017. https://www.neh .gov/news/press-release/2017-05-09.

National Institute of Justice. "Radicalization and Violent Extremism: Lessons Learned from Canada, the U.K. and the U.S." 2015. https://web .archive.org/web/20191231200635/https://www.ncjrs.gov/pdffiles1/ nij/249947.pdf.

Newfield, Christopher. "The Trouble with Numerical Culture." *Profession*, Fall 2019.

Newsom, Robert. *A Likely Story: Probability and Play in Fiction*. New Brunswick, N.J.: Rutgers University Press, 1989.

Ngai, Sianne. *Our Aesthetic Categories: Zany, Cute, Interesting.* Cambridge, Mass.: Harvard University Press, 2015.

Nguyen, Mimi Thi. *The Gift of Freedom: War, Debt, and Other Refugee Passages.* Durham, N.C.: Duke University Press, 2012.

Nguyen, Mimi Thi. "The Hoodie as Sign, Screen, Expectation, and Force." *Signs* 40, no. 4 (2015): 791–816. https://doi.org/10.1086/680326.

Nielsen, Henrik Skov, James Phelan, and Richard Walsh. "Ten Theses about Fictionality." *Narrative* 23, no. 1 (2014): 61–73. https://doi.org/10.1353/nar.2015.0005.

Nussbaum, Emily. "Tune in Next Week: The Curious Staying Power of the Cliffhanger." *New Yorker*, July 2012, 70–74.

Nussbaum, Martha C. *Cultivating Humanity: A Classical Defense of Reform in Liberal Education.* Cambridge, Mass.: Harvard University Press, 1998.

Nussbaum, Martha C. *Not for Profit: Why Democracy Needs the Humanities.* Princeton, N.J.: Princeton University Press, 2010.

Oakes, Guy. *The Imaginary War: Civil Defense and American Cold War.* Oxford: Oxford University Press, 1994.

Office of Public Health Preparedness and Response. "Zombie Preparedness." Centers for Disease Control and Prevention, June 2017. https://web.archive.org/web/20191231192455/https://www.cdc.gov/cpr/zombie/index.htm.

Office of the Press Secretary. "President Remembers 9/11 Heroes at Medal of Valor Award Ceremony." September 2005. https://web.archive.org/web/20191231190126/https://georgewbush-whitehouse.archives.gov/news/releases/2005/09/20050909-1.html.

Office of the Press Secretary. "President's Remarks to the Nation." September 2002. https://web.archive.org/web/20191231190201/https://georgewbush-whitehouse.archives.gov/news/releases/2002/09/20020911-3.html.

O'Malley, Pat. "Resilient Subjects: Uncertainty, Warfare and Liberalism." *Economy and Society* 39, no. 4 (2010): 488–509. https://doi.org/10.1080/03085147.2010.510681.

Orlemanski, Julie. "Scales of Reading." *Exemplaria* 26, no. 2–3 (2014): 215–33. https://doi.org/10.1179/1041257314Z.00000000051.

Orr, Jackie. *Panic Diaries: A Genealogy of Panic Disorder.* Durham, N.C.: Duke University Press, 2006.

Oyola-Yemaiel, Arthur, and Jennifer Wilson. "Three Essential Strategies for Emergency Management Professionalization in the U.S." *International Journal of Mass Emergencies and Disasters* 23, no. 1 (2005): 77–84.

Paige, Nicholas D. *Before Fiction: The Ancien Régime of the Novel.* Philadelphia: University of Pennsylvania Press, 2011.

Palumbo-Liu, David. "Preemption, Perpetual War, and the Future of the Imagination." *Boundary 2* 33, no. 1 (2006): 151–69. https://doi.org/10.1215/01903659-33-1-151.

Parks, Lisa. "Points of Departure: The Culture of US Airport Screening."

Journal of Visual Culture 6, no. 2 (2007): 183–200. https://doi
.org/10.1177/1470412907078559.

Patel, Faiza. *Rethinking Radicalization*. New York: Brennan Center for
Justice, NYU School of Law, 2011.

Patey, Douglas Lane. *Probability and Literary Form: Philosophic Theory and
Literary Practice in the Augustan Age*. Cambridge: Cambridge University
Press, 1984.

Patton, Elizabeth A. "*Get Out* and the Legacy of Sundown Suburbs in Post-
racial America." *New Review of Film and Television Studies* 17, no. 3
(2019): 349–63. https://doi.org/10.1080/17400309.2019.1622889.

Paul, Annie Murphy. "The Neuroscience of Your Brain on Fiction." *New
York Times*, March 17, 2012. https://www.nytimes.com/2012/03/18/
opinion/sunday/the-neuroscience-of-your-brain-on-fiction.html.

Pavel, Thomas. "Literary Genres as Norms and Good Habits." *New Literary
History* 34, no. 2 (2003): 201–10. https://doi.org/10.1353/nlh.2003.0021.

Pease, Donald E. *The New American Exceptionalism*. Minneapolis: University of Minnesota Press, 2009.

Peele, Jordan, dir. *Get Out*. Los Angeles: Universal Pictures, 2017. Amazon
Prime Video.

Peirce, Charles Sanders. *Philosophical Writings of Peirce*. Edited by Justus
Buchler. New York: Dover, 1955.

Perlin, Ken. "Can There Be a Form between a Game and a Story?" In *First
Person: New Media as Story, Performance, and Game*, edited by Noah
Wardrip-Fruin and Pat Harrigan, 12–18. Cambridge, Mass.: MIT Press,
2004.

Phillips, Amanda. "Shooting to Kill: Headshots, Twitch Reflexes, and the
Mechropolitics of Video Games." *Games and Culture* 13, no. 2 (2018):
136–52. https://doi.org/10.1177/1555412015612611.

Plant, Jeremy F., Thomas Arminio, and Paul Thompson. "A Matrix
Approach to Homeland Security Professional Education." *Journal of
Homeland Security and Emergency Management* 8, no. 2 (2011). https://
doi.org/10.2202/1547-7355.1883.

Politics and Prose. "Richard A. Clarke 'Sting of the Drone.'" June 2014.

Poot, Luke Terlaak. "On Cliffhangers." *Narrative* 24, no. 1 (2016): 50–67.
https://doi.org/10.1353/nar.2016.0001.

Potter, Margaret A., Kathleen R. Miner, Daniel J. Barnett, Rebecca Cadi-
gan, Laura Lloyd, Debra K. Olson, Cindy Parker, Elena Savoia, and
Kimberley Shoaf. "The Evidence Base for Effectiveness of Preparedness
Training: A Retrospective Analysis." *Public Health Reports* 125, no. 5_
suppl. (2010): 15–23. https://doi.org/10.1177/00333549101250S504.

Propp, Vladimir. *Morphology of the Folktale*. Edited by Louis A. Wagner.
Translated by Laurence Scott. 2nd ed. 1928. Reprint, Austin: University
of Texas Press, 1968.

Puar, Jasbir K. *Terrorist Assemblages: Homonationalism in Queer Times*.
Durham, N.C.: Duke University Press, 2007.

Raza v. City of New York. 998 F. Supp. 2d 70 (E.D.N.Y. 2013).

Reeves, Joshua. "If You See Something, Say Something: Lateral Surveillance and the Uses of Responsibility." *Surveillance and Society* 10, no. 3/4 (2012): 235–48. https://doi.org/10.24908/ss.v10i3/4.4209.

Ricoeur, Paul. *Freud and Philosophy: An Essay on Interpretation.* Translated by Denis Savage. New Haven, Conn.: Yale University Press, 1970.

Rieder, John. "On Defining SF, or Not: Genre Theory, SF, and History." *Science Fiction Studies* 37, no. 2 (2010): 191–209.

Rogers, Amanda. "'Think Again, Turn Away' . . . from Lousy Public Diplomacy." Middle East Research and Information Project, October 2014. https://www.merip.org/%E2%80%9Cthink-again-turn-away%E2%80%9D%E2%80%A6from-lousy-public-diplomacy.

Rose, Jacqueline. *States of Fantasy.* Oxford: Clarendon Press, 1996.

Rosen, Jeremy. *Minor Characters Have Their Day: Genre and the Contemporary Literary Marketplace.* New York: Columbia University Press, 2016.

Rumsfeld, Donald H. "Defense.Gov Transcript: DoD News Briefing—Secretary Rumsfeld and Gen. Myers." February 2002. https://web.archive.org/save/https://archive.defense.gov/transcripts/transcript.aspx?transcriptid=2636.

Rumsfeld, Donald H. "Transforming the Military." *Foreign Affairs*, May/June 2002. https://www.foreignaffairs.com/articles/2002-05-01/transforming-military.

Rutty, Guy N., and Jane E. Rutty. "Did the Participants of the Mass Fatality Exercise *Operation Torch* Learn Anything?" *Forensic Science, Medicine, and Pathology* 8 (2012): 88–93. https://doi.org/10.1007/s12024-010-9218-1.

Ryan, Marie-Laure. "Will New Media Produce New Narratives?" In *Narrative across Media: The Languages of Storytelling,* edited by Marie-Laure Ryan, 337–59. Lincoln: University of Nebraska Press, 2004.

Sawyer, Ben. *Serious Games: Improving Public Policy through Game-Based Learning and Simulation.* Washington, D.C.: Woodrow Wilson International Center for Scholars, 2002.

Sedgwick, Eve Kosofsky. "Paranoid Reading and Reparative Reading; or, You're So Paranoid, You Probably Think This Introduction Is about You." In *Novel Gazing: Queer Readings in Fiction,* edited by Eve Kosofsky Sedgwick, 1–40. Durham, N.C.: Duke University Press, 1997.

Select Bipartisan Committee to Investigate the Preparation for and Response to Hurricane Katrina. *A Failure of Initiative.* Washington, D.C.: Select Bipartisan Committee to Investigate the Preparation for and Response to Hurricane Katrina, February 15, 2006. https://web.archive.org/web/20191231193046/https://www.nrc.gov/docs/ML1209/ML12093A081.pdf.

Seltzer, Mark. *The Official World.* Durham, N.C.: Duke University Press, 2016.

Senate Committee on Homeland Security and Governmental Affairs. "Report on Violent Islamist Extremism, the Internet, and the Homegrown Terrorist Threat." Majority and Minority Staff Report, May 2008. https://web.archive.org/web/20191231200719/https://fas.org/irp/congress/2008_rpt/violent.pdf.

SF DEM. "Prepare to Prosper (with Audio Description)." February 8, 2012. YouTube video, 31:42. https://youtu.be/mRnqj1gAQTE.

Shapin, Steven, and Simon Schaffer. *Leviathan and the Air-Pump: Hobbes, Boyle, and the Experimental Life*. Princeton, N.J.: Princeton University Press, 1985.

Sharpe, Christina. "Black Studies: In the Wake." *Black Scholar* 44, no. 2 (2014): 59–69. https://doi.org/10.1080/00064246.2014.11413688.

Sharpe, Christina. *In the Wake: On Blackness and Being*. Durham, N.C.: Duke University Press, 2016.

SIGMA Forum. "SIGMA Members." https://web.archive.org/web/20191231190714/http://www.sigmaforum.org/?page_id=107.

SIGMA Forum. "What Is SIGMA?" https://web.archive.org/web/20191231192210/http://www.sigmaforum.org/.

Silber, Mitchell D., and Arvin Bhatt. "Radicalization in the West: The Homegrown Threat." New York City Police Department, 2007. https://web.archive.org/web/20191231200658/https://seths.blog/wp-content/uploads/2007/09/NYPD_Report-Radicalization_in_the_West.pdf.

Silver, Maggie, James Archer, Bob Hobbs, Alissa Eckert, and Mark Connor. *Preparedness 101: Zombie Pandemic*. Atlanta, Ga.: Centers for Disease Control and Prevention, 2011. https://web.archive.org/web/20191231195326/https://www.cdc.gov/cpr/documents/zombie_gn_final.pdf.

Smith, Susan. *Hitchcock: Suspense, Humour and Tone*. London: British Film Institute, 2000.

So, Richard Jean. "All Models Are Wrong." *PMLA* 132, no. 3 (2017): 668–73. https://doi.org/10.1632/pmla.2017.132.3.668.

Sobande, Francesca. "Dissecting Depictions of Black Masculinity in *Get Out*." In *Gender and Contemporary Horror in Film*, edited by Samantha Holland, Robert Shail, and Steven Gerrard, 237–50. Bingley, U.K.: Emerald, 2019.

Solomon, Akiba. "The 5-Year Fight to Shut down 'War Games Training' in the Bay Area." *Colorlines*, September 18, 2018. https://www.colorlines.com/articles/watch-5-year-fight-shut-down-war-games-training-bay-area.

Sontag, Susan. "Notes on 'Camp.'" In *Against Interpretation: And Other Essays*, 275–92. New York: Picador, 1966.

Sorensen, Leif. "Against the Post-apocalyptic: Narrative Closure in Colson Whitehead's *Zone One*." *Contemporary Literature* 55, no. 3 (2014): 559–92. https://doi.org/10.1353/cli.2014.0029.

Spillers, Hortense. "The Crisis of the Negro Intellectual: A Post-date." In *Black, White, and in Color: Essays on American Literature and Culture*, 428–70. Chicago: University of Chicago Press, 2003.

Spillers, Hortense. "'Mama's Baby, Papa's Maybe': An American Grammar

Book." In *Black, White, and in Color: Essays on American Literature and Culture*, 203–29. Chicago: University of Chicago Press, 2003.

Stop Urban Shield. "Infographic." http://stopurbanshield.org/resources/infographic/.

Stop Urban Shield. "Letters to the Alameda County Board of Supervisors." http://stopurbanshield.org/about-the-campaign/letters-to-the-alameda-county-board-of-supervisors/.

Stop Urban Shield. "Our Fight." http://stopurbanshield.org/about-the-campaign/our-fight/.

Stop Urban Shield. "Stop Urban Shield." http://stopurbanshield.org/.

Stop Urban Shield. "Stop Urban Shield Powerpoint." http://stopurbanshield.org/resources/stop-urban-shield-powerpoint/.

Stop Urban Shield. "Timeline—the Struggle against Urban Shield." http://stopurbanshield.org/about-the-campaign/timeline-the-struggle-against-urban-shield/.

Stop Urban Shield. "We Defended Our Victory against Urban Shield!" March 1, 2019. http://stopurbanshield.org/we-defended-our-victory-against-urban-shield/.

Stop Urban Shield. "We Put an End to Urban Shield!" March 28, 2018. http://stopurbanshield.org/we-put-an-end-to-urban-shield/.

Suvin, Darko. *Metamorphoses of Science Fiction: On the Poetics and History of a Literary Genre*. New Haven, Conn.: Yale University Press, 1979.

Taylor, Diana. *The Archive and the Repertoire: Performing Cultural Memory in the Americas*. Durham, N.C.: Duke University Press, 2003.

Taylor, Jesse Oak. "The Novel as Climate Model: Realism and the Greenhouse Effect in *Bleak House*." *Novel* 46, no. 1 (2013): 1–25. https://doi.org/10.1215/00295132-2019092.

Terdoslavich, William. *The Jack Ryan Agenda: Policy and Politics in the Novels of Tom Clancy: An Unauthorized Analysis*. New York: Macmillan, 2005.

Think AgainTurn Away (@ThinkAgain_DOS). Twitter, October 2014. https://web.archive.org/web/20141009064045/https://twitter.com/thinkagain_dos?lang=en.

Thomas, Lindsay. "Forms of Duration: Preparedness, the *Mars* Trilogy, and the Management of Climate Change." *American Literature* 88, no. 1 (2016): 159–84. https://doi.org/10.1215/00029831-3453696.

Thomas, Lindsay. "Preparedness Documents after the Fact." In *The Routledge Companion to Risk and Media*, edited by Bhaskar Sarkar and Bishnupriya Ghosh, 165–76. New York: Routledge, 2020.

Tolkien, J. R. R. "On Fairy-Stories." In *Tolkien on Fairy-Stories*, edited by Verlyn Flieger and Douglas A. Anderson, 27–84. London: HarperCollins, 2008.

Tomberg, Jaak. "On the 'Double Vision' of Realism and SF Estrangement in William Gibson's *Bigend Trilogy*." *Science Fiction Studies* 40, no. 2 (2013): 263–85. https://doi.org/10.5621/sciefictstud.40.2.0263.

Toon, Adam. *Models as Make-Believe: Imagination, Fiction and Scientific Representation*. London: Palgrave Macmillan, 2012.

uncertain commons. *Speculate This!* Durham, N.C.: Duke University Press, 2013. Kindle.

Underwood, Ted. "The Life Cycles of Genres." *Journal of Cultural Analytics,* May 2016. https://doi.org/10.22148/16.005.

Urban Shield. "Urban Shield." https://www.urbanshield.org/.

U.S. Department of Defense. "CONPLAN 8888 Counter-Zombie Dominance." April 2011. https://web.archive.org/web/20191231193455/https://documents.theblackvault.com/documents/controversies/CONPLAN8888-11.pdf.

U.S. Department of Homeland Security. "About the Campaign." December 19, 2014. https://web.archive.org/web/20191231180341/https://www.dhs.gov/see-something-say-something/about-campaign.

U.S. Department of Homeland Security. "Be a Hero! Youth Emergency Preparedness, Grades 9–12." 2014. https://www.hsdl.org/?abstract&did=798540.

U.S. Department of Homeland Security. "Campaign Materials." December 19, 2014. https://web.archive.org/web/20191231180642/https://www.dhs.gov/see-something-say-something/campaign-materials.

U.S. Department of Homeland Security. "Department of Homeland Security Strategy for Countering Violent Extremism." 2016. https://web.archive.org/web/20191231193522/https://www.dhs.gov/sites/default/files/publications/16_1028_S1_CVE_strategy.pdf.

U.S. Department of Homeland Security. "Disaster Master." 2013. https://web.archive.org/web/20191231181333/https://www.ready.gov/kids/games/data/dm-english/.

U.S. Department of Homeland Security. "FY 2019 Budget-in-Brief." February 2018. https://web.archive.org/web/20200114055306/https://www.dhs.gov/sites/default/files/publications/DHS%20BIB%202019.pdf.

U.S. Department of Homeland Security. "Homeland Security Exercise and Evaluation Program." April 2013. https://web.archive.org/web/20191231194046/https://www.fema.gov/media-library-data/20130726-1914-25045-8890/hseep_apr13_.pdf.

U.S. Department of Homeland Security. "Homeland Security Exercise and Evaluation Program (HSEEP), Vol II: Exercise Planning and Conduct." February 2007. http://www.enmagine.com/images/shared/Download_Central/Disaster_Exercises/Homeland%20Security%20Exercise%20and%20Evaluation%20Program%20(HSEEP)/HSEEP_VolumeII_ExercisePlanningandConduct_FEMA.pdf.

U.S. Department of Homeland Security. "If You See Something, Say Something Campaign Overview." Washington, D.C.: U.S. Department of Homeland Security, January 7, 2015. https://www.dhs.gov/publication/if-you-see-something-say-something%E2%84%A2-campaign-overview.

U.S. Department of Homeland Security. "'If You See Something, Say Something (TM)' Public Awareness Video." March 15, 2011. YouTube video, 9:55. https://youtu.be/6jAV1dbGPB4.

U.S. Department of Homeland Security. "Individual and Community

Preparedness Awards." https://web.archive.org/web/20191231182615/
https://www.fema.gov/individual-and-community-preparedness
-division.

U.S. Department of Homeland Security. "National Planning Scenarios."
March 2006. https://web.archive.org/web/20200111040846/https://
info.publicintelligence.net/DHS%20-%20National%20Planning%20
Scenarios%20March%202006.pdf.

U.S. Department of Homeland Security. "National Preparedness Goal."
September 2015. https://web.archive.org/web/20191231195000/https://
www.fema.gov/media-library-data/1443799615171-2aae90be5504174
0f97e8532fc680d40/National_Preparedness_Goal_2nd_Edition.pdf.

U.S. Department of Homeland Security. "NIPP 2013: Partnering for Critical Infrastructure Security and Resilience." 2013. https://web.archive
.org/web/20191231195136/https://www.dhs.gov/sites/default/files/
publications/national-infrastructure-protection-plan-2013-508.pdf.

U.S. Department of Homeland Security. "Our Mission." August 4, 2011.
https://web.archive.org/web/20191231185048/https://www.dhs.gov/
mission.

U.S. Department of Homeland Security. "Preventing Terrorism." June 19,
2012. https://web.archive.org/web/20191231105846/https://www.dhs
.gov/topic/preventing-terrorism.

U.S. Department of Homeland Security. "Protect Your Every Day Public
Service Announcement." March 29, 2016. https://www.dhs.gov/
see-something-say-something/campaign-materials/protect-your
-every-day-psa.

U.S. Department of Homeland Security. "Ready.Gov ESPN 'Hero.'" 2012.
https://web.archive.org/web/20190110173404/https://www.fema.gov/
media-library/assets/videos/80294.

U.S. Department of Homeland Security. "Resilience." September 12, 2018.
https://web.archive.org/web/20191231190637/https://www.dhs.gov/
topic/resilience.

U.S. Department of Homeland Security. "Take the Challenge." June 22,
2016. https://web.archive.org/save/https://www.dhs.gov/see
-something-say-something/take-challenge.

Vermeule, Blakey. *Why Do We Care about Literary Characters?* Baltimore:
Johns Hopkins University Press, 2011.

vlogger. *Welcome to the Islamic State Land.* Military.com, September 9, 2014.
Video. https://www.military.com/video/operations-and-strategy/
terrorism/welcome-to-the-islamic-state-land/3775821940001.

Voelz, Johannes. *The Poetics of Insecurity: American Fiction and the Uses of
Threat.* Cambridge: Cambridge University Press, 2018.

Volpp, Leti. "The Citizen and the Terrorist." *Immigration and Nationality
Law Review* 23 (2002): 1576–1600.

Waldo, Dwight. "Scope of the Theory of Public Administration." In *Theory
and Practice of Public Administration: Scope, Objectives, and Method,* ed-

ited by James C. Charlesworth, 1–26. Philadelphia: American Academy of Political and Social Science, 1968.

Walker, Jeremy, and Melissa Cooper. "Genealogies of Resilience: From Systems Ecology to the Political Economy of Crisis Adaptation." *Security Dialogue* 42, no. 2 (2011): 143–60. https://doi.org/10.1177/0967010611399616.

Walsh, Richard. *The Rhetoric of Fictionality: Narrative Theory and the Idea of Fiction*. 1st ed. Columbus: Ohio State University Press, 2007.

Warner, Michael. "The Mass Public and the Mass Subject." In *American Literary Studies: A Methodological Reader*, edited by Michael A. Elliott and Claudia Stokes, 243–63. New York: New York University Press, 2002.

Warner, Michael. *Publics and Counterpublics*. Brooklyn, N.Y.: Zone Books, 2002.

Waugh, William L., and Abdul-Akeem Sadiq. "Professional Education for Emergency Managers." *Journal of Homeland Security and Emergency Management* 8, no. 2 (2011). https://doi.org/10.2202/1547-7355.1891.

Weber, Max. *The Protestant Ethic and the Spirit of Capitalism*. Translated by Talcott Parsons. 1905. Reprint, London: Routledge, 1992.

Weheliye, Alexander G. *Habeas Viscus: Racializing Assemblages, Biopolitics, and Black Feminist Theories of the Human*. Durham, N.C.: Duke University Press, 2014.

White House. "International Strategy for Cyberspace: Prosperity, Security, and Openness in a Networked World." May 2011. https://web.archive.org/web/20191231194501/https://obamawhitehouse.archives.gov/sites/default/files/rss_viewer/international_strategy_for_cyberspace.pdf.

White House. "National Security Strategy of the United States." March 1990. https://web.archive.org/web/20191231195117/http://nssarchive.us/NSSR/1990.pdf.

Wiegman, Robyn. "Whiteness Studies and the Paradox of Particularity." *Boundary* 2 26, no. 3 (1999): 115–50.

Williams, Jefferson, Maryalice Nocera, and Carri Casteel. "The Effectiveness of Disaster Training for Health Care Workers: A Systematic Review." *Annals of Emergency Medicine* 52, no. 3 (2008): 211–222. https://doi.org/10.1016/j.annemergmed.2007.09.030.

Williamson, Elizabeth. "When Active-Shooter Drills Scare the Children They Hope to Protect." *New York Times*, September 4, 2019. https://www.nytimes.com/2019/09/04/us/politics/active-shooter-drills-schools.html.

Winant, Howard. *The New Politics of Race: Globalism, Difference, Justice*. Minneapolis: University of Minnesota Press, 2004.

Wolf, Mark J. P. *Building Imaginary Worlds*. 1st ed. New York: Routledge, 2012.

Woloch, Alex. *The One vs. the Many: Minor Characters and the Space of the*

Protagonist in the Novel. Princeton, N.J.: Princeton University Press, 2003.

World Health Organization. "Archived: WHO Timeline—COVID-19." https://www.who.int/news-room/detail/27-04-2020-who-timeline -covid-19.

Xin, Wendy Veronica. "Reading for the Plotter." *New Literary History* 49, no. 1 (2018): 93–118. https://doi.org/10.1353/nlh.2018.0004.

Yamato, Jen. "Jordan Peele on 'Get Out,' the Horror Film about Racism That Obama Would Love." *Los Angeles Times,* February 25, 2017. https:// www.latimes.com/entertainment/movies/la-et-get-out-jordan-peele -racism-horror-america-20170224-story.html.

Zhang, Dora. "Notes on Atmosphere." *Qui Parle* 27, no. 1 (2018): 121–55. https://doi.org/10.1215/10418385-4383010.

Zinoman, Jason. "Jordan Peele on a Truly Terrifying Monster: Racism." *New York Times,* February 16, 2017. https://www.nytimes.com/2017/ 02/16/movies/jordan-peele-interview-get-out.html.

Zunshine, Lisa. *Why We Read Fiction: Theory of Mind and the Novel.* Columbus: Ohio State University Press, 2006.

Zupančič, Alenka. *The Odd One In: On Comedy.* Cambridge, Mass.: MIT Press, 2008.

Index

Lindsay Thomas is assistant professor of English at the University of Miami.